# Praise for *Hypermodern Python Tooling*

For anyone managing existing Python projects—individually or within a company. Get to the forefront of Python's evolving ecosystem by using modern solutions and tools that turbocharge productivity and ensure code quality.

—*Karandeep Johar, Tech Lead Manager, Amplitude*

*Hypermodern Python Tooling* showcases some of the best Python tools in an ever-changing ecosystem, and, more importantly, provides a foundation for how to use them for any developer looking to level up their workflow.

—*Pat Viafore, Author of* Robust Python

A must-read for Python enthusiasts, offering comprehensive insights into modern developer tools and best practices.

—*William Jamir Silva, Senior Software Engineer, Adjust GmbH*

*Hypermodern Python Tooling* is the missing map for navigating Python's rich but overwhelming landscape of tools and practices. It's an indispensable companion for setting up and getting the most out of your project's tooling.

—*Thea Flowers, Creative Technologist*

A must-read for Python enthusiasts, this book provides invaluable insights and practical guidance for building robust Python workflows—perfect for both beginners and seasoned developers.

—*Ganesh Harke, Tech Lead, Citibank NA*

# Hypermodern Python Tooling

*Building Reliable Workflows*
*for an Evolving Python Ecosystem*

*Claudio Jolowicz*

Beijing · Boston · Farnham · Sebastopol · Tokyo

**Hypermodern Python Tooling**

by Claudio Jolowicz

Published by O'Reilly Media, Inc., 1005 Gravenstein Highway North, Sebastopol, CA 95472.

O'Reilly books may be purchased for educational, business, or sales promotional use. Online editions are also available for most titles (*https://oreilly.com*). For more information, contact our corporate/institutional sales department: 800-998-9938 or *corporate@oreilly.com*.

| | |
|---|---|
| **Acquisitions Editor:** Brian Guerin | **Indexer:** nSight, Inc. |
| **Development Editor:** Sarah Grey | **Interior Designer:** David Futato |
| **Production Editor:** Gregory Hyman | **Cover Designer:** Karen Montgomery |
| **Copyeditor:** Emily Wydeven | **Illustrator:** Kate Dullea |
| **Proofreader:** Piper Editorial Consulting, LLC | |

June 2024:          First Edition

**Revision History for the First Edition**
2024-06-19:    First Release

See *https://oreilly.com/catalog/errata.csp?isbn=9781098139582* for release details.

978-1-098-13958-2

[LSI]

*To Marianna*

# Table of Contents

## Part I.    Working with Python

## Part II.  Python Projects

## Part III.    Testing and Static Analysis

# Preface

This book is a guide to modern Python developer tools—the programs that help you perform tasks such as:

- Managing Python installations on your system
- Installing third-party packages for your current project
- Building a Python package for distribution on a package repository
- Running a test suite repeatedly across multiple environments
- Linting and type checking your code to catch bugs

You don't strictly need these tools to write Python software. Fire up your system's Python interpreter and get an interactive prompt. Save your Python code as a script for later. Why use anything beyond an editor and a shell?

This is not a rhetorical question. Every tool you add to your development workflow should have a clear purpose and bring benefits that outweigh the costs of using it. Generally, the benefits of development tooling become manifest when you need to make development sustainable *over time*. At some point, publishing your module on the Python Package Index will be easier than emailing it to your users.

Somewhere along the journey from writing one-off scripts to distributing and maintaining packages, challenges pop up:

- Supporting multiple versions of Python on multiple operating systems
- Keeping dependencies up-to-date and scanning them for vulnerabilities
- Keeping the code base readable and consistent
- Interacting with bug reports and external contributions from the community
- Keeping test coverage high to reduce the defect rate in code changes
- Automating repeated tasks to reduce friction and avoid surprises

This book will show you how developer tooling can help with such challenges. The tools described here greatly benefit the code quality, security, and maintainability of Python projects.

But tooling also adds complexity and overhead. This book strives to minimize that by forging tools into an easy-to-use toolchain and by automating workflows reliably and repeatably—whether they execute locally on a developer machine, or on a continuous integration server across a range of platforms and environments. As much as possible, you should be able to focus your attention on writing software, with your toolchain working in the background.

Laziness has been called "a programmer's greatest virtue,"[1] and this saying applies to development tooling, too: keep your workflow simple, and don't adopt tools for their own sake. At the same time, good programmers are also curious. Give the tools in this book a try to see what value they may bring to your projects.

The Python ecosystem constantly evolves: what we consider modern today inevitably yields to the *hypermodern* ways of tomorrow.[2] This book attempts to raise awareness for recent tools, standards, and best practices—not for newness' sake, but because they improve your productivity and developer experience. Understanding the whys and the hows of these tools and workflows—as well as their tradeoffs—will prepare you for when the next generation of Python tooling appears at the horizon.

## Who Should Read This Book?

If you're one of these people, you'll benefit from reading this book:

- You're proficient with Python, but you're not sure how to create a package.
- You've been doing this for years—setuptools, virtualenv, and pip are your friends. You're curious about recent developments in tooling and what they bring to the table.
- You maintain mission-critical code that runs in production. But there must be a better way to do all of this. You want to learn about state-of-the art tools and evolving best practices.
- You want to be more productive as a Python developer.
- You're an open source maintainer looking for a robust and modern project infrastructure.

---

1 Larry Wall, *Programming Perl* (Sebastopol: O'Reilly, 1991).

2 The title of this book is inspired by *Die hypermoderne Schachpartie* (The hypermodern chess game), written by Savielly Tartakower in 1924. It surveys the revolution that was taking place in chess theory during his time.

- You're using a bunch of Python tools in your projects, but it's hard to see how everything fits together. You want to reduce the friction that comes with all this tooling.
- "Things just keep breaking—why doesn't Python find my module now? Why can't I import the package I just installed?"

This book assumes that you have a basic knowledge of the Python programming language. The only tooling you need to be familiar with is the Python interpreter, an editor or IDE, and the command line of your operating system.

# How This Book Is Organized

This book is arranged in three parts:

*Part I, "Working with Python"*
- Chapter 1, "Installing Python", teaches you how to manage Python installations over time across different platforms. The chapter also introduces the Python Launchers for Windows and Unix—you'll use them throughout the book.
- Chapter 2, "Python Environments", zooms into a Python installation and discusses how your code interacts with it. You'll also learn about tools that help you work efficiently with virtual environments.

*Part II, "Python Projects"*
- Chapter 3, "Python Packages", teaches you how to set up your project as a Python package, and how to build and publish packaging artifacts. The chapter also introduces the example application used throughout the book.
- Chapter 4, "Dependency Management", describes how to add third-party packages to a Python project and how to keep track of your project dependencies over time.
- Chapter 5, "Managing Projects with Poetry", teaches you how to work with Python projects using Poetry. Poetry lets you manage environments, dependencies, and packaging at a higher level.

*Part III, "Testing and Static Analysis"*
- Chapter 6, "Testing with pytest", discusses how to test a Python project and how to work efficiently with the pytest framework and its ecosystem.
- Chapter 7, "Measuring Coverage with Coverage.py", teaches you how to discover untested code by measuring the code coverage of your test suite.
- Chapter 8, "Automation with Nox", introduces the Nox automation framework. You'll use it to run tests across Python environments and, more generally, to automate checks and other developer tasks in your projects.

- Chapter 9, "Linting with Ruff and pre-commit", shows you how to find and fix likely bugs, and how to format your code, with Ruff. You'll also learn about pre-commit, a cross-language linter framework with Git integration.

- Chapter 10, "Using Types for Safety and Inspection", teaches you how to verify type safety with static and runtime type checkers, and how to inspect types at runtime to perform actual magic (terms and conditions apply).

## References and Further Reading

Your first point of reference outside this book should be the official documentation of each tool. Besides those, many interesting packaging-related discussions take place on the Python Discourse (*https://oreil.ly/nS3hu*). Discussions in the Packaging category often shape the future of the Python packaging and tooling ecosystem in the form of packaging standards using the Python Enhancement Proposal (PEP) process (*https://oreil.ly/km1g3*). Finally, the Python Packaging Authority (PyPA) (*https://oreil.ly/YRd4-*) is a working group that maintains a core set of software projects used in Python packaging. Its website tracks the list of currently active interoperability standards governing Python packaging. The PyPA also publishes the Python Packaging User Guide (*https://oreil.ly/V2UBS*).

## Conventions Used in This Book

The following typographical conventions are used in this book:

*Italic*
> Indicates new terms, URLs, email addresses, filenames, and file extensions.

`Constant width`
> Used for program listings, as well as within paragraphs to refer to program elements such as variable or function names, databases, data types, environment variables, statements, and keywords.

**`Constant width bold`**
> Shows commands or other text that should be typed literally by the user.

*`Constant width italic`*
> Shows text that should be replaced with user-supplied values or by values determined by context.

This element signifies a tip or suggestion.

 This element signifies a general note.

 This element indicates a warning or caution.

# Using Code Examples

Supplemental material (code examples, exercises, etc.) is available for download at *https://oreil.ly/hmpt-code*.

If you have a technical question or a problem using the code examples, please email *bookquestions@oreilly.com*.

This book is here to help you get your job done. In general, if example code is offered with this book, you may use it in your programs and documentation. You do not need to contact us for permission unless you're reproducing a significant portion of the code. For example, writing a program that uses several chunks of code from this book does not require permission. Selling or distributing examples from O'Reilly books does require permission. Answering a question by citing this book and quoting example code does not require permission. Incorporating a significant amount of example code from this book into your product's documentation does require permission.

We appreciate, but generally do not require, attribution. An attribution usually includes the title, author, publisher, and ISBN. For example: "*Hypermodern Python Tooling* by Claudio Jolowicz (O'Reilly). Copyright 2024 Claudio Jolowicz, 978-1-098-13958-2."

If you feel your use of code examples falls outside fair use or the permission given above, feel free to contact us at *permissions@oreilly.com*.

# O'Reilly Online Learning

**O'REILLY**®  For more than 40 years, *O'Reilly Media* has provided technology and business training, knowledge, and insight to help companies succeed.

Our unique network of experts and innovators share their knowledge and expertise through books, articles, and our online learning platform. O'Reilly's online learning platform gives you on-demand access to live training courses, in-depth learning paths, interactive coding environments, and a vast collection of text and video from O'Reilly and 200+ other publishers. For more information, visit *https://oreilly.com*.

# How to Contact Us

Please address comments and questions concerning this book to the publisher:

> O'Reilly Media, Inc.
> 1005 Gravenstein Highway North
> Sebastopol, CA 95472
> 800-889-8969 (in the United States or Canada)
> 707-827-7019 (international or local)
> 707-829-0104 (fax)
> *support@oreilly.com*
> *https://oreilly.com/about/contact.html*

We have a web page for this book, where we list errata, examples, and any additional information. You can access this page at *https://oreil.ly/hypermodern-python-tooling*.

For news and information about our books and courses, visit *https://oreilly.com*.

Find us on LinkedIn: *https://linkedin.com/company/oreilly-media*

Watch us on YouTube: *https://youtube.com/oreillymedia*

# Acknowledgments

This book covers many open source Python projects. I am very grateful to their authors and maintainers, most of whom work on them in their free time, often over many years. In particular, I would like to acknowledge the unsung heroes of the PyPA, whose work on packaging standards lets the ecosystem evolve toward better tooling. Special thanks to Thea Flowers for writing Nox and building a welcoming community.

Before this book, there was the Hypermodern Python article series. I would like to thank Brian Okken, Michael Kennedy, and Paul Everitt for spreading the word, and Brian for giving me the courage to turn it into a book.

For their deep insights and opinionated feedback, I am indebted to my reviewers Pat Viafore, Jürgen Gmach, Hynek Schlawack, William Jamir Silva, Ganesh Hark, and Karandeep Johar. This book wouldn't be the same without them. I take responsibility for any errors that remain.

Making a book takes a village. I would like to thank my editors Zan McQuade, Brian Guerin, Sarah Grey, Greg Hyman, and Emily Wydeven, as well as all the team at O'Reilly. My special thanks go out to Sarah for keeping me on track and improving my writing during this journey. For giving me time to work on this book, I thank Jakub Borys, my manager at Cloudflare. Thank you, Gabriela Jolowicz, for creating such beautiful and compelling chapter vignettes featuring past visions of the future.

This book is dedicated to Marianna, the love of my life. Without her support, encouragement, and inspiration, I couldn't have written this book.

# Working with Python

# CHAPTER 1

# Installing Python

If you've picked up this book, you likely have Python installed on your machine already. Most common operating systems ship with a python3 command. This can be the interpreter used by the system itself; on Windows and macOS, it's a placeholder that installs Python for you when you invoke it for the first time.

Why dedicate an entire chapter to the topic if it's so easy to get Python onto a new machine? The answer is that installing Python for long-term development can be a complex matter, and there are several reasons for this:

- You generally need multiple versions of Python installed side by side. (If you're wondering why, we'll get to that shortly.)

- There are a few different ways to install Python across the common platforms, each with unique advantages, tradeoffs, and sometimes pitfalls.

- Python is a moving target: you need to keep existing installations up-to-date with the latest maintenance release, add installations when a new feature version is published, and remove versions that are no longer supported. You may even need to test a prerelease of the next Python.

- You may want your code to run on multiple platforms. While Python makes it easy to write portable programs, setting up a developer environment requires some familiarity with the idiosyncrasies of each platform.

- You may want to run your code with an alternative implementation of Python.[1]

In this first chapter, I'll show you how to install multiple Python versions on some of the major operating systems in a sustainable way—and how to keep your little snake farm in good shape.

---

1 While CPython is the reference implementation of Python, there are quite a few more to choose from: performance-oriented forks such as PyPy and Cinder, reimplementations such as RustPython and Micro-Python, and ports to other platforms like WebAssembly, Java, and .NET.

Even if you develop for only a single platform, I'd encourage you to learn about working with Python on other operating systems. It's fun—and familiarity with other platforms enables you to provide a better experience to your software's contributors and users.

# Supporting Multiple Versions of Python

Python programs often target several versions of the language and standard library at once. This may come as a surprise. Why would you run your code with anything but the latest Python? After all, this lets your programs benefit from new language features and library improvements immediately.

As it turns out, runtime environments often come with a variety of older versions of Python.[2] Even if you have tight control over your deployment environments, you may want to get into the habit of testing against multiple versions. The day the trusty Python in your production environment features in a security advisory had better not be the day you start porting your code to newer releases.

For these reasons, it's common to support both current and past versions of Python until their official end-of-life date and to set up installations for them side by side on a developer machine. With new feature versions coming out every year and support extending over five years, this gives you a testing matrix of five actively supported versions (see Figure 1-1). If that sounds like a lot of work, don't worry: the Python ecosystem comes with tooling that makes this a breeze.

---

## The Python Release Cycle

Python has an annual release cycle: feature releases happen every October. Each feature release gets a new minor version in Python's `major.minor.micro` scheme. By contrast, new major versions are rare and reserved for strongly incompatible changes—as I write this in early 2024, a Python 4 is not in sight. Python's backward compatibility policy allows incompatible changes in minor releases when preceded by a two-year deprecation period.

Feature versions are maintained for five years, after which they reach end-of-life. Bugfix releases for a feature version occur roughly every other month during the first 18 months after its initial release.[3] This is followed by security updates whenever necessary during the remainder of the five-year support period. Each maintenance release bumps the micro version.

---

2 At the time of writing in early 2024, the long-term support release of Debian Linux ships patched versions of Python 2.7.16 and 3.7.3—both released half a decade ago. (Debian's "testing" distribution, which is widely used for development, comes with a current version of Python.)

3 Starting with Python 3.13, bugfix releases are provided for two years after the initial release.

Prereleases for upcoming Python feature releases happen throughout the year before their publication. These prereleases fall into three consecutive phases: alphas, betas, and release candidates. You can recognize them by the suffix that gets appended to the upcoming Python version, indicating the release status and sequence number, such as a1, b3, rc2.

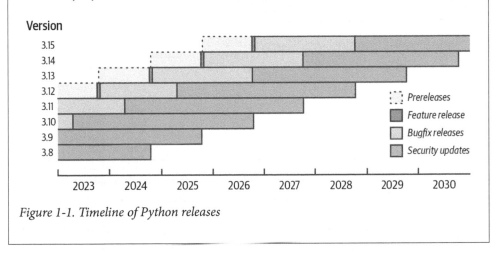

Figure 1-1. Timeline of Python releases

# Locating Python Interpreters

How do you select the correct Python interpreter if you have multiple ones on your system? Let's look at a concrete example. When you type python3 at the command line, the shell searches the directories in the PATH environment variable from left to right and invokes the first executable file named python3. Python installations on macOS and Linux also provide commands named python3.12, python3.11, and so on, to let you disambiguate between the different feature versions.

 On Windows, PATH-based interpreter discovery is less relevant because Python installations can be located via the Windows Registry (see "The Python Launcher for Windows" on page 10). Windows installers ship only an unversioned python.exe executable.

Figure 1-2 shows a macOS machine with several Python installations. Starting from the bottom, the first interpreter is located in */usr/bin/python3* and is part of Apple's Command Line Tools (Python 3.9 at time of writing). Next up, in */opt/homebrew/bin*, are several interpreters from the Homebrew distribution; the python3 command here is its main interpreter (Python 3.11). The Homebrew interpreters are followed by a prerelease from *python.org* (Python 3.13). The top entry contains the current release (Python 3.12 as of this writing), also from Homebrew.

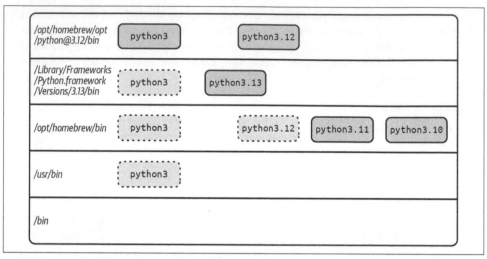

*Figure 1-2. A developer system with multiple Python installations. The search path is displayed as a stack of directories; commands at the top shadow those further down.*

The order of directories on the search path matters because earlier entries take precedence over, or "shadow," later ones. In Figure 1-2, `python3` refers to the current stable version (Python 3.12). If you omitted the top entry, `python3` would refer to the prerelease (Python 3.13). Without the top two entries, it would refer to Homebrew's default interpreter, which is still on the previous stable version (Python 3.11).

Locating Python interpreters on `PATH` is a common source of errors. Some installations overwrite the `python3` command in shared directories such as */usr/local/bin*. Others place `python3` in a distinct directory and alter the `PATH` to give it precedence, shadowing previously installed versions. To address these issues, this book uses the Python Launcher for Unix (see "The Python Launcher for Unix" on page 18). Nonetheless, understanding the `PATH` variable's mechanics will help you avoid issues with Python discovery on Windows, macOS, and Linux.

A common default for the `PATH` variable is `/usr/local/bin:/usr/bin:/bin` on Unix-like systems, usually combined with some OS-dependent locations. You can modify the variable using the `export` built-in of many shells. Here's how you would add a Python installation in */usr/local/opt/python* using the Bash shell:

```
export PATH="/usr/local/opt/python/bin:$PATH"
```

You're adding the *bin* subdirectory instead of the installation root because that's where the interpreter is normally located on these systems. We'll take a closer look at the layout of Python installations in Chapter 2. Also, you're adding the directory to the front of the `PATH` variable. I'll explain shortly why this is usually what you want.

The previous line also works with Zsh, which is the default shell on macOS. That said, there's a more idiomatic way to manipulate the search path on Zsh:

```
typeset -U path ❶
path=(/usr/local/opt/python/bin $path) ❷
```

❶ This instructs the shell to remove duplicate entries from the search path.

❷ The shell keeps the `path` array synchronized with the PATH variable.

The fish shell offers a function to uniquely and persistently prepend an entry to the search path:

```
fish_add_path /usr/local/opt/python/bin
```

It would be tedious to set up the search path manually at the start of every shell session. Instead, you can place the commands above in your *shell profile*—a file in your home directory that is read by the shell on startup. Table 1-1 shows the most common ones.

*Table 1-1. The startup files of some common shells*

| Shell | Startup file |
| --- | --- |
| Bash | *.bash_profile* (Debian and Ubuntu: *.profile*) |
| Zsh | *.zshrc* |
| fish | *.config/fish/fish.config* |

Why is it important to add new directories to the front of the PATH variable? On a pristine macOS or Linux installation, the `python3` command often points to an old version of Python. As a Python developer, your default interpreter should be the latest stable release of Python. Prepending to PATH lets you control which Python installation your shell chooses when faced with an ambiguous command like `python3`. You can guarantee that `python3` points to the latest stable release of Python and that each `python3.x` points to the latest bugfix or security release of the 3.x line.

 Unless your system already comes with a well-curated and up-to-date selection of interpreters, prepend Python installations to the PATH environment variable, with the latest stable version at the very front.

# Installing Python on Windows

The core Python team provides official binary installers in the Downloads for Windows section (*https://oreil.ly/yu-cN*) of the Python website. Locate the latest release of each Python version you wish to support, and download the 64-bit Windows installer for each.

 Depending on your domain and target environment, you may prefer to use the Windows Subsystem for Linux (WSL) for Python development. In this case, please refer to the section "Installing Python on Linux" on page 15 instead.

In general, there should be little need to customize the installation—with one exception: when installing the latest stable release (and only then), enable the option to add Python to your PATH environment variable on the first page of the installer dialog. This ensures that your default python command uses a well-known and up-to-date Python version.

The *python.org* installers are an efficient way to set up multiversion Python environments on Windows, for these reasons:

- They register each Python installation with the Windows Registry, making it easy for developer tools to discover interpreters on the system (see "The Python Launcher for Windows" on page 10).

- They don't have some of the disadvantages of redistributed versions of Python, such as lagging behind the official release or being subject to downstream modifications.

- They don't require you to build the Python interpreter, which—apart from taking precious time—involves setting up Python's build dependencies on your system.

Binary installers are provided only up to the last bugfix release of each Python version, which occurs around 18 months after the initial release. Security updates for older versions, on the other hand, are provided as source distributions only. If you don't want to build Python from source,[4] you can use one of the excellent Python Standalone Builds (*https://oreil.ly/xKU34*), a collection of self-contained, highly portable Python distributions.

Keeping Python installations up-to-date falls on your shoulders when you're using the binary installers from *python.org*. New releases are announced in many places, including the Python blog (*https://oreil.ly/IkLRO*) and the Python Discourse (*https://oreil.ly/BlYyt*). When you install a bugfix release for a Python version that is already present on the system, it will replace the existing installation. This preserves projects and developer tools on the upgraded Python version and should be a seamless experience.

When you install a new feature release of Python, be mindful of the following additional steps:

- Enable the option to add the new Python to the PATH environment variable.
- Remove the previous Python release from PATH. You can edit the environment variables for your account using the *System Settings* tool that is part of Windows.
- You may also wish to reinstall some of your developer tooling, to ensure that it runs on the latest Python version.

Eventually, a Python version will reach its end-of-life, and you may wish to uninstall it to free up resources. You can remove an existing installation using the *Installed Apps* tool. Choose the *Uninstall* action for its entry in the list of installed software. Beware that removing a Python version will break projects and tools that are still using it, so you should upgrade those to a newer Python beforehand.

---

### Microsoft Store Python

Windows systems ship with a python stub that redirects the user to the latest Python package on the Microsoft Store. The Microsoft Store package is intended mainly for educational purposes and does not have full write access to some shared locations on the filesystem and registry. While it's useful for teaching Python to beginners, I would not recommend it for most intermediate and advanced Python development.

---

4 Stack Overflow (*https://oreil.ly/m24jn*) has a good step-by-step guide to building Windows installers.

# The Python Launcher for Windows

Python development on Windows is special in that tooling can locate Python installations via the Windows Registry. The Python Launcher for Windows leverages this to provide a single entry point to interpreters on the system. It is a utility included with every *python.org* release and associated with Python file extensions, allowing you to launch scripts from the Windows File Explorer.

Running applications with a double-click is handy, but the Python Launcher is at its most powerful when you invoke it from a command-line prompt. Open a PowerShell window and run the py command to start an interactive session:

```
> py
Python 3.12.2 (tags/v3.12.2:6abddd9, Feb  6 2024, 21:26:36) [...] on win32
Type "help", "copyright", "credits" or "license" for more information.
>>>
```

By default, the Python Launcher selects the most recent version of Python installed on the system. It's worth noting that this may not be the same as the *most recently installed* version on the system. This is good—you don't want your default Python to change when you install a bugfix release for an older version.

If you want to launch a specific version of the interpreter, you can pass the feature version as a command-line option:

```
> py -3.11
Python 3.11.8 (tags/v3.11.8:db85d51, Feb  6 2024, 22:03:32) [...] on win32
Type "help", "copyright", "credits" or "license" for more information.
>>>
```

Any remaining arguments to py are forwarded to the selected interpreter. Let's see how you would display the versions of two interpreters on the system:

```
> py -V
Python 3.12.2

> py -3.11 -V
Python 3.11.8
```

Using the same mechanism, you can run a script on a specific interpreter:

```
> py -3.11 path\to\script.py
```

For historical reasons, py also inspects the first line of the script to see if a version is specified there. The canonical form is `#!/usr/bin/env python3`, which corresponds to py -3 and works across all major platforms.

As you have seen, the Python Launcher defaults to the newest version on the system. There is an exception to this rule: if a *virtual environment* is active, py defaults to the interpreter in the virtual environment.[5]

When you install a prerelease of Python, the Python Launcher will use it as the default interpreter instead of the current release—after all, it's the newest version on the system. In this case, you should override the default by setting the PY_PYTHON and PY_PYTHON3 environment variables to the current release:

```
> setx PY_PYTHON 3.12
> setx PY_PYTHON3 3.12
```

Restart the console for the setting to take effect. Don't forget to remove these variables once you upgrade from the prerelease to the final release.

To conclude our short tour of the Python Launcher, use the command py --list to enumerate the interpreters on your system:

```
> py --list
 -V:3.13          Python 3.13 (64-bit)
 -V:3.12 *        Python 3.12 (64-bit)
 -V:3.11          Python 3.11 (64-bit)
 -V:3.10          Python 3.10 (64-bit)
 -V:3.9           Python 3.9 (64-bit)
 -V:3.8           Python 3.8 (64-bit)
```

In this listing, the asterisk marks the default version of Python.

 Even if you always use the Python Launcher yourself, you should still keep your PATH up-to-date. Some third-party tools run the python.exe command directly—you don't want them to use an outdated Python version or fall back to the Microsoft Store shim.

# Installing Python on macOS

You can install Python on macOS in several ways. In this section, I'll take a look at the Homebrew package manager and the official *python.org* installers. Both provide multiversion binary distributions of Python. Some installation methods that are common on Linux—such as pyenv—also work on macOS. The Conda package manager even supports Windows, macOS, and Linux. I'll talk about them in later sections.

---

5 "Virtual Environments" on page 34 covers virtual environments in detail. For now, you can think of a virtual environment as a shallow copy of a full Python installation that lets you install a separate set of third-party packages.

## Homebrew Python

Homebrew is a third-party package manager for macOS and Linux. It provides an *overlay distribution*, an open source software collection that you install on top of the existing operating system. Installing the package manager is straightforward; refer to the official website (*https://brew.sh*) for instructions.

Homebrew distributes packages for every maintained feature version of Python. Use the `brew` command-line interface to manage them:

`brew install python@3.x`
> Install a new Python version.

`brew upgrade python@3.x`
> Upgrade a Python version to a maintenance release.

`brew uninstall python@3.x`
> Uninstall a Python version.

> Whenever you see names like `python3.x` or `python@3.x` in this section, replace `3.x` with the actual feature version. For example, use `python3.12` and `python@3.12` for Python 3.12.

You may find that you already have some Python versions installed for other Homebrew packages that depend on them. Nonetheless, it's important that you install every version explicitly. Automatically installed packages may get deleted when you run `brew autoremove` to clean up resources.

Homebrew places a `python3.x` command for each version on your `PATH`, as well as a `python3` command for its main Python package—which may be either the current or the previous stable release. You should override this to ensure `python3` points to the latest version. First, query the package manager for the installation root (which is platform-dependent):

```
$ brew --prefix python@3.12
/opt/homebrew/opt/python@3.12
```

Next, prepend the *bin* directory from this installation to your PATH. Here's an example that works on the Bash shell:

```
export PATH="/opt/homebrew/opt/python@3.12/bin:$PATH"
```

Homebrew has some advantages over the official *python.org* installers:

- You can use the command line to install, upgrade, and uninstall Python versions.
- Homebrew includes security releases for older versions—by contrast, *python.org* installers are provided up to the last bugfix release only.
- Homebrew Python is tightly integrated with the rest of the distribution. In particular, the package manager can satisfy Python dependencies like OpenSSL. This gives you the option to upgrade them independently when needed.

On the other hand, Homebrew Python also comes with some limitations:

- Homebrew doesn't package prereleases of upcoming Python versions.
- Packages generally lag a few days or weeks behind official releases. They also contain some downstream modifications, although these are quite reasonable. For example, Homebrew separates modules related to graphical user interfaces (GUI) from the main Python package.
- You can't install and uninstall Python packages system-wide unless they're also available as Homebrew packages. (See "Virtual Environments" on page 34 for why you shouldn't install packages system-wide for development anyway.)
- Homebrew upgrades Python to maintenance releases automatically and in a way that can break virtual environments installed on the previous version.[6]

 Personally, I recommend Hatch or Rye over Homebrew for managing Python on macOS (see "A Brave New World: Installing with Hatch and Rye" on page 22). Use the *python.org* installers to test your code against prereleases.

## The python.org Installers

The core Python team provides official binary installers in the downloads for macOS section of the Python website (*https://oreil.ly/jvZw0*). Download the 64-bit *universal2*

---

6 Justin Mayer, "Homebrew Python Is Not For You" (*https://oreil.ly/sYkpi*), February 3, 2021.

installer for the release you wish to install. The *universal2* binaries of the interpreter run natively on both Apple silicon and Intel chips.[7]

For multiversion development, I recommend a custom install—look for the *Customize* button in the installer dialog. In the resulting list of installable components, disable the *Unix command-line tools* and the *Shell profile updater*. Both options are designed to put the interpreter and some other commands on your PATH.[8] Instead, edit your shell profile manually. Prepend the directory */Library/Frameworks/Python.framework/Versions/3.x/bin* to PATH, replacing *3.x* with the actual feature version. Make sure the current stable release stays at the front of PATH.

 After installing a Python version, run the *Install Certificates* command located in the */Applications/Python 3.x/* folder. This command installs Mozilla's curated collection of root certificates, which are required to establish secure internet connections from Python.

When you install a bugfix release for a Python version that is already present on the system, it will replace the existing installation. You can uninstall a Python version by removing these two directories:

- */Library/Frameworks/Python.framework/Versions/3.x/*
- */Applications/Python 3.x/*

---

## Framework Builds on macOS

Most Python installations on Mac are so-called *framework builds*—a macOS concept for a "versioned bundle of shared resources." You may have come across bundles before in the form of apps in the *Applications* folder. A *bundle* is just a directory with a standard layout, keeping all the files in one place.

Frameworks contain multiple versions side by side in directories named *Versions/3.x*. One of these is designated as the current version using a *Versions/Current* symbolic link (symlink). Under each version in a Python Framework, you can find a conventional Python installation layout with `bin` and `lib` directories.

---

7 Do you have a Mac with Apple silicon, but programs that must run on Intel processors? You'll be pleased to know that the *python.org* installers also provide a `python3-intel64` binary using the x86_64 instruction set. You can run it on Apple silicon thanks to Apple's Rosetta translation environment.

8 The *Unix command-line tools* option places symbolic links in the */usr/local/bin* directory, which can conflict with Homebrew packages and other versions from *python.org*. A *symbolic link* (symlink) is a special kind of file that points to another file, much like a shortcut in Windows.

# Installing Python on Linux

The core Python team does not provide binary installers for Linux. Generally, the preferred way to install software on Linux distributions is using the official package manager. However, this isn't unequivocally true when installing Python for development—here are some important caveats:

- The system Python in a Linux distribution may be quite old, and not all distributions include alternate Python versions in their main package repositories.
- Linux distributions have mandatory rules about how applications and libraries may be packaged. For example, Debian's Python Policy mandates that the standard `ensurepip` module must be shipped in a separate package; as a result, you can't create virtual environments on a default Debian system (a situation commonly fixed by installing the `python3-full` package).
- The main Python package in a Linux distribution serves as the foundation for other packages that require a Python interpreter. These packages may include critical parts of the system, such as Fedora's package manager DNF. Distributions, therefore, apply safeguards to protect the integrity of the system; for example, most distributions prevent you from installing or uninstalling packages system-wide using pip.

In the next sections, I'll take a look at installing Python on two major Linux distributions, Fedora and Ubuntu. Afterward, I'll cover some generic installation methods that don't use the official package manager: Homebrew, Nix, pyenv, and Conda. I'll also introduce you to the Python Launcher for Unix, a third-party package that aims to bring the py utility to Linux, macOS, and similar systems.

## Fedora Linux

Fedora is an open source Linux distribution sponsored primarily by Red Hat and is the upstream source for Red Hat Enterprise Linux (RHEL). It aims to stay close to upstream projects and uses a rapid release cycle to foster innovation. Fedora is renowned for its excellent Python support, with Red Hat employing several Python core developers.

Python comes pre-installed on Fedora, and you can install additional Python versions using DNF:

```
sudo dnf install python3.x
```
Install a new Python version.

```
sudo dnf upgrade python3.x
```
Upgrade a Python version to a maintenance release.

```
sudo dnf remove python3.x
```
Uninstall a Python version.

Fedora has packages for all active feature versions and prereleases of CPython, the reference implementation of Python, as well as packages with alternative implementations like PyPy. A convenient shorthand to install all of these at once is to install the tox package:

```
$ sudo dnf install tox
```

In case you're wondering, tox is a test automation tool that makes it easy to run a test suite against multiple versions of Python; its Fedora package pulls in most available interpreters as recommended dependencies. Tox is also the spiritual ancestor of Nox, the subject of Chapter 8.

## Ubuntu Linux

Ubuntu is a popular Linux distribution based on Debian and funded by Canonical Ltd. Ubuntu ships only a single version of Python in its main repositories; other versions of Python, including prereleases, are provided by a *Personal Package Archive* (PPA). A PPA is a community-maintained software repository on Launchpad, the software collaboration platform run by Canonical.

Your first step on an Ubuntu system should be to add the deadsnakes PPA:

```
$ sudo apt update && sudo apt install software-properties-common
$ sudo add-apt-repository ppa:deadsnakes/ppa && sudo apt update
```

You can now install Python versions using the APT package manager:

```
sudo apt install python3.x-full
```
Install a new Python version.

```
sudo apt upgrade python3.x-full
```
Upgrade a Python version to a maintenance release.

```
sudo apt remove python3.x-full
```
Uninstall a Python version.

 Always remember to include the -full suffix when installing Python on Debian and Ubuntu. The python3.x-full packages pull in the entire standard library and up-to-date root certificates. In particular, they ensure that you can create virtual environments.

## Other Linux Distributions

What do you do if your Linux distribution doesn't package multiple versions of Python? The traditional answer is "roll your own Python." This may seem scary, but we'll see how straightforward building Python has become these days in "Installing Python with pyenv" on page 19. However, it turns out that building from source is not your only option. Several cross-platform package managers provide binary packages of Python; in fact, you've already seen one of them.

The Homebrew distribution (see "Homebrew Python" on page 12) is available on Linux and macOS, and most of what I said above applies to Linux as well. The main difference between both platforms is the installation root: Homebrew on Linux installs packages under *$/home/linuxbrew/.linuxbrew$* by default instead of *$/opt/homebrew$*. Keep this in mind when adding Homebrew's Python installations to your PATH.

A popular cross-platform way to install Python is the Anaconda distribution, which is targeted at scientific computing and supports Windows, macOS, and Linux. I'll cover Anaconda in a separate section at the end of this chapter (see "Installing Python from Anaconda" on page 21).

---

### The Nix Package Manager

Another fascinating option for both macOS and Linux is Nix (*https://nixos.org*), a purely functional package manager with reproducible builds of thousands of software packages. Nix makes it fast and easy to set up isolated environments with arbitrary versions of software packages. Here's how you would set up a development environment with two Python versions:

```
$ nix-shell --packages python312 python311
[nix-shell]$ python3 -V
Python 3.12.1
[nix-shell]$ python3.11 -V
Python 3.11.7
[nix-shell]$ exit
```

Before dropping you into the environment, Nix transparently downloads prebuilt Python binaries from the Nix Packages collection and adds them to your PATH. Each package gets a unique subdirectory on the local filesystem, using a cryptographic hash that captures all its dependencies.

You can install the Nix package manager using its official installer (*https://oreil.ly/ 9jPdt*). If you're not ready to install Nix permanently, you can get a taste of what's possible using the Docker image for NixOS, a Linux distribution built entirely using Nix:

```
$ docker run --rm -it nixos/nix
```

---

# The Python Launcher for Unix

The Python Launcher for Unix (*https://oreil.ly/Jxz0X*) is a port of the official py utility to Linux and macOS, as well as any other operating system supporting the Rust programming language. Its key benefit is to offer a unified, cross-platform way to launch Python, with a well-defined default when no version is specified: the newest interpreter on the system.

The py command is a convenient, portable method for launching interpreters that avoids some pitfalls of invoking Python directly (see "Locating Python Interpreters" on page 5). For this reason, I'll use it throughout this book. You can install the python-launcher package with a number of package managers, including Homebrew, DNF, and Cargo.

The Python Launcher for Unix discovers interpreters by scanning the PATH environment variable for python*x.y* commands. Otherwise, it works much like its Windows counterpart (see "The Python Launcher for Windows" on page 10). While py on its own launches the newest Python, you can also request a specific version—for example, py -3.12 is equivalent to running python3.12.

The following is an example session using the macOS system from Figure 1-2. (Python 3.13 was a prerelease at the time of writing this, so I've changed the default interpreter by setting PY_PYTHON and PY_PYTHON3 to 3.12.)

```
$ py -V
3.12.1
$ py -3.11 -V
3.11.7
$ py --list
 3.13 | /Library/Frameworks/Python.framework/Versions/3.13/bin/python3.13
 3.12 | /opt/homebrew/bin/python3.12
 3.11 | /opt/homebrew/bin/python3.11
 3.10 | /opt/homebrew/bin/python3.10
```

If a virtual environment is active, py defaults to the interpreter in that environment instead of the system-wide interpreter (see "Virtual Environments" on page 34). A special rule in the Python Launcher for Unix makes working with virtual environments more convenient: if the current directory (or one of its parents) contains a virtual environment with the standard name *.venv*, you don't need to activate it explicitly.

You can run many third-party tools by passing their import name to the -m interpreter option. Suppose you have installed pytest (a test framework) on multiple Python versions. Using py -m pytest lets you determine which interpreter should run the tool. By contrast, a bare pytest uses the command that happens to appear first on your PATH.

---

If you invoke py with a Python script but don't specify a version, py inspects the first line of the script for a *shebang*—a line specifying the interpreter for the script. Stick with the canonical form here: #!/usr/bin/env python3. *Entry-point scripts* are a more sustainable way to link a script to a specific interpreter, because package installers can generate the correct interpreter path during installation (see "Entry-point scripts" on page 32).

For compatibility with the Windows version, the Python Launcher uses only the Python version from shebangs, not the full interpreter path. As a result, you can end up with a different interpreter than if you were to invoke the script directly without py.

# Installing Python with pyenv

Pyenv is a Python version manager for macOS and Linux. It includes a build tool—also available as a stand-alone program named python-build—that downloads, builds, and installs Python versions in your home directory. Pyenv allows you to activate and deactivate these installations globally, per project directory, or per shell session.

In this section, you'll use pyenv as a build tool. If you're interested in using pyenv as a version manager, please refer to the official documentation (*https://oreil.ly/ANNeg*) for additional setup steps. I'll discuss some of the trade-offs in "Managing Python Versions with pyenv" on page 20.

The best way to install pyenv on macOS and Linux is using Homebrew:

```
$ brew install pyenv sqlite3 xz zlib tcl-tk
```

Besides pyenv itself, this command also installs the build dependencies of Python. If you use a different installation method, check the pyenv wiki (*https://oreil.ly/VFIaJ*) for platform-specific instructions on how to set up your build environment.

Display the available Python versions using the following command:

```
$ pyenv install --list
```

The list of interpreters is impressive. Not only does it cover all active feature versions of Python, but it also includes prereleases, unreleased development versions, almost every point release published over the past two decades, and a wealth of alternative implementations, such as PyPy, GraalPy, MicroPython, Jython, IronPython, and Stackless Python.

You can build and install any of these versions by passing them to `pyenv install`:

```
$ pyenv install 3.x.y
```

When using pyenv as a mere build tool, as we're doing here, you need to add each installation to `PATH` manually. You can find its location using the command `pyenv prefix 3.x.y` and append */bin* to that. Here's an example for the Bash shell:

```
export PATH="$HOME/.pyenv/versions/3.x.y/bin:$PATH"
```

Installing a maintenance release with pyenv does *not* implicitly upgrade existing virtual environments and developer tools on the same feature version, so you'll have to recreate these environments using the new release.

When you no longer need an installation, you can remove it like this:

```
$ pyenv uninstall 3.x.y
```

By default, pyenv does not enable profile-guided optimization (PGO) or link-time optimization (LTO) when building the interpreter. According to the Python Performance Benchmark Suite (*https://oreil.ly/OkzM9*), these optimizations can lead to a significant speedup for CPU-bound Python programs—between 10% and 20%. You can enable them using the `PYTHON_CONFIGURE_OPTS` environment variable:

```
$ export PYTHON_CONFIGURE_OPTS='--enable-optimizations --with-lto'
```

Unlike most macOS installers, pyenv defaults to a POSIX installation layout instead of the framework builds typical for this platform. If you are on macOS, I advise you to enable framework builds for consistency.[9] You can do so by adding the configuration option `--enable-framework` to the previous list.

---

### Managing Python Versions with pyenv

Version management in pyenv works by placing small wrapper scripts called *shims* on your `PATH`. These shims intercept invocations of the Python interpreter and other Python-related tools and delegate to the actual commands in the appropriate Python installation. This can be seen as a more powerful method of interpreter discovery than the `PATH` mechanism of the operating system, and it avoids polluting the search path with a plethora of Python installations.

Pyenv's shim-based approach to version management is convenient, but it also comes with a tradeoff in runtime and complexity: shims add to the startup time of the Python interpreter. They also put deactivated commands on `PATH`, which can interfere with other tools that perform interpreter discovery, such as `py`, `virtualenv`, `tox`, and

---

[9] For historical reasons, framework builds use a different path for the *per-user site directory*, the location where packages are installed if you invoke pip outside of a virtual environment and without administrative privileges. This different installation layout can prevent you from importing a previously installed package.

Nox. When installing packages with entry-point scripts, you need to run pyenv rehash for the scripts to become visible.

If the practical advantages of the shim mechanism convince you, you may also like asdf (*https://asdf-vm.com*), a generic version manager for multiple language runtimes; its Python plugin uses python-build internally. If you like per-directory version management but don't like shims, take a look at direnv (*https://direnv.net*), which can update your PATH whenever you enter a directory. (It can even create and activate virtual environments for you.)

# Installing Python from Anaconda

Anaconda (*https://oreil.ly/a4rH1*) is an open source software distribution for scientific computing, maintained by Anaconda Inc. Its centerpiece is Conda (*https://oreil.ly/9l9_G*), a cross-platform package manager for Windows, macOS, and Linux. Conda packages can contain software written in any language, such as C, C++, Python, R, or Fortran.

In this section, you'll use Conda to install Python. Conda does not install software packages globally on your system. Each Python installation is contained in a Conda environment and isolated from the rest of your system. A typical Conda environment is centered around the dependencies of a particular project—say, a set of libraries for machine learning or data science—of which Python is only one among many.

Before you can create Conda environments, you'll need to bootstrap a base environment containing Conda itself. There are a few ways to go about this: you can install the full Anaconda distribution, or you can use the Miniconda installer with just Conda and a few core packages. Both Anaconda and Miniconda download packages from the *defaults* channel, which may require a commercial license for enterprise use.

Miniforge is a third alternative—it is similar to Miniconda but installs packages from the community-maintained *conda-forge* channel. You can get Miniforge using its official installers from GitHub (*https://oreil.ly/5zmRC*), or you can install it from Homebrew on macOS and Linux:

```
$ brew install miniforge
```

Conda requires shell integration to update the search path and shell prompt when you activate or deactivate an environment. If you've installed Miniforge from Homebrew, update your shell profile using the conda init command with the name of your shell. For example:

```
$ conda init bash
```

By default, the shell initialization code activates the base environment automatically in every session. You may want to disable this behavior if you also use Python installations that are not managed by Conda:

```
$ conda config --set auto_activate_base false
```

The Windows installer does not activate the base environment globally. Interact with Conda using the Miniforge Prompt from the Windows Start menu.

Congratulations, you now have a working Conda installation on your system! Let's use Conda to create an environment with a specific version of Python:

```
$ conda create --name=name python=3.x
```

Before you can use this Python installation, you need to activate the environment:

```
$ conda activate name
```

Upgrading Python to a newer release is simple:

```
$ conda update python
```

This command will run in the active Conda environment. What's great about Conda is that it won't upgrade Python to a release that's not yet supported by the Python libraries in the environment.

When you're done working in the environment, deactivate it like this:

```
$ conda deactivate
```

Conda doesn't install Python system-wide; rather, every Python installation is part of an isolated Conda environment. Conda takes a holistic view of an environment: Python is but one dependency of your projects, on par with system libraries, third-party Python packages, and even software packages from other language ecosystems.

# A Brave New World: Installing with Hatch and Rye

While I was writing this book, the Python project managers Rye (*https://oreil.ly/O5R5E*) and Hatch (*https://oreil.ly/nZ3mA*) added support for installing Python interpreters on all major platforms. Both use interpreters from the Python Standalone Builds collection (*https://oreil.ly/xKU34*) and the PyPy project (*https://oreil.ly/dtg8T*).

Both Rye and Hatch are distributed as stand-alone executables—in other words, you can easily install them on a system that doesn't already have Python. Please refer to their official documentation for detailed installation instructions.

Hatch lets you install all CPython and PyPy interpreters compatible with your platform with a single command:

```
$ hatch python install all
```

This command also adds the installation directories to your PATH.[10] Re-run the command with the `--update` option to upgrade the interpreters to newer versions. Hatch organizes interpreters by feature version, so patch releases overwrite the existing installation.

Rye fetches interpreters into the *~/.rye/py* directory. Normally, this happens behind the scenes when you synchronize the dependencies of your project. But it's also available as a dedicated command:

```
$ rye fetch 3.12
$ rye fetch 3.11.8
$ rye fetch pypy@3.10
```

The second example places the interpreter in *~/.rye/py/cpython@3.11.8/bin* (Linux and macOS). You can install to another directory using the option `--target-path=<dir>`. This puts the interpreter in *<dir>* on Windows and *<dir>*/bin on Linux and macOS. Rye doesn't add the interpreter to your PATH when you're working outside of a project.

# An Overview of Installers

Figure 1-3 provides an overview of the main Python installation methods for Windows, macOS, and Linux.

Here's some case-by-case guidance on how to choose an installer:

- As a general rule, install Python stand-alone builds using Hatch.
- For scientific computing, I recommend using Conda instead.
- Get preleases from *python.org* if you're on Windows or macOS. If you're on Linux, build them from source with pyenv.
- On Fedora Linux, always use DNF.
- On Ubuntu Linux, always use the deadsnakes PPA with APT.

Choose Nix on macOS and Linux if you need a reproducible build of Python.

---

10 In a future release, Hatch will add interpreters to the Windows registry as well, letting you use them with the Python Launcher.

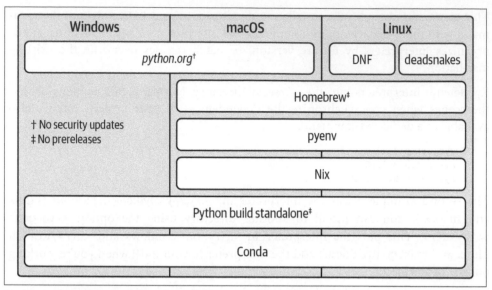

*Figure 1-3. Python installers for Windows, macOS, and Linux*

## Summary

In this chapter, you've learned how to manage Python installations on Windows, macOS, and Linux. Use the Python Launcher to select interpreters installed on your system. Additionally, audit your search path to ensure you have well-defined `python` and `python3` commands.

The next chapter zooms into a Python installation: its contents and structure, and how your code interacts with it. You'll also learn about its lightweight cousins, virtual environments, and the tooling that has evolved around those.

# CHAPTER 2

# Python Environments

At its core, every Python installation consists of two things: an interpreter and modules. The modules, in turn, come from the standard library and from third-party packages, if you've installed any. Together, these provide the essential components you need to execute a Python program: a *Python environment* (Figure 2-1).

Python installations aren't the only kind of Python environment. *Virtual environments* are stripped-down environments that share the interpreter and the standard library with a full installation. You use them to install third-party packages for a specific project or application while keeping the system-wide environment pristine.

 This book uses *Python environment* as an umbrella term that includes both system-wide installations and virtual environments. Beware that some people only use the term for project-specific environments, like virtual environments or Conda environments.

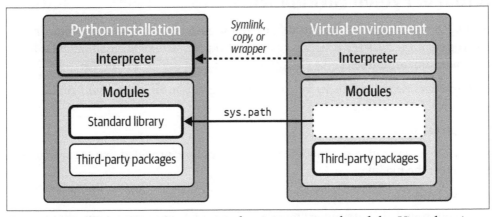

*Figure 2-1. Python environments consist of an interpreter and modules. Virtual environments share the interpreter and the standard library with their parent environment.*

Managing environments is a crucial aspect of Python development. You'll want to make sure your code works on your users' systems, particularly across the language versions you support, and possibly across major versions of an important third-party package. A Python environment can contain only a single version of each third-party package—if two projects require different versions of the same package, they can't be installed side by side. That's why it's considered good practice to install every Python application, and every project you work on, in a dedicated virtual environment.

In this chapter, you'll build a deeper understanding of what Python environments are and how they work. The chapter has three parts:

- The first part introduces the three kinds of Python environments—Python installations, the per-user environment, and virtual environments—as well as two fundamental tools: the Python package installer pip and the standard venv module.

- The second part introduces two modern tools that let you manage environments more efficiently: pipx, an installer for Python applications, and uv, a drop-in replacement for Python packaging tools written in Rust.

- The final part of this chapter dives deep into how and where Python finds the modules you import—feel free to skip it unless you're curious how this works.

 This chapter uses the Python Launcher to invoke the interpreter (see "The Python Launcher for Windows" on page 10 and "The Python Launcher for Unix" on page 18). If you don't have it installed, replace py with python3 when running the examples.

# A Tour of Python Environments

Every Python program runs "inside" a Python environment: the interpreter in the environment executes the program's code, and import statements load modules from the environment. You select the environment by launching its interpreter.

Python offers two mechanisms for running a program on an interpreter. You can pass a Python script as an argument:

```
$ py hello.py
```

Alternatively, you can pass a module with the -m option, provided that the interpreter can import the module:

```
$ py -m hello
```

Most commonly, the interpreter imports *hello.py* from the environment—but for the sake of this example, placing it in the current directory will also work.

Additionally, many Python applications install an entry-point script in your PATH (see "Entry-point scripts" on page 32). This mechanism allows you to launch the application without specifying an interpreter. Entry-point scripts always use the interpreter from the environment in which they're installed:

```
$ hello
```

This method is convenient, but there's also a drawback: if you've installed the program in multiple environments, the first environment on PATH "wins." In such a scenario, the form `py -m hello` offers you more control.

"The interpreter determines the environment." As mentioned previously, this rule applies when you import modules. It also applies in the complementary situation: when you install a package into an environment. Pip, the Python package installer, installs packages into its own environment by default. In other words, you select the target environment for a package by running pip on the interpreter in that environment.

For this reason, the canonical way to install a package with pip uses the `-m` form:

```
$ py -m pip install <package>
```

Alternatively, you can provide a virtual environment or interpreter to pip using its `--python` option:

```
$ pip --python=<env> install <package>
```

The second method has the advantage of not requiring pip in every environment.

## Python Installations

This section takes you on a tour of a Python installation. Feel free to follow along on your own system. Table 2-1 shows the most common locations—replace 3.*x* and 3*x* with the Python feature version, such as 3.12 and 312.

*Table 2-1. Locations of Python installations*

| Platform | Python installation |
| --- | --- |
| Windows (single-user) | *%LocalAppData%\Programs\Python\Python3x* |
| Windows (multi-user) | *%ProgramFiles%\Python3x* |
| macOS (Homebrew) | */opt/homebrew/Frameworks/Python.framework/Versions/3.x*[a] |
| macOS (python.org) | */Library/Frameworks/Python.framework/Versions/3.x* |
| Linux (generic) | */usr/local* |
| Linux (package manager) | */usr* |

[a] Homebrew on macOS Intel uses */usr/local* instead of */opt/homebrew*.

An installation might be cleanly separated from the rest of your system, but not necessarily. On Linux, it goes into a shared location like */usr* or */usr/local*, with its files scattered across the filesystem. Windows systems, on the other hand, keep all files in a single place. Framework builds on macOS are similarly self-contained, although distributions may also install symbolic links into the traditional Unix locations.

In the following sections, you'll take a closer look at the core parts of Python installations—the interpreter and the modules, as well as some other components such as entry-point scripts and shared libraries.

The layout of Python installations varies quite a bit from system to system. The good news is, you rarely have to care—a Python interpreter knows its environment. For reference, Table 2-2 provides a baseline for installation layouts on the major platforms. All paths are relative to the installation root.

*Table 2-2. Layout of Python installations*

| Files | Windows | Linux and macOS | Notes |
|---|---|---|---|
| Interpreter | *python.exe* | *bin/python3.x* | |
| Standard library | *Lib* and *DLLs* | *lib/python3.x* | Extension modules are located under *DLLs* on Windows. Fedora places the standard library under *lib64* instead of *lib*. |
| Third-party packages | *Lib\site-packages* | *lib/python3.x/site-packages* | Debian and Ubuntu put packages in *dist-packages*. Fedora places extension modules under *lib64* instead of *lib*. |
| Entry-point scripts | *Scripts* | *bin* | |

### The interpreter

The executable that runs Python programs is named *python.exe* on Windows and located at the root of a full installation.[1] On Linux and macOS, the interpreter is named *python3.x* and stored in the *bin* directory with a *python3* symbolic link.

The Python interpreter ties the environment to three things:

- A specific version of the Python language
- A specific implementation of Python
- A specific build of the interpreter

---

1 There's also a *pythonw.exe* executable that runs programs without a console window, like GUI applications.

The implementation might be CPython (*https://oreil.ly/7eb5R*), the reference implementation of Python, but it could also be any of a number of alternative implementations—such as PyPy (*https://oreil.ly/dtg8T*), a fast interpreter with just-in-time compilation, written in Python itself; or GraalPy (*https://oreil.ly/ctx6J*), a highly performant implementation with Java interoperability, using the GraalVM development kit.

Builds differ in their CPU architecture—for example, 32-bit versus 64-bit, or Intel versus Apple silicon—and their build configuration, which determines things like compile-time optimizations or the installation layout.

---

## Querying the Interpreter About the Python Environment

In an interactive session, import the `sys` module and inspect the following variables:

`sys.version_info`
   The version of the Python language, represented as a *named tuple* with the major, minor, and micro versions, as well as the release level and serial number for prereleases

`sys.implementation.name`
   The implementation of Python, such as `"cpython"` or `"pypy"`

`sys.implementation.version`
   The version of the implementation, same as `sys.version_info` for CPython

`sys.executable`
   The location of the Python interpreter

`sys.prefix`
   The location of the Python environment

`sys.path`
   The list of directories searched when importing Python modules

The command `py -m sysconfig` prints a great deal of metadata compiled into the Python interpreter, such as the instruction set architecture, the build configuration, and the installation layout.

---

## Python modules

Modules are containers of Python objects that you load via the `import` statement. They're organized below *Lib* (Windows) or *lib/python3.x* (Linux and macOS) with some platform-dependent variations. Third-party packages go into a subdirectory named *site-packages*.

Modules come in various forms and shapes. If you've worked with Python, you've likely used most of them already. Let's go over the different kinds:

*Simple modules*
> In the simplest case, a *module* is a single file containing Python source code. The statement `import string` executes the code in *string.py* and binds the result to the name `string` in the local scope.

*Packages*
> Directories with *\_\_init\_\_.py* files are known as *packages*—they allow you to organize modules in a hierarchy. The statement `import email.message` loads the `message` module from the `email` package.

*Namespace packages*
> Directories with modules but no *\_\_init\_\_.py* are known as *namespace packages*. You use them to organize modules in a common namespace such as a company name (say `acme.unicycle` and `acme.rocketsled`). Unlike with regular packages, you can distribute each module in a namespace package separately.

*Extension modules*
> Extension modules, such as the `math` module, contain native code compiled from low-level languages like C. They're shared libraries[2] with a special entry point that lets you import them as modules from Python. People write them for performance reasons or to make existing C libraries available as Python modules. Their names end in *.pyd* on Windows, *.dylib* on macOS, and *.so* on Linux.

*Built-in modules*
> Some modules from the standard library, such as the `sys` and `builtins` modules, are compiled into the interpreter. The variable `sys.builtin_module_names` lists all of these modules.

*Frozen modules*
> Some modules from the standard library are written in Python but have their bytecode embedded in the interpreter. Originally, only core parts of `importlib`

---

2 A *shared library* is a file with executable code that multiple programs can use at runtime. The operating system keeps only a single copy of the code in memory.

---

got this treatment. Recent versions of Python freeze every module that's imported during interpreter startup, such as os and io.

 The term *package* carries some ambiguity in the Python world. It refers both to modules and to the artifacts used for distributing modules, also known as *distributions*. Unless stated otherwise, this book uses *package* as a synonym for *distribution*.

*Bytecode* is an intermediate representation of Python code that is platform-independent and optimized for fast execution. The interpreter compiles pure Python modules to bytecode when it loads them for the first time. Bytecode modules are cached in the environment in *.pyc* files under *__pycache__* directories.

## Inspecting Modules and Packages with importlib

You can find out where a module comes from using importlib from the standard library. Every module has an associated ModuleSpec object whose origin attribute contains the location of the source file or dynamic library for the module, or a fixed string like "built-in" or "frozen". The cached attribute stores the location of the bytecode for a pure Python module. Example 2-1 shows the origin of each module in the standard library.

*Example 2-1. Listing standard library modules and their origin*

```
import importlib.util
import sys

for name in sorted(sys.stdlib_module_names):
    if spec := importlib.util.find_spec(name):
        print(f"{name:30} {spec.origin}")
```

Environments also store metadata about installed third-party packages, such as their authors, licenses, and versions. Example 2-2 shows the version of each package in the environment using importlib.metadata from the standard library.

*Example 2-2. Listing packages installed in the environment*

```
import importlib.metadata

distributions = importlib.metadata.distributions()
for distribution in sorted(distributions, key=lambda d: d.name):
    print(f"{distribution.name:30} {distribution.version}")
```

### Entry-point scripts

An *entry-point script* is an executable file in *Scripts* (Windows) or *bin* (Linux and macOS) with a single purpose: it launches a Python application by importing the module with its entry-point function and calling that function.

This mechanism has two key benefits. First, you can launch the application in a shell by running a simple command—say, pydoc3 for Python's built-in documentation browser.[3] Second, entry-point scripts use the interpreter and modules from their environment, sparing you surprises about wrong Python versions or missing third-party packages.

Package installers, like pip, can generate entry-point scripts for third-party packages they install. Package authors only need to designate the function that the script should invoke. This is a handy method to provide an executable for a Python application (see "Entry-Point Scripts" on page 78).

Platforms differ in how they let you execute entry-point scripts directly. On Linux and macOS, they're regular Python files with *execute* permission, such as the one shown in Example 2-3. Windows embeds the Python code in a binary file in the Portable Executable (PE) format—more commonly known as a *.exe* file. The binary launches the interpreter with the embedded code.

*Example 2-3. The entry-point script pydoc3 from a Linux installation*

```
#!/usr/local/bin/python3.12  ❶
import pydoc  ❷
if __name__ == "__main__":  ❸
    pydoc.cli()  ❹
```

❶  Request the interpreter from the current environment.

❷  Load the module containing the designated entry-point function.

❸  Check that the script wasn't imported from another module.

❹  Finally, call the entry-point function to start up the program.

 The #! line is known as a *shebang* on Unix-like operating systems. When you run the script, the program loader uses the line to locate and launch the interpreter. The *program loader* is the part of the operating system that loads a program into main memory.

---

3  Windows installations don't include an entry-point script for pydoc—launch it using py -m pydoc instead.

### Other components

Besides the interpreter, modules, and scripts, Python environments can include some additional components:

*Shared libraries*

Python environments sometimes contain shared libraries that aren't extension modules, named *.dll* on Windows, *.dylib* on macOS, and *.so* on Linux. Third-party packages may bundle shared libraries they use so you don't need to install them separately. Python installations may also bundle shared libraries—for example, the standard `ssl` module uses OpenSSL, an open source library for secure communication.

*Header files*

Python installations contain header files for the *Python/C API*, an application programming interface for writing extension modules or embedding Python as a component in a larger application. They're located under *Include* (Windows) or *include/python3.x* (Linux and macOS).

*Static data*

Python installations also contain static data in various locations. This includes configuration files, documentation, and any resource files shipped with third-party packages.

*Tcl/Tk*

By default, Python installations also include *Tcl/Tk*, a toolkit for creating graphical user interfaces (GUIs) written in Tcl. The standard `tkinter` module allows you to use this toolkit from Python.

## The Per-User Environment

The *per-user environment* allows you to install third-party packages for a single user. It offers two main benefits over installing packages system-wide: you don't need administrative privileges to install packages, and you don't affect other users on a multiuser system.

The per-user environment is located in the home directory on Linux and macOS and in the app data directory on Windows (see Table 2-3). It contains a *site-packages* directory for every Python version. Entry-point scripts are shared across Python versions, except on macOS, where the entire per-user installation is kept under a version-specific directory.[4]

---

4 Historically, macOS framework builds pioneered per-user installation before it became a standard in 2008.

*Table 2-3. Location of per-user directories*

| Platform | Third-party packages | Entry-point scripts |
|---|---|---|
| Windows | %AppData%\Python\Python3x\site-packages | %AppData%\Python\Scripts |
| macOS | ~/Library/Python/3.x/lib/python/site-packages | ~/Library/Python/3.x/bin |
| Linux | ~/.local/lib/python3.x/site-packages[a] | ~/.local/bin |

[a] Fedora places extension modules under *lib64*.

You install a package into the per-user environment using `py -m pip install --user <package>`. If you invoke `pip` outside a virtual environment and pip finds that it can't write to the system-wide installation, it will also default to this location. If the per-user environment doesn't exist yet, pip creates it for you.

> The per-user script directory may not be on PATH by default. If you install applications into the per-user environment, remember to edit your shell profile to update the search path. Pip issues a friendly reminder when it detects this situation.

Per-user environments have an important shortcoming: by design, they're not isolated from the global environment. You can still import system-wide site packages if they're not shadowed by per-user modules with the same name. Applications in the per-user environment also aren't isolated from each other—in particular, they can't depend on incompatible versions of another package. Even applications in the system-wide environment can import modules from the per-user environment.

And there's another drawback: you can't install packages into the per-user environment if the Python installation is marked as *externally managed*—for example, if you installed Python using the package manager of your distribution.

In "Installing Applications with pipx" on page 38, I'll introduce pipx, which lets you install applications in isolated environments. It uses the per-user script directory to put applications onto your search path but relies on virtual environments under the hood.

## Virtual Environments

When you're working on a Python project that uses third-party packages, it's usually a bad idea to install these packages into the system-wide or per-user environments. First, you're polluting a global namespace. Testing and debugging your projects gets a lot easier when you run them in isolated and reproducible environments. Second, if two projects depend on conflicting versions of the same package, a single environment isn't even an option. Third, as mentioned in the previous section, you can't install packages into environments marked as *externally managed*. This is a good thing: installing and uninstalling Python packages behind your package manager's back introduces a real chance of breaking your system.

Virtual environments were invented to solve these problems. They're isolated from the system-wide installation and from each other. Under the hood, a virtual environment is a lightweight Python environment that stores third-party packages and delegates most other things to a full installation. Packages in virtual environments are visible only to the interpreter in the environment.

You create a virtual environment with the command py -m venv <directory>. The last argument is the location where you want the environment to exist—its root directory—and conventionally named .venv.

The directory tree of a virtual environment looks much like a Python installation, except that some files are missing, most notably the entire standard library. Table 2-4 shows the standard locations within a virtual environment.

*Table 2-4. Layout of a virtual environment*

| Files | Windows | Linux and macOS |
|---|---|---|
| Interpreter | *Scripts* | *bin* |
| Entry-point scripts | *Scripts* | *bin* |
| Third-party packages | *Lib\site-packages* | *lib/python3.x/site-packages*[a] |
| Environment configuration | *pyvenv.cfg* | *pyvenv.cfg* |

[a] Fedora places third-party extension modules under *lib64* instead of *lib*.

Virtual environments have their own python command, which is located next to the entry-point scripts. On Linux and macOS, the command is a symbolic link to the interpreter you used to create the environment. On Windows, it's a small wrapper executable that launches the parent interpreter.[5]

## Installing packages

Virtual environments include pip as a means to install packages into them.[6] Let's create a virtual environment, install httpx (an HTTP client library), and launch an interactive session. On Windows, enter the following commands:

---

5 You could force the use of symbolic links on Windows via the --symlinks option—but don't. There are subtle differences in the way these work on Windows. For example, the File Explorer resolves the symbolic link before it launches Python, which prevents the interpreter from detecting the virtual environment.

6 Before Python 3.12, the venv module also pre installed setuptools for the benefit of legacy packages that don't declare it as a build dependency.

```
> py -m venv .venv
> .venv\Scripts\python -m pip install httpx
> .venv\Scripts\python
```

On Linux and macOS, enter the following commands. There's no need to spell out the path to the interpreter if the environment uses the well-known name *.venv*. The Python Launcher for Unix selects its interpreter by default:

```
$ py -m venv .venv
$ py -m pip install httpx
$ py
```

In the interactive session, use `httpx.get` to perform a GET request to a web host:

```
>>> import httpx
>>> httpx.get("https://example.com/")
<Response [200 OK]>
```

Virtual environments come with the version of pip that was current when Python was released. This can be a problem when you're working with an old Python release. Create the environment with the option `--upgrade-deps` to ensure you get the latest pip release from the Python Package Index.

You can also create a virtual environment without pip using the option `--without-pip` and install packages with an external installer. If you have pip installed globally, you can pass the target environment using its `--python` option, like this:

```
$ pip --python=.venv install httpx
```

It's easy to install a package into the Python installation or per-user environment by accident—especially if you're used to invoking `pip` directly. If your Python installation isn't marked as externally managed, you may not even notice. Fortunately, you can configure pip to always require a virtual environment when installing packages:

```
$ pip config set global.require-virtualenv true
```

### Activation scripts

Virtual environments come with *activation scripts* in the *bin* or *Scripts* directory—these scripts make it more convenient to use a virtual environment from the command line, and they're provided for a number of supported shells and command interpreters. Here's the Windows example again, this time using the activation script:

```
> py -m venv .venv
> .venv\Scripts\activate
(.venv) > py -m pip install httpx
(.venv) > py
```

Activation scripts bring three features to your shell session:

- They prepend the script directory to the PATH variable. This allows you to invoke python, pip, and entry-point scripts without prefixing them with the path to the environment.

- They set the VIRTUAL_ENV environment variable to the location of the virtual environment. Tools like the Python Launcher use this variable to detect that the environment is active.

- They update your shell prompt to provide a visual reference for which environment is active, if any. By default, the prompt uses the name of the directory where the environment is located.

 You can provide a custom prompt using the option --prompt when creating the environment. The special value . designates the current directory; it's particularly useful when you're inside a project repository.

On macOS and Linux, you need to *source* the activation script to allow it to affect your current shell session. Here's an example for Bash and similar shells:

```
$ source .venv/bin/activate
```

Environments come with activation scripts for some other shells as well. For example, if you use the fish shell, source the supplied *activate.fish* script instead.

On Windows, you can invoke the activation script directly. There's an *Activate.ps1* script for PowerShell and an *activate.bat* script for *cmd.exe*. You don't need to provide the file extension; each shell selects the script appropriate for it:

```
> .venv\Scripts\activate
```

PowerShell on Windows doesn't allow you to execute scripts by default, but you can change the execution policy to something more suited to development: the Remote Signed policy allows scripts written on the local machine or signed by a trusted publisher. On Windows servers, this policy is already the default. You only need to do this once—the setting is stored in the registry:

```
> Set-ExecutionPolicy -ExecutionPolicy RemoteSigned -Scope CurrentUser
```

Activation scripts provide you with a deactivate command to revert the changes to your shell environment. It's usually implemented as a shell function and works the same on Windows, macOS, and Linux:

```
$ deactivate
```

### A look under the hood

How does Python know to import a third-party package like httpx from the virtual environment instead of the Python installation? The location can't be hardcoded in the interpreter binary, given that virtual environments share the interpreter with the Python installation. Instead, Python looks at the location of the python command you used to launch the interpreter. If its parent directory contains a *pyvenv.cfg* file, Python treats that file as a *landmark* for a virtual environment and imports third-party modules from the *site-packages* directory beneath.

This explains how you import third-party modules from the virtual environment, but how does Python find modules from the standard library? After all, they're neither copied nor linked into the virtual environment. Again, the answer lies in the *pyvenv.cfg* file: when you create a virtual environment, the interpreter records its own location under the home key in this file. If it later finds itself in a virtual environment, it looks for the standard library relative to that home directory.

 The name *pyvenv.cfg* is a remnant of the pyvenv script that used to ship with Python. The py -m venv form makes it clearer which interpreter you use to create the virtual environment—and thus which interpreter the environment itself will use.

While the virtual environment has access to the standard library in the system-wide environment, it's isolated from its third-party modules. (Although not recommended, you can give the environment access to those modules as well, using the --system-site-packages option when creating the environment.)

How does pip know where to install packages? The short answer is that pip asks the interpreter it's running on, and the interpreter derives the location from its own path—just like when you import a module.[7] This is why it's best to run pip with an explicit interpreter using the py -m pip idiom. If you invoke pip directly, the system searches your PATH and may come up with the entry-point script from a different environment.

# Installing Applications with pipx

In "Virtual Environments" on page 34, you saw why it makes good sense to install your projects in separate virtual environments: unlike system-wide and per-user environments, virtual environments isolate your projects, avoiding dependency conflicts.

---

[7] Internally, pip queries the sysconfig module for an appropriate *installation scheme*—a Python environment layout. This module constructs the installation scheme using the build configuration of Python and the location of the interpreter in the filesystem.

The same reasoning applies when you install third-party Python applications—say, a code formatter like Black or a packaging manager like Hatch. Applications tend to depend on more packages than libraries, and they can be quite picky about the versions of their dependencies.

Unfortunately, managing and activating a separate virtual environment for every application is cumbersome and confusing—and it limits you to using only a single application at a time. Wouldn't it be great if we could confine applications to virtual environments and still have them available globally?

That's precisely what pipx (*https://oreil.ly/zlOVW*) does, and it leverages a simple idea to make it possible: it copies or symlinks the entry-point script for the application from its virtual environment into a directory on your search path. Entry-point scripts contain the full path to the environment's interpreter, so you can copy them anywhere you want, and they'll still work.

## pipx in a Nutshell

Let me show you how this works in a nutshell—the following commands are for Linux or macOS. First, you create a shared directory for the entry-point scripts of your applications and add it to your PATH environment variable:

```
$ mkdir -p ~/.local/bin
$ export PATH="$HOME/.local/bin:$PATH"
```

Next, you install an application in a dedicated virtual environment—I've chosen the Black code formatter as an example:

```
$ py -m venv black
$ black/bin/python -m pip install black
```

Finally, you copy the entry-point script into the directory you created in the first step—that would be a script named black in the *bin* directory of the environment:

```
$ cp black/bin/black ~/.local/bin
```

Now you can invoke black even though the virtual environment is not active:

```
$ black --version
black, 24.2.0 (compiled: yes)
Python (CPython) 3.12.2
```

On top of this simple idea, the pipx project has built a cross-platform package manager for Python applications with a great developer experience.

> If there's a single Python application that you should install on a development machine, pipx is probably it. It lets you install, run, and manage all the other Python applications in a way that's convenient and avoids trouble.

## Installing pipx

If your system package manager distributes pipx as a package, I recommend using that as the preferred installation method, as it's more likely to provide good integration out of the box:

```
$ apt install pipx
$ brew install pipx
$ dnf install pipx
```

As a post-installation step, update your PATH environment variable to include the shared script directory, using the ensurepath subcommand. (If you've modified your PATH variable when running the commands above, open a new terminal first.)

```
$ pipx ensurepath
```

On Windows, and if your system package manager doesn't distribute pipx, I recommend installing pipx into the per-user environment, like this:

```
$ py -m pip install --user pipx
$ py -m pipx ensurepath
```

The second step also puts the pipx command itself on your search path.

If you don't already have shell completion for pipx, activate it by following the instructions for your shell, which you can print with this command:

```
$ pipx completions
```

## Managing Applications with pipx

With pipx installed on your system, you can use it to install and manage applications from the Python Package Index (PyPI). For example, here's how you would install Black with pipx:

```
$ pipx install black
```

You can also use pipx to upgrade an application to a new release, reinstall it, or uninstall it from your system:

```
$ pipx upgrade black
$ pipx reinstall black
$ pipx uninstall black
```

As a package manager, pipx keeps track of the applications it installs and lets you perform bulk operations across all of them. This is particularly useful to keep your development tools updated to the latest version and to reinstall them on a new version of Python:

```
$ pipx upgrade-all
$ pipx reinstall-all
$ pipx uninstall-all
```

You can also list the applications you've installed previously:

```
$ pipx list
```

Some applications support plugins that extend their functionality. These plugins must be installed in the same environment as the application. For example, the packaging managers Hatch and Poetry both come with plugin systems. Here's how you would install Hatch with a plugin that determines the package version from the version control system (see "Single-Sourcing the Project Version" on page 76):

```
$ pipx install hatch
$ pipx inject hatch hatch-vcs
```

## Running Applications with pipx

The previous commands provide all the primitives to manage global developer tools efficiently, but it gets better. Most of the time, you just want to use recent versions of your developer tools. You don't want the responsibility of keeping the tools updated, reinstalling them on new Python versions, or removing them when you no longer need them. Pipx allows you to run an application directly from PyPI without an explicit installation step. Let's use the classic Cowsay app to try it:

```
$ pipx run cowsay moo
  ___
| moo |
  ===
    \
     \
       ^__^
      (oo)_____
      (__)\       )\/\
         ||----w |
         ||     ||
```

Behind the scenes, pipx installs Cowsay in a temporary virtual environment and runs it with the arguments you've provided. It keeps the environment around for a while,[8] so you don't end up reinstalling applications on every run. Use the `--no-cache` option to force pipx to create a new environment and reinstall the latest version.

You may have noticed an implicit assumption in the `run` command: that the PyPI package must have the same name as the command it provides. This may seem a reasonable expectation—but what if a Python package provides multiple commands? For example, the pip-tools package (see "Compiling Requirements with pip-tools and uv" on page 105) provides commands named `pip-compile` and `pip-sync`.

---

8 At the time of writing in 2024, pipx caches temporary environments for 14 days.

If you find yourself in this situation, provide the PyPI name using the `--spec` option, like this:

```
$ pipx run --spec pip-tools pip-sync
```

 Use `pipx run <app>` as the default method to install and run developer tools from PyPI. Use `pipx install <app>` if you need more control over application environments; for example, if you need to install plugins. (Replace `<app>` with the name of the app.)

## Configuring pipx

By default, pipx installs applications on the same Python version that it runs on itself. This may not be the latest stable version, particularly if you installed pipx using a system package manager like APT. I recommend setting the environment variable `PIPX_DEFAULT_PYTHON` to the latest stable Python if that's the case. Many developer tools you run with pipx create their own virtual environments; for example, virtualenv, Nox, tox, Poetry, and Hatch all do. It's worthwhile to ensure that all downstream environments use a recent Python version by default:

```
$ export PIPX_DEFAULT_PYTHON=python3.12 # Linux and macOS
> setx PIPX_DEFAULT_PYTHON python3.12   # Windows
```

Under the hood, pipx uses pip as a package installer. This means that any configuration you have for pip also carries over to pipx. A common use case is installing Python packages from a private index instead of PyPI, such as a company-wide package repository.

You can use `pip config` to set the URL of your preferred package index persistently:

```
$ pip config set global.index-url https://example.com
```

Alternatively, you can set the package index for the current shell session only. Most pip options are also available as environment variables:

```
$ export PIP_INDEX_URL=https://example.com
```

Both methods cause pipx to install applications from the specified index.

## Managing Environments with uv

The tool uv is a drop-in replacement for core Python packaging tools, written in the Rust programming language. It offers order-of-magnitude performance improvements over the Python tools it replaces, in a single static binary without dependencies. While its `uv venv` and `uv pip` subcommands aim for compatibility with virtualenv and pip, uv also embraces evolving best practices, such as operating in a virtual environment by default.

Install uv with pipx:

```
$ pipx install uv
```

By default, uv creates a virtual environment using the well-known name *.venv* (you can pass another location as an argument):

```
$ uv venv
```

Specify the interpreter for the virtual environment using the `--python` option with a specification like `3.12` or `python3.12`; a full path to an interpreter also works. Uv discovers available interpreters by scanning your PATH. On Windows, it also inspects the output of `py --list-paths`. If you don't specify an interpreter, uv defaults to `python3` on Linux and macOS, and `python.exe` on Windows.

 Despite its name, uv venv emulates the Python tool virtualenv, not the built-in venv module. Virtualenv creates environments with any Python interpreter on your system. It combines interpreter discovery with aggressive caching to make this fast and flawless.

By default, uv installs packages into the environment named *.venv* in the current directory or one of its parent directories (using the same logic as the Python Launcher for Unix):

```
$ uv pip install httpx
```

You can install packages into another environment by activating it—this works for both virtual environments (VIRTUAL_ENV) and Conda environments (CONDA_PREFIX). If there's neither an active environment nor a *.venv* directory, uv bails out with an error. It will never install or uninstall packages from your global environment unless you explicitly ask it to do so using the `--system` option.

While uv's initial development has focused on providing drop-in replacements for standard Python tooling, its ultimate goal is to grow into that one unified packaging tool that has eluded Python for so long—with the kind of developer experience that Rust developers love about Cargo. Even at this early stage, uv gives you a unified and streamlined workflow, thanks to a cohesive feature set with good defaults. And it's blazingly fast.

# Finding Python Modules

Python environments consist, first and foremost, of a Python interpreter and Python modules. Consequently, there are two mechanisms that play a key role in linking a Python program to an environment: interpreter discovery and module import.

*Interpreter discovery* is the process of locating the Python interpreter to execute a program. You've already seen the most important methods for locating interpreters:

- Entry-point scripts reference the interpreter in their environment directly, using a shebang or a wrapper executable (see "Entry-point scripts" on page 32).

- Shells locate the interpreter by searching directories on PATH for commands like python, python3, or python3.x (see "Locating Python Interpreters" on page 5).

- The Python Launcher locates interpreters using the Windows Registry, PATH (on Linux and macOS), and the VIRTUAL_ENV variable (see "The Python Launcher for Windows" on page 10 and "The Python Launcher for Unix" on page 18).

- When you activate a virtual environment, the activation script puts its interpreter and entry-point scripts on PATH. It also sets the VIRTUAL_ENV variable for the Python Launcher and other tools (see "Virtual Environments" on page 34).

This section takes a deep dive into the other mechanism that links programs to an environment: *module import*, which is the process of locating and loading Python modules for a program.

 In a nutshell, just like the shell searches PATH for executables, Python searches sys.path for modules. This variable holds a list of locations from where Python can load modules—most commonly, directories on the local filesystem.

The machinery behind the import statement lives in importlib from the standard library (see "Inspecting Modules and Packages with importlib" on page 31). The interpreter translates every use of the import statement into an invocation of the __import__ function from importlib. The importlib module also exposes an import_module function that allows you to import modules whose names are only known at runtime.

Having the import system in the standard library lets you inspect and customize the import mechanism from within Python. For example, the import system supports loading modules from directories and from zip archives out of the box. But entries on sys.path can be anything really—say, a URL or a database query—as long as you register a function in sys.path_hooks that knows how to find and load modules from these path entries.

## Module Objects

When you import a module, the import system returns a *module object*, an object of type types.ModuleType. Any global variable defined by the imported module

---

becomes an attribute of the module object. This allows you to access the module variable in dotted notation (`module.var`) from the importing code.

Under the hood, module variables are stored in a dictionary in the `__dict__` attribute of the module object. (This is the standard mechanism used to store attributes of any Python object.) When the import system loads a module, it creates a module object and executes the module's code using `__dict__` as the global namespace. To simplify somewhat, it invokes the built-in `exec` function like this:

```
exec(code, module.__dict__)
```

Additionally, module objects have some special attributes. For instance, the `__name__` attribute holds the fully qualified name of the module, like `email.message`. The `__spec__` module holds the *module spec*, which I'll talk about shortly. Packages also have a `__path__` attribute, which contains locations to search for submodules.

 Most commonly, the `__path__` attribute of a package contains a single entry: the directory holding its *__init__.py* file. Namespace packages, on the other hand, can be distributed across multiple directories.

## The Module Cache

When you first import a module, the import system stores the module object in the `sys.modules` dictionary, using its fully qualified name as a key. Subsequent imports return the module object directly from `sys.modules`. This mechanism brings a number of benefits:

*Performance*
> Imports are expensive because the import system loads most modules from disk. Importing a module also involves executing its code, which can further increase startup time. The `sys.modules` dictionary functions as a cache to speed things up.

*Idempotency*
> Importing modules can have side effects; for example, when executing module-level statements. Caching modules in `sys.modules` ensures that these side effects happen only once. The import system also uses locks to ensure that multiple threads can safely import the same module.

*Recursion*
> Modules can end up importing themselves recursively. A common case is *circular imports*, where module a imports module b, and b imports a. The import system supports this by adding modules to `sys.modules` *before* they're executed. When b

imports a, the import system returns the (partially initialized) module a from the sys.modules dictionary, thereby preventing an infinite loop.

## Module Specs

Conceptually, Python imports a module in two steps: *finding* and *loading*. First, given the fully qualified name of a module, the import system locates the module and produces a module spec (importlib.machinery.ModuleSpec). Second, the import system creates a module object from the module spec and executes the module's code.

The module spec is the link between those two steps. A *module spec* contains metadata about a module such as its name and location, as well as an appropriate loader for the module (Table 2-5). You can also access most of the metadata from the module spec using special attributes directly on the module object.

*Table 2-5. Attributes of module specs and module objects*

| Spec attribute | Module attribute | Description |
| --- | --- | --- |
| name | __name__ | The fully qualified name of the module |
| loader | __loader__ | A loader object that knows how to execute the module's code |
| origin | __file__ | The location of the module |
| submodule_search_locations | __path__ | Where to search for submodules, if the module is a package |
| cached | __cached__ | The location of the compiled bytecode for the module |
| parent | __package__ | The fully qualified name of the containing package |

The __file__ attribute of a module typically holds the filename of the Python module. In special cases, it's a fixed string, like "builtin" for built-in modules, or None for namespace packages (which don't have a single location).

## Finders and Loaders

The import system finds and loads modules using two kinds of objects. *Finders* (importlib.abc.MetaPathFinder) are responsible for locating modules given their fully qualified names. When successful, their find_spec method returns a module spec with a loader; otherwise, it returns None. *Loaders* (importlib.abc.Loader) are objects with an exec_module function that load and execute the module's code. The function takes a module object and uses it as a namespace when executing the module. The finder and loader can be the same object, which is then known as an *importer*.

Finders are registered in the sys.meta_path variable, and the import system tries each finder in turn. When a finder has returned a module spec with a loader, the import system creates and initializes a module object, then passes it to the loader for execution.

By default, the `sys.meta_path` variable contains three finders, which handle different kinds of modules (see "Python modules" on page 30):

- `importlib.machinery.BuiltinImporter` for built-in modules
- `importlib.machinery.FrozenImporter` for frozen modules
- `importlib.machinery.PathFinder` to search modules on `sys.path`

The `PathFinder` is the central hub of the import machinery. It's responsible for every module that's not embedded into the interpreter, and searches `sys.path` to locate it.[9] The path finder uses a second level of finder objects known as *path entry finders* (`importlib.abc.PathEntryFinder`), each of which finds modules under a specific location on `sys.path`. The standard library provides two types of path entry finders, registered under `sys.path_hooks`:

- `zipimport.zipimporter` to import modules from zip archives
- `importlib.machinery.FileFinder` to import modules from a directory

Typically, modules are stored in directories on the filesystem, so `PathFinder` delegates its work to a `FileFinder`. The latter scans the directory for the module and uses its file extension to determine the appropriate loader. There are three loaders for the different kinds of modules:

- `importlib.machinery.SourceFileLoader` for pure Python modules
- `importlib.machinery.SourcelessFileLoader` for bytecode modules
- `importlib.machinery.ExtensionFileLoader` for binary extension modules

The zip importer works similarly, except that it doesn't support extension modules because current operating systems don't allow loading dynamic libraries from a zip archive.

## The Module Path

When your program can't find a specific module or imports the wrong version of a module, it can help to look at `sys.path`, the module path. But where do the entries on `sys.path` come from in the first place? Let's unravel some of the mysteries of the module path.

---

9 For modules located within a package, the __path__ attribute of the package takes the place of `sys.path`.

When the interpreter starts up, it constructs the module path in two steps. First, it builds an initial module path using some built-in logic. Most importantly, this initial path includes the standard library. Second, the interpreter imports the `site` module from the standard library. The `site` module extends the module path to include the site packages from the current environment.

In this section, we'll take a look at how the interpreter constructs the initial module path with the standard library. The next section explains how the `site` module appends directories with site packages.

 You can find the built-in logic for constructing `sys.path` in *Modules/getpath.py* in the CPython source code. Despite appearances, this is not an ordinary module. When you build Python, its code is frozen to bytecode and embedded in the executable.

The locations on the initial module path fall into three categories, and they occur in this order:

1. The current directory or the directory containing the Python script (if any)
2. The locations in the `PYTHONPATH` environment variable (if set)
3. The locations of the standard library

Let's look at each in more detail.

### The current directory or the directory containing the script

The first item on `sys.path` can be any of the following:

- If you ran `py <script>`, the directory where the script is located
- If you ran `py -m <module>`, the current directory
- Otherwise, the empty string, which also denotes the current directory

Traditionally, this mechanism has long provided a convenient way to structure an application: just put the main entry-point script and all application modules in the same directory. During development, launch the interpreter from within that directory for interactive debugging, and your imports will still work.

Unfortunately, having the working directory on `sys.path` is quite unsafe, as an attacker (or you, mistakenly) can override the standard library by placing Python files in the victim's directory. To avoid this, starting with Python 3.11, you can use the `-P` interpreter option or the `PYTHONSAFEPATH` environment variable to omit the current directory from `sys.path`. If you invoke the interpreter with a script, this option also omits the directory where the script is located.

Installing your application into a virtual environment is a safer and more flexible approach than putting its modules in the current directory. This requires packaging the application, which is the topic of Chapter 3.

### The PYTHONPATH variable

The PYTHONPATH environment variable provides another way to add locations before the standard library on sys.path. It uses the same syntax as the PATH variable. Avoid this mechanism for the same reasons as the current working directory and use a virtual environment instead.

### The standard library

Table 2-6 shows the remaining entries on the initial module path, which are dedicated to the standard library. Locations are prefixed with the path to the installation, and may differ in details on some platforms. Notably, Fedora places the standard library under *lib64* instead of *lib*.

*Table 2-6. The standard library on sys.path*

| Windows | Linux and macOS | Description |
|---|---|---|
| *python3x.zip* | *lib/python3x.zip* | For compactness, the standard library can be installed as a zip archive. This entry is present even if the archive doesn't exist (which it normally doesn't). |
| *Lib* | *lib/python3.x* | Pure Python modules |
| *DLLs* | *lib/python3.x/lib-dynload* | Binary extension modules |

The location of the standard library is not hardcoded in the interpreter (see "Virtual Environments" on page 34). Rather, Python looks for landmark files on the path to its own executable and uses them to locate the current environment (sys.prefix) and the Python installation (sys.base_prefix). One such landmark file is *pyvenv.cfg*, which marks a virtual environment and points to its parent installation via the home key. Another landmark is *os.py*, the file containing the standard os module: Python uses *os.py* to discover the prefix outside a virtual environment and to locate the standard library itself.

## Site Packages

The interpreter constructs the initial sys.path early on during initialization using a fairly fixed process. By contrast, the remaining locations on sys.path—known as *site packages*—are highly customizable and under the responsibility of a Python module named site.

The site module adds the following path entries if they exist on the filesystem:

*User site packages*
> This directory holds third-party packages from the per-user environment. It's in a fixed location that depends on the OS (see "The Per-User Environment" on page 33). On Fedora and some other systems, there are two path entries: for pure Python modules and extension modules, respectively.

*Site packages*
> This directory holds third-party packages from the current environment, which is either a virtual environment or a system-wide installation. On Fedora and some other systems, pure Python modules and extension modules are in separate directories. Many Linux systems also separate distribution-owned site packages under */usr* from local site packages under */usr/local*.

In the general case, the site packages are in a subdirectory of the standard library named *site-packages*. If the site module finds a *pyvenv.cfg* file on the interpreter path, it uses the same relative path as in a system installation but starts from the virtual environment marked by that file. The site module also modifies sys.prefix to point to the virtual environment.

The site module provides a few hooks for customization:

*.pth files*
> Within site packages directories, any file with a *.pth* extension can list additional directories for sys.path, one directory per line. This works similarly to PYTHON PATH, except that modules in these directories will never shadow the standard library. Additionally, *.pth* files can import modules directly—the site module executes any line starting with import as Python code. Third-party packages can ship *.pth* files to configure sys.path in an environment. Some packaging tools use *.pth* files behind the scenes to implement editable installs. An *editable install* places the source directory of your project on sys.path, making code changes instantly visible inside the environment.

*The sitecustomize module*
> After setting up sys.path as described previously, the site module attempts to import the sitecustomize module, typically located in the *site-packages* directory. This provides a hook for the system administrator to run site-specific customizations when the interpreter starts up.

*The usercustomize module*
> If there is a per-user environment, the site module also attempts to import the usercustomize module, typically located in the user *site-packages* directory. You can use this module to run user-specific customizations when the interpreter starts up. Contrast this with the PYTHONSTARTUP environment variable, which

allows you to specify a Python script to run before interactive sessions, within the same namespace as the session.

If you run the `site` module as a command, it prints out your current module path as well as some information about the per-user environment:

```
$ py -m site
sys.path = [
    '/home/user',
    '/usr/local/lib/python312.zip',
    '/usr/local/lib/python3.12',
    '/usr/local/lib/python3.12/lib-dynload',
    '/home/user/.local/lib/python3.12/site-packages',
    '/usr/local/lib/python3.12/site-packages',
]
USER_BASE: '/home/user/.local' (exists)
USER_SITE: '/home/user/.local/lib/python3.12/site-packages' (exists)
ENABLE_USER_SITE: True
```

## Back to the Basics

If you've read this far, the module path may seem a little—*byzantine*?

Here's a good, solid intuition of how Python locates a module: the interpreter searches the directories on `sys.path` for the module—first the directories that contain the modules of the standard library, then the *site-packages* directory with third-party packages. An interpreter in a virtual environment uses the *site-packages* directory from that environment.

As you've seen in this section, the truth is far more complex than that simple story. But I've got good news for you: Python lets you *make* that story true. The `-P` interpreter option omits the directory containing your script from the module path (or the current directory, if you're running your program with `py -m <module>`). The `-I` interpreter option omits the per-user environment from the module path as well as any directories set with `PYTHONPATH`. Use both options when running your Python programs if you want a more predictable module path.

If you re-run the `site` module with the `-I` and `-P` options, the module path is cut down to just the standard library and site packages:

```
$ py -IPm site
sys.path = [
    '/usr/local/lib/python312.zip',
    '/usr/local/lib/python3.12',
    '/usr/local/lib/python3.12/lib-dynload',
    '/usr/local/lib/python3.12/site-packages',
]
USER_BASE: '/home/user/.local' (exists)
USER_SITE: '/home/user/.local/lib/python3.12/site-packages' (exists)
ENABLE_USER_SITE: False
```

The current directory no longer appears on the module path, and the per-user site packages are gone, too—even though the directory exists on this system.

## Summary

In this chapter, you've learned what Python environments are, where to find them, and how they look on the inside. At the core, a Python environment consists of the Python interpreter and Python modules, as well as entry-point scripts to run Python applications. Environments are tied to a specific version of the Python language.

There are three kinds of Python environments. *Python installations* are complete, stand-alone environments with an interpreter and the full standard library. *Per-user environments* are annexes to an installation where you can install modules and scripts for a single user. *Virtual environments* are lightweight environments for project-specific modules and entry-point scripts, which reference their parent environment via a *pyvenv.cfg* file. They come with an interpreter, which is typically a symbolic link or small wrapper for the parent interpreter, and with activation scripts for shell integration. You create a virtual environment using the command `py -m venv`.

Install Python applications with pipx to make them available globally while keeping them in separate virtual environments. You can install and run an application using a single command, such as `pipx run black`. Set the `PIPX_DEFAULT_PYTHON` variable to ensure pipx installs tools on the current Python release.

Uv is a blazingly fast drop-in replacement for virtualenv and pip with better defaults. Use `uv venv` to create a virtual environment, and `uv pip` to install packages into it. Both commands use the *.venv* directory by default, just like the `py` tool on Unix. The `--python` option lets you select the Python version for the environment.

In the final section of this chapter, you've learned how Python uses `sys.path` to locate modules when you import them and how the module path is constructed during interpreter startup. You've also learned how module import works under the hood, using finders and loaders as well as the module cache. Interpreter discovery and module import are the key mechanisms that link Python programs to an environment at runtime.

# PART II

# Python Projects

# CHAPTER 3
# Python Packages

In this chapter, you'll learn how to package your Python projects for distribution. A *package* is a single file containing an archive of your code along with metadata that describes it, like the project name and version.

Python folks use the word *package* for two distinct concepts. *Import packages* are modules that contain other modules. *Distribution packages* are archive files for distributing Python software—they're the subject of this chapter.

You can install a package into a Python environment using a package installer like pip. You can also upload it to a package repository for the benefit of others. The Python Software Foundation (PSF) operates a package repository known as the Python Package Index (PyPI) (*https://pypi.org*). If your package is on PyPI, anyone can install it by passing its project name to pip install.

Packaging your project makes it easy to share with others, but there's another benefit. When you install your package, it becomes a first-class citizen of a Python environment:

- The interpreter imports your modules from the environment—rather than an arbitrary directory on your filesystem, which may or may not work depending on how you invoke Python.

- Installers use the package metadata to ensure the environment matches the prerequisites of your package, such as the minimum Python version and any third-party packages it depends on.

- Installers can generate entry-point scripts that ensure your code always runs on the interpreter in the environment. Compare this to hand-written Python scripts, which may run on the wrong Python version, or without the required third-party packages, or be unable to import their own modules.

In this chapter, I'll explain how you can package your Python projects and introduce you to tools that help with packaging tasks. The chapter has three parts:

- In the first part, I'll talk about the life of a Python package. I'll also introduce an example application that you'll use throughout this book. And I'll ask: why would you want to package your code at all?

- In the second part, I'll introduce Python's package configuration file, *pyproject .toml*, and tools for working with packages: build, hatchling, and Twine. The tools pip, uv, and pipx also make a reappearance. Finally, I'll introduce Rye, a project manager that ties these packaging tools together into a unified workflow. Along the way, you'll learn about build frontends and backends, wheels and sdists, editable installs, and the *src* layout.

- In the third part, I'll look at project metadata in detail—the various fields you can specify in *pyproject.toml* to define and describe your package, and how to make efficient use of them.

## The Package Lifecycle

Figure 3-1 shows the typical lifecycle of a package.

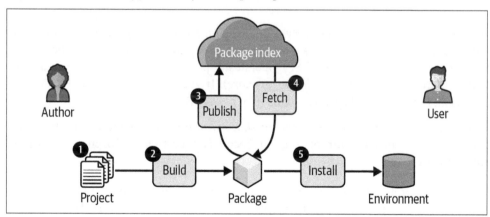

*Figure 3-1. The package lifecycle: an author builds a project into a package and uploads it to a package index, and then a user downloads and installs the package into an environment.*

❶ Everything starts with a *project*: the source code of an application, library, or other piece of software.

❷ As an author, your first step is to build a package from the project. The package is an installable artifact with a snapshot of your project at this point in time, identified by a unique name and version.

❸ Next, you publish the package to a well-known repository, such as PyPI.

❹ A user can now fetch your package by specifying its name and version.

❺ Finally, the user installs your package into their environment.

You can install a freshly built package directly into an environment without uploading it to a package repository first—for example, when you're testing your package or when you're its only user.

In real life, tools often combine fetching and installing, building and installing, and even building and publishing, into a single command.

## An Example Application

Many applications start out as small, ad-hoc scripts. Example 3-1 fetches a random article from Wikipedia and displays its title and summary in the console. The script restricts itself to the standard library, so it runs in any Python 3 environment.

*Example 3-1. Displaying an extract from a random Wikipedia article*

```
import json
import textwrap
import urllib.request

API_URL = "https://en.wikipedia.org/api/rest_v1/page/random/summary" ❶

def main():
    with urllib.request.urlopen(API_URL) as response: ❷
        data = json.load(response) ❸

    print(data["title"], end="\n\n") ❹
    print(textwrap.fill(data["extract"])) ❹

if __name__ == "__main__":
    main()
```

❶ The `API_URL` constant points to the REST API of the English Wikipedia—or more specifically, its `/page/random/summary` endpoint.

❷ The `urllib.request.urlopen` invocation sends an HTTP GET request to the Wikipedia API. The `with` statement ensures that the connection is closed at the end of the block.

❸ The response body contains the resource data in JSON format. Conveniently, the response is a file-like object, so the `json` module can load it like a file from disk.

❹ The `title` and `extract` keys hold the title of the Wikipedia page and a short plain text extract, respectively. The `textwrap.fill` function wraps the text so that every line is at most 70 characters long.

Store this script in a file called *random_wikipedia_article.py* and take it for a spin. Here's a sample run:

```
> py -m random_wikipedia_article
Jägersbleeker Teich

The Jägersbleeker Teich in the Harz Mountains of central Germany
is a storage pond near the town of Clausthal-Zellerfeld in the
county of Goslar in Lower Saxony. It is one of the Upper Harz Ponds
that were created for the mining industry.
```

# Why Packaging?

Sharing a script like Example 3-1 doesn't require packaging. You can publish it on a blog or a hosted repository, or send it to friends by email or chat. Python's ubiquity, the "batteries included" approach of its standard library, and its nature as an interpreted language make this possible.

The ease of sharing modules with the world was a boon to Python's adoption in the early days. The Python programming language predates the advent of language-specific package repositories—PyPI didn't come about for more than a decade.[1]

Distributing self-contained modules without packaging them seems like a great idea at first: you keep your projects free of packaging cruft. They require no separate artifacts, no intermediate steps like building, and no dedicated tooling. But using modules as the unit of distribution comes with limitations:

---

[1] Even the venerable Comprehensive Perl Archive Network (CPAN) didn't exist in February 1991, when Guido van Rossum published the first release of Python on Usenet.

*Projects composed of multiple modules*

When your project outgrows a single-file script, you should break it up—but installing a collection of files is cumbersome for your users. Packaging lets you keep everything in a single file for distribution.

*Projects with third-party dependencies*

Python has a rich ecosystem of third-party packages, so you're standing on the shoulders of giants. But your users shouldn't need to worry about installing the correct version of every package you require. Packaging lets you declare dependencies on other packages, which installers satisfy automatically.

*Finding the project*

What's the repository URL of that useful module again? Or was it on a blog? If you publish a package on PyPI, your users only need to know its name to install the latest version. The situation is similar in a corporate environment, where developers' machines are configured to use a company-wide package repository.

*Installing the project*

Downloading and double-clicking a script won't work much of the time. You shouldn't need to place modules in arcane directories and perform a special dance so your script executes on the correct interpreter. Packaging lets users install your project with a single command, in a portable and safe way.

*Updating the project*

Users need to determine if the project is up-to-date and upgrade it to the latest version if it isn't. As an author, you need a way to let your users benefit from new features, bug fixes, and improvements. Package repositories let you publish a stream of releases for your project (a subset of the development snapshots you'd get from its code repository).

*Running the project in the correct environment*

Don't leave it to chance whether your program runs on a supported Python version with the required third-party packages. Package installers check and, where possible, satisfy your prerequisites. They also ensure that your code runs in the environment intended for it.

*Binary extensions*

Python modules written in a compiled language like C or Rust require a build step. Packaging lets you distribute prebuilt binaries for common platforms. Additionally, it lets you publish a source archive as a fallback; installers run the build step on the end user's machine.

*Metadata*

You can embed metadata inside a module, using attributes like `__author__`, `__version__`, or `__license__`. But then tools have to execute the module to read those attributes. Packages contain static metadata that any tool can read without running Python.

As you've seen, packaging solves many problems, but what's the overhead? In short, you drop a declarative file named *pyproject.toml* into your project—a standard file that specifies the project metadata and its build system. In return, you get commands to build, publish, and install your package.

In summary, Python packages come with many advantages:

- You can easily install and upgrade them.
- You can publish them in a package repository.
- They can depend on other packages.
- They run in an environment that satisfies their requirements.
- They can contain multiple modules.
- They can contain prebuilt binary extensions.
- They can contain source distributions with automated build steps.
- They come with metadata that describes the package.

# The pyproject.toml File

Example 3-2 shows how to package the script from Example 3-1 with a bare minimum of metadata—the project name and version—as well as an entry-point script. The project and the script use hyphens (random-wikipedia-article), while the module uses underscores (random_wikipedia_article). Place the module and the *pyproject.toml* file side by side in an empty directory.

*Example 3-2. A minimal pyproject.toml file*

```
[project]
name = "random-wikipedia-article"
version = "0.1"

[project.scripts]
random-wikipedia-article = "random_wikipedia_article:main"

[build-system]
requires = ["hatchling"]
build-backend = "hatchling.build"
```

PyPI projects share a single namespace—their names aren't scoped by the users or organizations owning the projects. Choose a unique name such as `random-wikipedia-article-{your-name}`, and rename the Python module accordingly.

At the top level, the *pyproject.toml* file can contain up to three sections—or *tables*, as the TOML standard calls them:

`[project]`

    The `project` table holds the project metadata. The `name` and `version` fields are mandatory. For real projects, you should provide additional information, such as a description, the license, and the required Python version (see "Project Metadata" on page 73). The `scripts` section declares the name of the entry-point script and the function it should call.

`[build-system]`

    The `build-system` table specifies how to build packages for the project (see "Building Packages with build" on page 62)—specifically, which build tool your project uses. I've opted for `hatchling` here, which comes with Hatch (*https://oreil.ly/nZ3mA*), a modern and standards-compliant Python project manager.

`[tool]`

    The `tool` table stores configurations for each tool used by the project. For example, the Ruff linter reads its configuration from the `[tool.ruff]` table, while the type checker mypy uses `[tool.mypy]`.

---

## The TOML Format

Python's project specification file uses *TOML* (Tom's Obvious Minimal Language), a cross-language format for configuration files that's both unambiguous and human-readable. The TOML website (*https://toml.io*) has a good introduction to the format.

Lists are termed *arrays* in TOML and use the same notation as Python:

```
requires = ["hatchling", "hatch-vcs"]
```

Dictionaries are known as *tables* and come in several equivalent forms. You can put the key/value pairs on separate lines, preceded by the table name in square brackets:

```
[project]
name = "foo"
version = "0.1"
```

Inline tables contain all key/value pairs on the same line:

```
project = { name = "foo", version = "0.1" }
```

---

You can also use dotted notation to create a table implicitly:

```
project.name = "foo"
project.version = "0.1"
```

You can load a TOML file using the standard tomllib module:

```
import tomllib

with open("pyproject.toml", mode="rb") as io:  ❶
    data = tomllib.load(io)
```

❶ Always open the file in binary mode. TOML mandates UTF-8 character encoding; on older platforms, opening the file in text mode can lead to garbled text (or *mojibake*, as it's affectionately known).

Python represents a TOML file as a dictionary, where keys are strings and values can be strings, integers, floats, dates, times, lists, or dictionaries. Here's what a *pyproject.toml* file looks like in Python:

```
{
  "project": {
    "name": "random-wikipedia-article",
    "version": "0.1",
    "scripts": {
        "random-wikipedia-article": "random_wikipedia_article:main"
    }
  },
  "build-system": {
    "requires": ["hatchling"],
    "build-backend": "hatchling.build"
  }
}
```

# Building Packages with build

Let's create a package for your new project using build, a dedicated build frontend maintained by the Python Packaging Authority (PyPA). The PyPA is a group of volunteers that maintains a core set of software projects used in Python packaging.

A *build frontend* is an application that orchestrates the build process for a Python package. Build frontends don't know how to assemble packaging artifacts from source trees. The tool that does the actual building is known as the *build backend*.

Open a terminal, change to the project directory, and invoke build with pipx:

```
$ pipx run build
* Creating isolated environment: venv+pip...
* Installing packages in isolated environment:
  - hatchling
* Getting build dependencies for sdist...
* Building sdist...
* Building wheel from sdist
* Creating isolated environment: venv+pip...
* Installing packages in isolated environment:
  - hatchling
* Getting build dependencies for wheel...
* Building wheel...
Successfully built random_wikipedia_article-0.1.tar.gz
  and random_wikipedia_article-0.1-py2.py3-none-any.whl
```

By default, build creates two kinds of packages for a project, an sdist and a wheel (see "Wheels and Sdists" on page 70). You can find these files in the *dist* directory of your project.

As you can see in the previous output, build delegates the actual work to hatchling, the build backend you designated in Example 3-2. A build frontend uses the build-system table to determine the build backend for the project (Table 3-1).

Table 3-1. The build-system table

| Field | Type | Description |
|---|---|---|
| requires | Array of strings | The list of packages required to build the project |
| build-backend | String | The import name of the build backend in the format package.module:object |
| build-path | String | An entry for sys.path needed to import the build backend (optional) |

Figure 3-2 shows how the build frontend and the build backend collaborate to build a package.

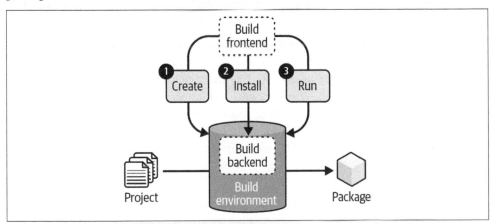

*Figure 3-2. Build frontend and build backend*

❶ The build frontend creates a virtual environment, the *build environment*.

❷ The build frontend installs the packages listed under `requires`: the build backend itself as well as, optionally, plugins for that backend. These packages are known as the *build dependencies*.

❸ The build frontend triggers the actual package build, in two steps. First, it imports the module or object declared in `build-backend`. Second, it invokes well-known functions for creating packages and related tasks, known as *build hooks*.

Here's a simplified version of the commands the build frontend performs when you build a wheel for your project:[2]

```
$ py -m venv buildenv
$ buildenv/bin/python -m pip install hatchling
$ buildenv/bin/python
>>> import hatchling.build as backend
>>> backend.get_requires_for_build_wheel()
[]  # no additional build dependencies requested
>>> backend.build_wheel("dist")
'random_wikipedia_article-0.1-py2.py3-none-any.whl'
```

Some build frontends let you build in your current environment. If you disable build isolation, the frontend only checks for build dependencies. If it installed them, the build and runtime dependencies of different packages might conflict.

Why separate the build frontend from the build backend? It means that tools can trigger package builds without knowing the intricacies of the build process. For example, package installers like pip and uv build packages on the fly when you install from a source directory (see "Installing Projects from Source" on page 66).

Standardizing the contract between build frontends and build backends has brought tremendous diversity and innovation to the packaging ecosystem. Build frontends include build, pip, and uv, the backend-agnostic Python project managers Rye, Hatch, and PDM (*https://oreil.ly/sydmt*), and test automation tools like tox (*https:// oreil.ly/EFWsN*). Build backends include those shipped with the project managers Flit (*https://oreil.ly/QSaej*), Hatch, PDM, and Poetry (*https://oreil.ly/4us6n*), the traditional build backend setuptools (*https://oreil.ly/R-eAj*), as well as exotic builders like

---

2 By default, the `build` tool builds the wheel from the sdist instead of the source tree to ensure that the sdist is valid. Build backends can request additional build dependencies using the `get_requires_for_build_wheel` and `get_requires_for_build_sdist` build hooks.

Maturin (*https://oreil.ly/i1mXW*), a build backend for Python modules written in the Rust programming language, and Sphinx Theme Builder (*https://oreil.ly/btnWl*), a build backend for Sphinx documentation themes (Table 3-2).

*Table 3-2. Build backends*

| Project | requires[a] | build-backend |
|---|---|---|
| Flit | flit-core | flit_core.buildapi |
| Hatch | hatchling | hatchling.build |
| Maturin | maturin | maturin |
| PDM | pdm-backend | pdm.backend |
| Poetry | poetry-core | poetry.core.masonry.api |
| Setuptools | setuptools | setuptools.build_meta |
| Sphinx Theme Builder | sphinx-theme-builder | sphinx_theme_builder |

[a] See the official documentation of each tool for any recommended version bounds.

# Uploading Packages with Twine

It's time to publish your package. In this section, you'll use TestPyPI (*https://test.pypi.org*), a separate instance of the Python Package Index intended for testing and experimentation. Just omit the `--repository` and `--index-url` options below to use the real PyPI.

First, register an account using the link on the front page of TestPyPI. Second, create an API token from your account page and copy the token to your preferred password manager. You can now upload the packages in *dist* using Twine, the official PyPI upload tool:

```
$ pipx run twine upload --repository=testpypi dist/*
Uploading distributions to https://test.pypi.org/legacy/
Enter your API token: *********
Uploading random_wikipedia_article-0.1-py2.py3-none-any.whl
Uploading random_wikipedia_article-0.1.tar.gz

View at:
https://test.pypi.org/project/random-wikipedia-article/0.1/
```

Congratulations, you have published your first Python package! Let's install the package from TestPyPI:

```
$ pipx install --index-url=https://test.pypi.org/simple random-wikipedia-article
  installed package random-wikipedia-article 0.1, installed using Python 3.12.2
  These apps are now globally available
    - random-wikipedia-article
done!
```

You're now able to invoke your application from anywhere:

```
$ random-wikipedia-article
```

# Installing Projects from Source

If you distribute packages for your project, it's a good idea to install these packages locally for development and testing. Running tests against an installed package rather than the source code means you're testing your project the way your users see it. And if you're working on a service, it helps keep development, staging, and production as similar as possible.

You *could* build a wheel with `build` and install it into a virtual environment:

```
$ pipx run build
$ uv venv
$ uv pip install dist/*.whl
```

There's a shortcut for this, though. Both pip and uv can install your project directly from a source directory, such as . for the current directory. Behind the scenes, they use the project's build backend to create a wheel for installation—they're build frontends just like `build`:

```
$ uv venv
$ uv pip install .
```

If your project comes with an entry-point script, you can also install it with pipx:

```
$ pipx install .
  installed package random-wikipedia-article 0.1, installed using Python 3.12.2
  These apps are now globally available
    - random-wikipedia-article
```

During development, it saves time to see code changes reflected in the environment immediately, without repeatedly installing the project. You could import your modules directly from the source tree—but you'd lose all the benefits of packaging your project.

*Editable installs* achieve the best of both worlds by installing your package in a special way that redirects imports to the source tree (see "Site Packages" on page 49). You can think of this mechanism as a kind of "hot reloading" for Python packages. The `--editable` option (`-e`) works with uv, pip, and pipx:

```
$ uv pip install --editable .
$ py -m pip install --editable .
$ pipx install --editable .
```

Once you've installed your package in this way, you won't need to reinstall it to see changes to the source code—only when you edit *pyproject.toml* to change the project metadata or add a third-party dependency.

---

Editable installs are modeled after the *development mode* feature from setuptools, if you've been around long enough to be familiar with it. But unlike `setup.py develop`, they rely on standard build hooks that any build backend can provide.

# Project Layout

Dropping a *pyproject.toml* next to a single-file module is an appealingly simple approach. Unfortunately, this project layout comes with a serious footgun, as you'll see in this section. Let's start by breaking something in the project:

```
def main():
    raise Exception("Boom!")
```

Before publishing your package, run a last smoke test with a locally built wheel:

```
$ pipx run build
$ uv venv
$ uv pip install dist/*.whl
$ py -m random_wikipedia_article
Exception: Boom!
```

A bug found is a bug fixed. After removing the offending line, verify that the program works as expected:

```
$ py -m random_wikipedia_article
Cystiscus viaderi

Cystiscus viaderi is a species of very small sea snail, a marine
gastropod mollusk or micromollusk in the family Cystiscidae.
```

All good, time to cut a release! First, push your fix and a Git tag for the new version to your code repository. Next, use Twine to upload the wheel to PyPI:

```
$ pipx run twine upload dist/*
```

But, oh no—you never rebuilt the wheel. That bug is now in a public release! How could that happen?

Running your application with `py -m` protects you from inadvertently running an entry-point script from another installation (and it has the advantage of not requiring an active environment on macOS and Linux). But it also adds the current directory to the front of `sys.path` (see "Site Packages" on page 49). All along, you've been testing the module in your source tree, not the wheel you were going to publish!

You could set the `PYTHONSAFEPATH` environment variable and never think about this again—it's an alias for `py -P` and omits the current directory from the module path. But that would leave your contributors out in the cold—and yourself, whenever you're working on another machine.

Instead, move your module out of the top-level directory so folks can't import it by mistake. By convention, Python source trees go into the *src* directory—which is why the arrangement is known as *src layout* in the Python community.

At this point, it also makes sense to convert your single-file module into an import package. Replace the *random_wikipedia_article.py* file by a *random_wikipedia_article* directory with a *__init__.py* module.

Placing your code in an import package is mostly equivalent to having it in a single-file module—but there's one difference: you can't run the application with `py -m random_wikipedia_article` unless you also add the special *__main__.py* module to the package (Example 3-3).

*Example 3-3. The __main__.py module*

```
from random_wikipedia_article import main

main()
```

The *__main__.py* module replaces the `if __name__ == "__main__"` block in *__init__.py*. Remove that block from the module.

This leaves you with a classic initial project structure:

```
random-wikipedia-article
├── pyproject.toml
└── src
    └── random_wikipedia_article
        ├── __init__.py
        └── __main__.py
```

An import package makes it easier for your project to grow: you can move code into separate modules and import it from there. For example, you could extract the code that talks to the Wikipedia API into a function `fetch`. Next, you might move the function to a module *fetch.py* in the package. Here's how you'd import the function from *__init__.py*:

```
from random_wikipedia_article.fetch import fetch
```

Eventually, *__init__.py* will contain only `import` statements for your public API.

# Managing Packages with Rye

Many modern programming languages come with a single tool for building, packaging, and other development tasks. You may wonder how the Python community ended up with so many packaging tools with disjoint responsibilities.

The answer has to do with the nature and history of the Python project: Python is a decentralized open source project driven by a community of thousands of volunteers, with a history spanning more than three decades of organic growth. This makes it hard for a single packaging tool to cater to all demands and become firmly established.[3]

Python's strength lies in its rich ecosystem—and interoperability standards promote this diversity. As a Python developer, you have a choice of small single-purpose tools that play well together. This approach ties in with the Unix philosophy of "Do one thing, and do it well."

But the Unix approach is no longer your only choice. *Python project managers* provide a more integrated workflow. Among the first, Poetry (see Chapter 5) has set itself the goal of reinventing Python packaging and pioneered ideas such as static metadata and cross-platform lock files.

Rye, a Python project manager written in Rust, chooses a different path. It provides a unified development experience on top of the widely used single-purpose tools you've already seen (and are about to see) in this book. Started by Armin Ronacher as a private project and first released to the public in 2023, it's now under the stewardship of Astral, the company behind Ruff and uv. Please see Rye's official documentation (*https://rye-up.com*) for installation instructions.

Your first step with Rye is initializing a new project with `rye init`. If you don't pass the project name, Rye uses the name of the current directory. Use the `--script` option to include an entry-point script:

```
$ rye init random-wikipedia-article --script
```

Rye initializes a Git repository in *random-wikipedia-article* and populates it with a *pyproject.toml* file, an import package `random_wikipedia_article` in the *src* directory, a *README.md* with the project description, a *.python-version* file with the default Python version, and a virtual environment in *.venv*. Rye supports various build backends, with `hatchling` as the default choice:

```
random-wikipedia-article
├── .git
├── .gitignore
├── .python-version
├── .venv
├── README.md
├── pyproject.toml
└── src
```

---

3 Python's packaging ecosystem is also a great demonstration of *Conway's law*. In 1967, Melvin Conway—an American computer scientist also known for developing the concept of coroutines—observed that organizations will design systems that are copies of their communication structure.

```
└── random_wikipedia_article
    ├── __init__.py
    └── __main__.py
```

Many of Rye's commands are frontends to tools that have become a de facto standard in the Python world—or that promise to become one in the future. The command `rye build` creates packages with `build`, the command `rye publish` uploads them using Twine, and the command `rye sync` performs an editable install using uv:

```
$ rye build
$ rye publish -r testpypi --repository-url https://test.pypi.org/legacy/
$ rye sync
```

There's much more to `rye sync`, though. Rye manages private Python installations using the Python Standalone Builds project (see "A Brave New World: Installing with Hatch and Rye" on page 22), and `rye sync` fetches each Python version on first use. The command also generates a lock file for the project dependencies and synchronizes the environment with that file (see Chapter 4).

# Wheels and Sdists

In "Building Packages with build" on page 62, `build` created two packages for your project:

- *random_wikipedia_article-0.1.tar.gz*
- *random_wikipedia_article-0.1-py2.py3-none-any.whl*

These artifacts are known as *wheels* and *sdists*. Wheels are ZIP archives with a *.whl* extension, and they're *built distributions*—for the most part, installers extract them into the environment as-is. Sdists, by contrast, are *source distributions*: they're compressed archives of the source code with packaging metadata. Sdists require an additional build step to produce an installable wheel.

 The name "wheel" for a Python package is a reference to wheels of cheese. PyPI was originally known as the *Cheese Shop*, after the Monty Python sketch about a cheese shop with no cheese whatsoever. (These days, PyPI serves over a petabyte of packages per day.)

The distinction between source distributions and built distributions may seem strange for an interpreted language like Python. But you can also write Python modules in a compiled language. In this situation, source distributions provide a useful fallback when no prebuilt wheels are available for a platform.

As a package author, you should build and publish both sdists and wheels for your releases. This gives users a choice: they can fetch and install the wheel if their environment is compatible (which is always the case for a pure Python package)—or they can fetch the sdist and build a wheel from it locally (see Figure 3-3).

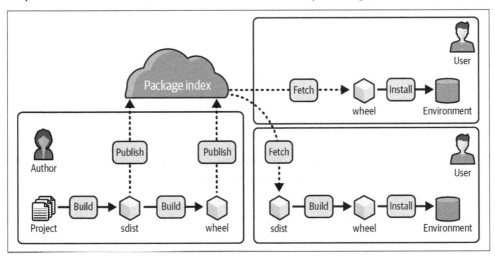

*Figure 3-3. Wheels and sdists*

For consumers of packages, sdists come with a few caveats. First, the build step involves arbitrary code execution, which can be a security concern.[4] Second, installing wheels is much faster than installing sdists, especially for legacy *setup.py*-based packages. Lastly, users may encounter confusing build errors for extension modules if they don't have the required build toolchain on their system.

Generally, a pure Python package has a single sdist and a single wheel for a given release. Binary extension modules, on the other hand, commonly come in wheels for a range of platforms and environments.

If you're an author of extension modules, check out the `cibuild wheel` project: it automates the building and testing of wheels across multiple platforms, with support for GitHub Actions and various other continuous integration (CI) systems.

---

4 This is especially true given the existence of *typosquatting*—where an attacker uploads a malicious package whose name is similar to a popular package—and *dependency confusion attacks*—where a malicious package on a public server uses the same name as a package on a private company repository.

## Wheel Compatibility Tags

Installers select the appropriate wheel for an environment using three so-called *compatibility tags* that are embedded in the name of each wheel file:

*Python tag*
> The target Python implementation

*ABI tag*
> The target *application binary interface* (ABI) of Python, which defines the set of symbols that binary extension modules can use to interact with the interpreter

*Platform tag*
> The target platform, including the processor architecture

Pure Python wheels are usually compatible with any Python implementation, do not require a particular ABI, and are portable across platforms. Wheels express such wide compatibility using the tags py3-none-any.

Wheels with binary extension modules, on the other hand, have more stringent compatibility requirements. Take a look at the compatibility tags of these wheels, for example:

*numpy-1.24.0-cp311-cp311-macosx_10_9_x86_64.whl*
> NumPy is a fundamental library for scientific computing. Its wheel targets a specific Python implementation and version (CPython 3.11), operating system release (macOS 10.9 and above), and processor architecture (x86-64).

*cryptography-38.0.4-cp36-abi3-manylinux_2_28_x86_64.whl*
> Cryptography is another fundamental library, with an interface to cryptographic algorithms. Its wheel demonstrates two ways to reduce the build matrix for binary distributions: the *stable ABI* is a restricted set of symbols that are guaranteed to persist across Python feature versions (abi3), and the manylinux tag advertises compatibility with a particular C standard library implementation (glibc 2.28 and above) across a wide range of Linux distributions.

If you're curious, you can extract a wheel using the unzip utility to see the files that installers place in the *site-packages* directory. Execute the following commands in a shell on Linux or macOS—preferably inside an empty directory. If you're on Windows, you can follow along using the Windows Subsystem for Linux (WSL):

```
$ py -m pip download attrs
$ unzip *.whl
$ ls -1
attr
attrs
attrs-23.2.0.dist-info
```

```
attrs-23.2.0-py3-none-any.whl

$ head -n4 attrs-23.2.0.dist-info/METADATA
Metadata-Version: 2.1
Name: attrs
Version: 23.2.0
Summary: Classes Without Boilerplate
```

Besides the import packages (named `attr` and `attrs` in this case), the wheel contains a *.dist-info* directory with administrative files. The *METADATA* file in this directory contains the *core metadata* for the package, a standardized set of attributes that describe the package for the benefit of installers and other packaging tools. You can access the core metadata of installed packages at runtime using the standard library:

```
$ uv pip install attrs
$ py
>>> from importlib.metadata import metadata
>>> metadata("attrs")["Version"]
23.2.0
>>> metadata("attrs")["Summary"]
Classes Without Boilerplate
```

In the next section, you'll see how to embed core metadata in your own packages, using the `project` table in *pyproject.toml*.

The core metadata standards predate *pyproject.toml* by many years. Most project metadata fields correspond to a core metadata field, but their names and syntax differ slightly. As a package author, you can safely ignore this translation and focus on the project metadata.

# Project Metadata

Build backends write out core metadata fields based on what you specify in the `project` table of *pyproject.toml*. Table 3-3 provides an overview of all the fields you can use in the `project` table.

*Table 3-3. The project table*

| Field | Type | Description |
| --- | --- | --- |
| name | String | The project name |
| version | String | The version of the project |
| description | String | A short description of the project |
| keywords | Array of strings | A list of keywords for the project |
| readme | String or table | A file with a long description of the project |
| license | Table | The license governing the use of this project |
| authors | Array of tables | The list of authors |

| Field | Type | Description |
|---|---|---|
| `maintainers` | Array of tables | The list of maintainers |
| `classifiers` | Array of strings | A list of classifiers describing the project |
| `urls` | Table of strings | The project URLs |
| `dependencies` | Array of strings | The list of required third-party packages |
| `optional-dependencies` | Table of arrays of strings | Named lists of optional third-party packages (*extras*) |
| `scripts` | Table of strings | Entry-point scripts |
| `gui-scripts` | Table of strings | Entry-point scripts providing a graphical user interface |
| `entry-points` | Table of tables of strings | Entry-point groups |
| `requires-python` | String | The Python version required by this project |
| `dynamic` | Array of strings | A list of dynamic fields |

Two fields are essential and mandatory for every package: `project.name` and `project.version`. The project name uniquely identifies the project itself. The project version identifies a *release*—a published snapshot of the project during its lifetime. Besides the name and version, there are a number of optional fields you can provide, such as the author and license, a short text describing the project, or third-party packages used by the project (see Example 3-4).

*Example 3-4. A pyproject.toml file with project metadata*

```
[project]
name = "random-wikipedia-article"
version = "0.1"
description = "Display extracts from random Wikipedia articles"
keywords = ["wikipedia"]
readme = "README.md"  # only if your project has a README.md file
license = { text = "MIT" }
authors = [{ name = "Your Name", email = "you@example.com" }]
classifiers = ["Topic :: Games/Entertainment :: Fortune Cookies"]
urls = { Homepage = "https://yourname.dev/projects/random-wikipedia-article" }
requires-python = ">=3.8"
dependencies = ["httpx>=0.27.0", "rich>=13.7.1"]
```

In the following sections, I'll take a closer look at the various project metadata fields.

## Naming Projects

The `project.name` field contains the official name of your project:

```
[project]
name = "random-wikipedia-article"
```

Your users specify this name to install the project with pip. This field also determines your project's URL on PyPI. You can use any ASCII letter or digit to name your project, interspersed with periods, underscores, and hyphens. Packaging tools normalize project names for comparison: all letters are converted to lowercase, and punctuation runs are replaced by a single hyphen (or underscore, in the case of package filenames). For example, `Awesome.Package`, `awesome_package`, and `awesome-package` all refer to the same project.

Project names are distinct from *import names*, the names users specify to import your code. Import names must be valid Python identifiers, so they can't have hyphens or periods and can't start with a digit. They're case-sensitive and can contain any Unicode letter or digit. As a rule of thumb, you should have a single import package per distribution package and use the same name for both (or a straightforward translation, like `random-wikipedia-article` and `random_wikipedia_article`).

## Versioning Projects

The `project.version` field stores the version of your project at the time you publish the release:

```
[project]
version = "0.1"
```

The Python community has a specification for version numbers to ensure that automated tools can make meaningful decisions, such as picking the latest release of a project. At the core, versions are a dotted sequence of numbers. These numbers may be zero, and trailing zeros can be omitted: `1`, `1.0`, and `1.0.0` all refer to the same version. Additionally, you can append certain kinds of suffixes to a version (Table 3-4). The most common ones identify prereleases: `1.0.0a2` is the second alpha release, `1.0.0b3` is the third beta release, `1.0.0rc1` is the first release candidate. Each of these precedes the next, and all of them precede the final release: `1.0.0`. Python versions can use additional components as well as alternate spellings; refer to PEP 440 (*https://oreil.ly/Dcc_F*) for the full specification.

*Table 3-4. Version identifiers*

| Release type | Description | Examples |
| --- | --- | --- |
| Final release | A stable, public snapshot (default) | `1.0.0`, `2017.5.25` |
| Prerelease | Preview of a final release to support testing | `1.0.0a1`, `1.0.0b1`, `1.0.0rc1` |
| Developmental release | A regular internal snapshot, such as a nightly build | `1.0.0.dev1` |
| Post-release | Corrects a minor error outside of the code | `1.0.0.post1` |

The Python version specification is intentionally permissive. Two widely adopted cross-language standards attach additional meaning to version numbers: Semantic Versioning (*https://semver.org*) uses the scheme `major.minor.patch`, where `patch` designates bugfix releases, `minor` designates compatible feature releases, and major designates releases with breaking changes. Calendar Versioning (*https://calver.org*) uses date-based versions of various forms, such as year.month.day, year.month.sequence, or year.quarter.sequence.

## Dynamic Fields

The *pyproject.toml* standard encourages projects to define their metadata statically rather than rely on the build backend to compute the fields during the package build. Static metadata benefits the packaging ecosystem because it makes the fields accessible to other tools. It also reduces cognitive overhead: build backends use the same configuration format and populate the fields in a straightforward and transparent way.

But sometimes it's useful to let the build backend fill in a field dynamically. For example, "Single-Sourcing the Project Version" shows how you can derive the package version from a Python module or Git tag instead of duplicating it in *pyproject.toml*.

For this reason, the project metadata standard provides an escape hatch in the form of *dynamic fields*. Projects are allowed to use a backend-specific mechanism to compute a field on the fly if they list its name under the dynamic key:

```
[project]
dynamic = ["version", "readme"]
```

### Single-Sourcing the Project Version

Many projects declare their version at the top of a Python module, like this:

```
__version__ = "0.1"
```

Updating a frequently changing item in several locations is tedious and error-prone. Some build backends, therefore, allow you to extract the version number from the code instead of repeating it in project.version. This mechanism is specific to your build backend, so you configure it in the tool table. Example 3-5 demonstrates how this works with Hatch.

*Example 3-5. Deriving the project version from a Python module*

```
[project]
name = "random-wikipedia-article"
dynamic = ["version"] ❶

[tool.hatch.version]
path = "src/random_wikipedia_article/__init__.py" ❷

[build-system]
requires = ["hatchling"]
build-backend = "hatchling.build"
```

❶ Mark the version field as dynamic.

❷ Tell Hatch where to look for the __version__ attribute.

You can also avoid the duplication by going in the other direction: declare the version statically in *pyproject.toml* and read it from the installed metadata at runtime, as shown in Example 3-6.

*Example 3-6. Reading the version from the installed metadata*

```
from importlib.metadata import version

__version__ = version("random-wikipedia-article")
```

But don't go and add this boilerplate to all your projects yet. Reading the metadata from the environment isn't something you want to do during program startup. Third-party libraries like click perform the metadata lookup on demand—for example, when the user specifies a command-line option like --version. You can read the version on demand by providing a __getattr__ function for your module (Example 3-7).[5]

*Example 3-7. Reading the version from the installed metadata on demand*

```
def __getattr__(name):
    if name != "__version__":
        msg = f"module {__name__} has no attribute {name}"
        raise AttributeError(msg)

    from importlib.metadata import version

    return version("random-wikipedia-article")
```

Alas, you still haven't truly single-sourced the version. Most likely, you also tag releases in your version control system (VCS) using a command like git tag v1.0.0. (If you don't, you should—if a release has a bug, the version tags help you find the commit that introduced it.)

Luckily, a number of build backends come with plugins that extract the version number from Git, Mercurial, and similar systems. This technique was pioneered by the setuptools-scm plugin. For Hatch, you can use the hatch-vcs plugin, which is a wrapper around setuptools-scm (Example 3-8).

---

5 This nifty technique comes courtesy of my reviewer Hynek Schlawack.

*Example 3-8. Deriving the project version from the version control system*

```
[project]
name = "random-wikipedia-article"
dynamic = ["version"]

[tool.hatch.version]
source = "vcs"

[build-system]
requires = ["hatchling", "hatch-vcs"]
build-backend = "hatchling.build"
```

If you build this project from a repository and you've checked out the tag v1.0.0, Hatch will use the version 1.0.0 for the metadata. If you've checked out an untagged commit, Hatch will instead generate a developmental release like 0.1.dev1+g6b80314.[6] In other words, you read the project version from Git during the package build and from the package metadata at runtime.

# Entry-Point Scripts

*Entry-point scripts* are small executables that launch the interpreter from their environment, import a module, and invoke a function (see "Entry-point scripts" on page 32). Installers like pip generate them on the fly when they install a package.

The project.scripts table lets you declare entry-point scripts. Specify the name of the script as the key and the module and function that the script should invoke as the value, using the format *package.module:function*:

```
[project.scripts]
random-wikipedia-article = "random_wikipedia_article:main"
```

This declaration allows users to invoke the program using its given name:

```
$ random-wikipedia-article
```

The project.gui-scripts table uses the same format as the project.scripts table—use it if your application has a graphical user interface (GUI):

```
[project.gui-scripts]
random-wikipedia-article-gui = "random_wikipedia_article:gui_main"
```

---

6 In case you're wondering, the +g6b80314 suffix is a *local version identifier* that designates downstream changes, in this case using output from the command git describe.

# Entry Points

Entry-point scripts are a special case of a more general mechanism called *entry points*. Entry points allow you to register a Python object in your package under a public name. Python environments come with a registry of entry points, and any package can query this registry to discover and import modules using the function `importlib.metadata.entry_points` from the standard library. Applications commonly use this mechanism to support third-party plugins.

The `project.entry-points` table contains these generic entry points. They use the same syntax as entry-point scripts but are grouped in subtables known as *entry-point groups*. If you want to write a plugin for another application, you register a module or object in its designated entry-point group:

```
[project.entry-points.some_application]
my-plugin = "my_plugin"
```

You can also register submodules using dotted notation, as well as objects within modules, using the format `module:object`:

```
[project.entry-points.some_application]
my-plugin = "my_plugin.submodule:plugin"
```

Let's look at an example to see how this works. Random Wikipedia articles make for fun little fortune cookies, but they can also serve as *test fixtures*[7] for developers of Wikipedia viewers and similar apps. Let's turn the app into a plugin for the pytest testing framework. (Don't worry if you haven't worked with pytest yet; I'll cover testing in depth in Chapter 6.)

Pytest allows third-party plugins to extend its functionality with test fixtures and other features. It defines an entry-point group for such plugins named `pytest11`. You can provide a plugin for pytest by registering a module in this group. Let's also add pytest to the project dependencies:

```
[project]
dependencies = ["pytest"]

[project.entry-points.pytest11]
random-wikipedia-article = "random_wikipedia_article"
```

Next, extend pytest with a test fixture returning a random Wikipedia article, as shown in Example 3-9. Place this code in the *__init__.py* module of your package.

---

7 *Test fixtures* set up objects that you need to run repeatable tests against your code.

*Example 3-9. Test fixture with a random Wikipedia article*

```python
import json
import urllib.request

import pytest

API_URL = "https://en.wikipedia.org/api/rest_v1/page/random/summary"

@pytest.fixture
def random_wikipedia_article():
    with urllib.request.urlopen(API_URL) as response:
        return json.load(response)
```

A developer of a Wikipedia viewer can now install your plugin next to pytest. Test functions use your test fixture by referencing it as a function argument (see Example 3-10). Pytest recognizes that the function argument is a test fixture and invokes the test function with the return value of the fixture.

*Example 3-10. A test function that uses the random article fixture*

```python
# test_wikipedia_viewer.py
def test_wikipedia_viewer(random_wikipedia_article):
    print(random_wikipedia_article["extract"])  ❶
    assert False  ❷
```

❶  A real test would run the viewer instead of `print()`.

❷  Fail the test so we get to see the full output.

You can try this out yourself in an active virtual environment in the project directory:

```
$ uv pip install .
$ py -m pytest
============================== test session starts ==============================
platform darwin -- Python 3.12.2, pytest-8.1.1, pluggy-1.4.0
rootdir: ...
plugins: random-wikipedia-article-0.1
collected 1 item

test_wikipedia_viewer.py F                                              [100%]

=================================== FAILURES ====================================
_____ test_wikipedia_viewer _____

    def test_wikipedia_viewer(random_wikipedia_article):
        print(random_wikipedia_article["extract"])
>       assert False
E       assert False
```

```
test_wikipedia_viewer.py:4: AssertionError
--------------------------- Captured stdout call ----------------------------
Halgerda stricklandi is a species of sea slug, a dorid nudibranch, a shell-less
marine gastropod mollusk in the family Discodorididae.
=========================== short test summary info ===========================
FAILED test_wikipedia_viewer.py::test_wikipedia_viewer - assert False
============================== 1 failed in 1.10s ==============================
```

## Authors and Maintainers

The `project.authors` and `project.maintainers` fields contain the list of authors and maintainers for the project. Each item in these lists is a table with `name` and `email` keys—you can specify either of these keys or both:

```
[project]
authors = [{ name = "Your Name", email = "you@example.com" }]
maintainers = [
  { name = "Alice", email = "alice@example.com" },
  { name = "Bob", email = "bob@example.com" },
]
```

The meaning of the fields is somewhat open to interpretation. If you start a new project, I recommend including yourself under `authors` and omitting the `maintainers` field. Long-lived open source projects typically list the original author under `authors`, while the people in charge of ongoing project maintenance appear as `maintainers`.

## The Description and README

The `project.description` field contains a short description as a string. This field will appear as the subtitle of your project page on PyPI. Some packaging tools also use this field when displaying a compact list of packages with human-readable descriptions:

```
[project]
description = "Display extracts from random Wikipedia articles"
```

The `project.readme` field is typically a string with the relative path to the file with the long description of your project. Common choices are *README.md* for a description written in Markdown format and *README.rst* for the reStructuredText format. The contents of this file appear on your project page on PyPI:

```
[project]
readme = "README.md"
```

Instead of a string, you can also specify a table with `file` and `content-type` keys:

```
[project]
readme = { file = "README", content-type = "text/plain" }
```

You can even embed the long description in the *pyproject.toml* file using the `text` key:

```
[project.readme]
content-type = "text/markdown"
text = """
# random-wikipedia-article

Display extracts from random Wikipedia articles
"""
```

Writing a README that renders well is not trivial—often, the project description appears in disparate places, like PyPI, a repository hosting service like GitHub, and inside official documentation on services like Read the Docs (*https://readthedocs.org*). If you need more flexibility, you can declare the field dynamic and use a plugin like `hatch-fancy-pypi-readme` to assemble the project description from multiple fragments.

## Keywords and Classifiers

The `project.keywords` field contains a list of strings that people can use to search for your project on PyPI:

```
[project]
keywords = ["wikipedia"]
```

The `project.classifiers` field contains a list of classifiers to categorize the project in a standardized way:

```
[project]
classifiers = [
    "Development Status :: 3 - Alpha",
    "Environment :: Console",
    "Topic :: Games/Entertainment :: Fortune Cookies",
]
```

PyPI maintains the official registry of classifiers for Python projects (*https://oreil.ly/6-XGL*). They're known as *Trove classifiers* and consist of hierarchically organized labels separated by double colons (Table 3-5). The Trove project, initiated by Eric S. Raymond, was an early design for an open source software repository.

*Table 3-5. Trove classifiers*

| Classifier group | Description | Example |
| --- | --- | --- |
| Development Status | How mature this release is | `Development Status :: 5 - Production/Stable` |
| Environment | The environment in which the project runs | `Environment :: No Input/Output (Daemon)` |
| Operating System | The operating systems supported by the project | `Operating System :: OS Independent` |
| Framework | Any framework used by the project | `Framework :: Flask` |

| Classifier group | Description | Example |
| --- | --- | --- |
| Audience | The kind of users served by the project | `Intended Audience :: Developers` |
| License | The license under which the project is distributed | `License :: OSI Approved :: MIT License` |
| Natural Language | The natural languages supported by the project | `Natural Language :: English` |
| Programming Language | The programming language the project is written in | `Programming Language :: Python :: 3.12` |
| Topic | Various topics related to the project | `Topic :: Utilities` |

Classifiers are entirely optional. I recommend indicating the development status and the supported operating systems, which aren't covered by other metadata fields. If you'd like to include more classifiers, provide one from each classifier group.

## The Project URLs

The `project.urls` table allows you to point users to your project homepage, source code, documentation, issue tracker, and similar project-related URLs. Your project page on PyPI links to these pages using the provided key as the display text for each link. It also displays an appropriate icon for many common names and URLs:

```
[project.urls]
Homepage = "https://yourname.dev/projects/random-wikipedia-article"
Source = "https://github.com/yourname/random-wikipedia-article"
Issues = "https://github.com/yourname/random-wikipedia-article/issues"
Documentation = "https://readthedocs.io/random-wikipedia-article"
```

## The License

The `project.license` field is a table where you can specify your project license under the **text** key or by reference to a file under the **file** key. You may also want to add the corresponding Trove classifier for the license:

```
[project]
license = { text = "MIT" }
classifiers = ["License :: OSI Approved :: MIT License"]
```

I recommend using the **text** key with a SPDX license identifier (*https://oreil.ly/ XNMEP*) such as "MIT" or "Apache-2.0." The Software Package Data Exchange (SPDX) is an open standard backed by the Linux Foundation for communicating software bill of material information, including licenses.

> As of this writing, a Python Enhancement Proposal (PEP) is under discussion that changes the `license` field to a string using SPDX syntax and adds a `license-files` key for license files distributed with the package: PEP 639 (*https://oreil.ly/RydcA*)

If you're unsure which open source license to use for your project, *choosealicense.com* provides some useful guidance. For a proprietary project, it's common to specify "proprietary." You can also add the special classifier `Private :: Do Not Upload` to prevent accidental upload to PyPI:

```
[project]
license = { text = "proprietary" }
classifiers = [
    "License :: Other/Proprietary License",
    "Private :: Do Not Upload",
]
```

## The Required Python Version

Use the `project.requires-python` field to specify the versions of Python that your project supports:[8]

```
[project]
requires-python = ">=3.8"
```

Most commonly, people specify the minimum Python version as a lower bound, using a string with the format >=3.x. The syntax of this field is more general and follows the same rules as *version specifiers* for project dependencies (see Chapter 4).

Tools like Nox and tox make it easy to run checks across multiple Python versions, helping you ensure that the field reflects reality. As a baseline, I recommend requiring the oldest Python version that still receives security updates. You can find the end-of-life dates for all current and past Python versions on the Python Developer Guide (*https://oreil.ly/n3ztQ*).

There are three main reasons to be more restrictive about the Python version. First, your code may depend on newer language features—for example, structural pattern matching was introduced in Python 3.10. Second, your code may depend on newer features in the standard library—look out for the "Changed in version 3.x" notes in the official documentation. Third, it could depend on third-party packages with more restrictive Python requirements.

Some packages declare upper bounds on the Python version, such as >=3.8,<4. This practice is discouraged, but depending on such a package may force you to declare the same upper bound for your own package. Dependency solvers can't downgrade the Python version in an environment; they will either fail or, worse, downgrade the package to an old version with a looser Python constraint. A future Python 4 is unlikely to introduce the kind of breaking changes that people associate with the transition from Python 2 to 3.

---

8 You can also add Trove classifiers for each supported Python version. Some backends backfill classifiers for you—Poetry does this out of the box for Python versions and project licenses.

Don't specify an upper bound for the required Python version unless you *know* that your package is not compatible with any higher version. Upper bounds cause disruption in the ecosystem when a new version is released.

## Dependencies and Optional Dependencies

The remaining fields, `project.dependencies` and `project.optional-dependencies`, list any third-party packages on which your project depends. You'll take a closer look at these fields—and dependencies in general—in the next chapter.

# Summary

Packaging allows you to publish releases of your Python projects, using source distributions (*sdists*) and built distributions (*wheels*). These artifacts contain your Python modules, together with project metadata, in an archive format that end users can easily install into their environments. The standard *pyproject.toml* file defines the build system for a Python project as well as the project metadata. Build frontends like `build`, pip, and uv use the build system information to install and run the build backend in an isolated environment. The build backend assembles an sdist and wheel from the source tree and embeds the project metadata. You can upload packages to the Python Package Index (PyPI) or a private repository, using a tool like Twine. The Python project manager Rye provides a more integrated workflow on top of these tools.

# CHAPTER 4

# Dependency Management

Python programmers benefit from a rich ecosystem of third-party libraries and tools. Standing on the shoulders of giants comes at a price: the packages you depend on for your projects generally depend on a number of packages themselves. All of these are moving targets—as long as any project is alive, its maintainers will publish a stream of releases to fix bugs, add features, and adapt to the evolving ecosystem.

Managing dependencies is a major challenge when you maintain software over time. You need to keep your project up-to-date, if only to close security vulnerabilities in a timely fashion. Often this requires updating your dependencies to the latest version—few open source projects have the resources to distribute security updates for older releases. You'll be updating dependencies all the time! Making the process as frictionless, automated, and reliable as possible comes with a huge payoff.

*Dependencies* of a Python project are the third-party packages that must be installed in its environment.[1] Most commonly, you incur a dependency on a package because it distributes a module you import. We also say that the project *requires* a package.

Many projects also use third-party tools for developer tasks—like running the test suite or building documentation. These packages are known as *development dependencies*: end users don't need them to run your code. A related case is the build dependencies from Chapter 3, which let you create packages for your project.

Dependencies are like relatives. If you depend on a package, its dependencies are your dependencies, too—no matter how much you like them. These packages are known as *indirect dependencies*; you can think of them as a tree with your project at its root.

---

1 In a wider sense, the dependencies of a project consist of all software packages that users require to run its code—including the interpreter, the standard library, third-party packages, and system libraries. Conda and distro package managers like APT, DNF, and Homebrew support this generalized notion of dependencies.

This chapter explains how to manage dependencies effectively. In the next section, you'll learn how to specify dependencies in *pyproject.toml* as part of the project metadata. Afterward, I'll talk about development dependencies and requirements files. Finally, I'll explain how you can *lock* dependencies to precise versions for reliable deployments and repeatable checks.

# Adding Dependencies to the Example Application

As a working example, let's enhance `random-wikipedia-article` from Example 3-1 with the HTTPX library (*https://oreil.ly/4lJmF*), a fully featured HTTP client that supports both synchronous and asynchronous requests as well as the newer (and far more efficient) protocol version HTTP/2. You'll also improve the output of the program using Rich (*https://oreil.ly/1UKRb*), a library for rich text and beautiful formatting in the terminal.

## Consuming an API with HTTPX

Wikipedia asks developers to set a `User-Agent` header with contact details. That's not so they can send out postcards to congratulate folks on their proficient use of the Wikipedia API. It gives them a way to reach out if a client inadvertently hammers their servers.

Example 4-1 shows how you can use `httpx` to send a request to the Wikipedia API with the header. You could also use the standard library to send a `User-Agent` header with your requests. But `httpx` offers a more intuitive, explicit, and flexible interface, even when you're not using any of its advanced features.

*Example 4-1. Using httpx to consume the Wikipedia API*

```
import textwrap
import httpx

API_URL = "https://en.wikipedia.org/api/rest_v1/page/random/summary"
USER_AGENT = "random-wikipedia-article/0.1 (Contact: you@example.com)"

def main():
    headers = {"User-Agent": USER_AGENT}

    with httpx.Client(headers=headers) as client:  ❶
        response = client.get(API_URL, follow_redirects=True)  ❷
        response.raise_for_status()  ❸
        data = response.json()  ❹

    print(data["title"], end="\n\n")
    print(textwrap.fill(data["extract"]))
```

**❶** When creating a client instance, you can specify headers that it should send with every request—like the User-Agent header. Using the client as a context manager ensures that the network connection is closed at the end of the with block.

**❷** This line performs two HTTP GET requests to the API. The first one goes to the *random* endpoint, which responds with a redirect to the actual article. The second one follows the redirect.

**❸** The raise_for_status method raises an exception if the server response indicates an error via its status code.

**❹** The json method abstracts the details of parsing the response body as JSON.

## Console Output with Rich

While you're at it, let's improve the look and feel of the program. Example 4-2 uses Rich, a library for console output, to display the article title in bold. That hardly scrapes the surface of Rich's formatting options. Modern terminals are surprisingly capable, and Rich lets you leverage their potential with ease. Take a look at its official documentation (*https://oreil.ly/1UKRb*) for details.

*Example 4-2. Using Rich to enhance console output*

```
import httpx
from rich.console import Console

def main():
    ...
    console = Console(width=72, highlight=False)  ❶
    console.print(data["title"], style="bold", end="\n\n")  ❷
    console.print(data["extract"])
```

**❶** Console objects provide a featureful print method for console output. Setting the console width to 72 characters replaces our earlier call to textwrap.fill. You'll also want to disable automatic syntax highlighting, since you're formatting prose rather than data or code.

**❷** The style keyword allows you to set the title apart using a bold font.

# Specifying Dependencies for a Project

If you haven't done so yet, create and activate a virtual environment for the project, and perform an editable install from the current directory:

```
$ uv venv
$ uv pip install --editable .
```

You may be tempted to install httpx and rich manually into the environment. Instead, add them to the project dependencies in *pyproject.toml*. This ensures that whenever you install your project, the two packages are installed along with it:

```
[project]
name = "random-wikipedia-article"
version = "0.1"
dependencies = ["httpx", "rich"]
...
```

If you reinstall the project, you'll see that uv installs its dependencies as well:

```
$ uv pip install --editable .
```

Each entry in the dependencies field is a *dependency specification*. Besides the package name, it lets you supply additional information: version specifiers, extras, and environment markers. The following sections explain what these are.

## Version Specifiers

*Version specifiers* define the range of acceptable versions for a package. When you add a new dependency, it's a good idea to include its current version as a lower bound—unless your project needs to be compatible with older releases. Update the lower bound whenever you start relying on newer features of the package:

```
[project]
dependencies = ["httpx>=0.27.0", "rich>=13.7.1"]
```

Why declare lower bounds on your dependencies? Installers choose the latest version for a dependency by default. There are three reasons why you should care. First, libraries are typically installed alongside other packages, which may have additional version constraints. Second, even applications aren't always installed in isolation—for example, Linux distros may package your application for the system-wide environment. Third, lower bounds help you detect version conflicts in your own dependency tree—such as when you require a recent release of a package, but another dependency only works with its older releases.

Avoid speculative upper version bounds—you shouldn't guard against newer releases unless you know they're incompatible with your project. See "Upper Version Bounds in Python" on page 91 about issues with version capping.

*Lock files* are a much better solution to dependency-induced breakage than upper bounds—they request "known good" versions of your dependencies when deploying a service or running automated checks (see "Locking Dependencies" on page 101).

If a botched release breaks your project, publish a bugfix release to exclude that specific broken version:

```
[project]
dependencies = ["awesome>=1.2,!=1.3.1"]
```

Use an upper bound as a last resort if a dependency breaks compatibility permanently. Lift the version cap once you're able to adapt your code:

```
[project]
dependencies = ["awesome>=1.2,<2"]
```

 Excluding versions after the fact has a pitfall that you need to be aware of. Dependency resolvers can decide to downgrade your project to a version without the exclusion and upgrade the dependency anyway. Lock files can help with this.

## Upper Version Bounds in Python

Some people routinely include upper bounds in version constraints. Packages following the Semantic Versioning scheme use major versions to signal a *breaking change*: an incompatible change to their public API.

As engineers, we err on the side of safety to build robust products. At first glance, guarding against major releases seems like something any responsible person would do. Even if most of them don't break your project, isn't it better to opt in after you have a chance to test the release?

Unfortunately, upper version bounds quickly lead to unsolvable dependency conflicts.[2] Python environments (unlike Node.js environments, in particular) can contain only a single version of each package. Libraries that put upper bounds on their dependencies prevent downstream projects from receiving security and bug fixes. Before adding an upper version bound, carefully consider the costs and benefits.

What exactly constitutes a breaking change is less defined than it may seem. For example, should a project increment its major version every time it drops support for an old Python version?

---

2 Henry Schreiner, "Should You Use Upper Bound Version Constraints?" (*https://oreil.ly/IYXYy*), December 9, 2021.

Even in clear cases, a breaking change will break your project only if it affects the part of the public API that your project uses. By contrast, many changes that will break your project aren't marked by a version number: they're just bugs. In the end, you'll still rely on automated tests to discover "bad" versions and deal with them after the fact.

Version specifiers support several operators, as shown in Table 4-1. In short, use the equality and comparison operators you know from Python: ==, !=, <=, >=, <, and >.

*Table 4-1. Version specifiers*

| Operator | Name | Description |
| --- | --- | --- |
| == | Version matching | Versions must compare equal after normalization. Trailing zeros are stripped off. |
| != | Version exclusion | The inverse of the == operator |
| <=, >= | Inclusive ordered comparison | Performs lexicographical comparison. Prereleases precede final releases. |
| <, > | Exclusive ordered comparison | Similar to inclusive, but the versions must not compare equal |
| ~= | Compatible release | Equivalent to >=x.y,==x.* to the specified precision |
| === | Arbitrary equality | Simple string comparison for nonstandard versions |

Three operators merit additional discussion:

- The == operator supports wildcards (*), albeit only at the end of the version string. In other words, you can require the version to match a particular prefix, such as 1.2.*.

- The === operator lets you perform a simple character-by-character comparison. It's best used as a last resort for nonstandard versions.

- The ~= operator for compatible releases specifies that the version should be greater than or equal to the given value, while still starting with the same prefix. For example, ~=1.2.3 is equivalent to >=1.2.3,==1.2.*, and ~=1.2 is equivalent to >=1.2,==1.*.

You don't need to guard against prereleases—version specifiers exclude them by default. Prereleases are valid candidates in three situations only: when they're already installed, when no other releases satisfy the dependency specification, and when you request them explicitly, using a clause like >=1.0.0rc1.

## Extras

Suppose you want to use the newer HTTP/2 protocol with httpx. This requires only a small change to the code that creates the HTTP client:

```
def main():
    headers = {"User-Agent": USER_AGENT}
    with httpx.Client(headers=headers, http2=True) as client:
        ...
```

Under the hood, httpx delegates the gory details of speaking HTTP/2 to another package, h2. That dependency is not pulled in by default, however. This way, users who don't need the newer protocol get away with a smaller dependency tree. You do need it here, so activate the optional feature using the syntax httpx[http2]:

```
[project]
dependencies = ["httpx[http2]>=0.27.0", "rich>=13.7.1"]
```

Optional features that require additional dependencies are known as *extras*, and you can have more than one. For example, you could specify httpx[http2,brotli] to allow decoding responses with *Brotli compression*, which is a compression algorithm developed at Google that's common in web servers and content delivery networks.

## Optional dependencies

Let's look at this situation from the point of view of httpx. The h2 and brotli dependencies are optional, so httpx declares them under optional-dependencies instead of dependencies (Example 4-3).

*Example 4-3. Optional dependencies of httpx (simplified)*

```
[project]
name = "httpx"

[project.optional-dependencies]
http2 = ["h2>=3,<5"]
brotli = ["brotli"]
```

The optional-dependencies field is a TOML table. It can hold multiple lists of dependencies, one for each extra provided by the package. Each entry is a dependency specification and uses the same rules as the dependencies field.

If you add an optional dependency to your project, how do you use it in your code? Don't check if your package was installed with the extra—just import the optional package. You can catch the ImportError exception if the user didn't request the extra:

```
try:
    import h2
except ImportError:
    h2 = None

# Check h2 before use.
if h2 is not None:
    ...
```

This is a common pattern in Python—so common it comes with a name and an acronym: "Easier to Ask Forgiveness than Permission" (EAFP). Its less Pythonic counterpart is dubbed "Look Before You Leap" (LBYL).

## Environment Markers

The third piece of metadata you can specify for a dependency is environment markers. Before I explain what these markers are, let me show you an example of where they come in handy.

If you looked at the `User-Agent` header in Example 4-1 and thought, "I shouldn't have to repeat the version number in the code," you're absolutely right. As you saw in "Single-Sourcing the Project Version" on page 76, you can read the version of your package from its metadata in the environment.

Example 4-4 shows how you can use the function `importlib.metadata.metadata` to construct the `User-Agent` header from the core metadata fields `Name`, `Version`, and `Author-email`. These fields correspond to `name`, `version`, and `authors` in the project metadata.[3]

*Example 4-4. Using `importlib.metadata` to build a `User-Agent` header*

```
from importlib.metadata import metadata

USER_AGENT = "{Name}/{Version} (Contact: {Author-email})"

def build_user_agent():
    fields = metadata("random-wikipedia-article")  ❶
    return USER_AGENT.format_map(fields)  ❷

def main():
    headers = {"User-Agent": build_user_agent()}
    ...
```

❶ The `metadata` function retrieves the core metadata fields for the package.

❷ The `str.format_map` function looks up each placeholder in the mapping.

The `importlib.metadata` library was introduced in Python 3.8. While it's now available in all supported versions, that wasn't always so. Were you out of luck if you had to support an older Python version?

---

3 For simplicity, the code doesn't handle multiple authors—which one ends up in the header is undefined.

---

Not quite. Fortunately, many additions to the standard library come with *backports* —third-party packages that provide the functionality for older interpreters. For `importlib.metadata`, you can fall back to the `importlib-metadata` backport from PyPI. The backport remains useful because the library changed several times after its introduction.

You need backports only in environments that use specific Python versions. An environment marker lets you express this as a conditional dependency:

```
importlib-metadata; python_version < '3.8'
```

Installers will install the package only on interpreters older than Python 3.8.

More generally, an *environment marker* expresses a condition that an environment must satisfy for the dependency to apply. Installers evaluate the condition on the interpreter of the target environment.

Environment markers let you request dependencies for specific operating systems, processor architectures, Python implementations, or Python versions. Table 4-2 lists all the environment markers at your disposal, as specified in PEP 508.[4]

*Table 4-2. Environment markers[a]*

| Environment marker | Standard library | Description | Examples |
| --- | --- | --- | --- |
| os_name | os.name() | The operating system family | posix, nt |
| sys_platform | sys.platform() | The platform identifier | linux, darwin, win32 |
| platform_system | platform.system() | The system name | Linux, Darwin, Windows |
| platform_release | platform.release() | The operating system release | 23.2.0 |
| platform_version | platform.version() | The system release | Darwin Kernel Version 23.2.0: ... |
| platform_machine | platform.machine() | The processor architecture | x86_64, arm64 |
| python_version | platform.python _version_tuple() | The Python feature version in the format x.y | 3.12 |
| python_full_version | platform.python _version() | The full Python version | 3.12.0, 3.13.0a4 |
| platform_python _implementation | platform.python _implementation() | The Python implementation | CPython, PyPy |

---

4 Robert Collins, "PEP 508 – Dependency specification for Python Software Packages" (*https://oreil.ly/BWXc7*), November 11, 2015.

| Environment marker | Standard library | Description | Examples |
|---|---|---|---|
| implementation_name | sys.implementation<br>.name | The Python implementation | cpython, pypy |
| implementation<br>_version | sys.implementation<br>.version | The Python implementation<br>version | 3.12.0, 3.13.0a4 |

[a] The python_version and implementation_version markers apply transformations. See PEP 508 for details.

Going back to Example 4-4, here are the `requires-python` and `dependencies` fields to make the package compatible with Python 3.7:

```
[project]
requires-python = ">=3.7"
dependencies = [
    "httpx[http2]>=0.24.1",
    "rich>=13.7.1",
    "importlib-metadata>=6.7.0; python_version < '3.8'",
]
```

The import name for the backport is `importlib_metadata`, while the standard library module is named `importlib.metadata`. You can import the appropriate module in your code by checking the Python version in `sys.version_info`:

```
if sys.version_info >= (3, 8):
    from importlib.metadata import metadata
else:
    from importlib_metadata import metadata
```

Did I just hear somebody shout "EAFP"? If your imports depend on the Python version, it's better to avoid the technique from "Optional dependencies" on page 93 and "look before you leap." An explicit version check communicates your intent to static analyzers, such as the mypy type checker (see Chapter 10). EAFP may result in errors from these tools because they can't detect when each module is available.

Markers support the same equality and comparison operators as version specifiers (Table 4-1). Additionally, you can use `in` and `not in` to match a substring against the marker. For example, the expression `'arm' in platform_version` checks if `platform.version()` contains the string `'arm'`.

You can also combine multiple markers using the Boolean operators `and` and `or`. Here's a rather contrived example combining all these features:

```
[project]
dependencies = ["""                                                        \
  awesome-package; python_full_version <= '3.8.1'                          \
    and (implementation_name == 'cpython' or implementation_name == 'pypy') \
    and sys_platform == 'darwin'                                           \
    and 'arm' in platform_version                                          \
"""]
```

The example also relies on TOML's support for multiline strings, which uses triple quotes just like Python. Dependency specifications cannot span multiple lines, so you have to escape the newlines with a backslash.

# Development Dependencies

Development dependencies are third-party packages that you require during development. As a developer, you might use the pytest testing framework to run the test suite for your project, the Sphinx documentation system to build its docs, or a number of other tools to help with project maintenance. Your users, on the other hand, don't need to install any of these packages to run your code.

## An Example: Testing with pytest

As a concrete example, let's add a small test for the build_user_agent function from Example 4-4. Create a directory *tests* with two files: an empty *__init__.py* and a module *test_random_wikipedia_article.py* with the code from Example 4-5.

*Example 4-5. Testing the generated* User-Agent *header*

```
from random_wikipedia_article import build_user_agent

def test_build_user_agent():
    assert "random-wikipedia-article" in build_user_agent()
```

Example 4-5 uses only built-in Python features, so you could just import and run the test manually. But even for this tiny test, pytest adds three useful features. First, it discovers modules and functions whose names start with test, so you can run your tests by invoking pytest without arguments. Second, pytest shows tests as it executes them, as well as a summary with the test results at the end. Third, pytest rewrites assertions in your tests to give you friendly, informative messages when they fail.

Let's run the test with pytest. I'm assuming you already have an active virtual environment with an editable install of your project. Enter the commands below to install and run pytest in that environment:

```
$ uv pip install pytest
$ py -m pytest
========================= test session starts =========================
platform darwin -- Python 3.12.2, pytest-8.1.1, pluggy-1.4.0
rootdir: ...
plugins: anyio-4.3.0
collected 1 item

tests/test_random_wikipedia_article.py .                    [100%]

========================= 1 passed in 0.22s =========================
```

For now, things look great. Tests help your project evolve without breaking things. The test for `build_user_agent` is a first step in that direction. Installing and running pytest is a small infrastructure cost compared to these long-term benefits.

Setting up a project environment becomes harder as you acquire more development dependencies—documentation generators, linters, code formatters, type checkers, or other tools. Even your test suite may require more than pytest: plugins for pytest, tools for measuring code coverage, or just packages that help you exercise your code.

You also need compatible versions of these packages—your test suite may require the latest version of pytest, while your documentation may not build on the new Sphinx release. Each of your projects may have slightly different requirements. Multiply this by the number of developers working on each project, and it becomes clear that you need a way to track your development dependencies.

As of this writing, Python doesn't have a standard way to declare the development dependencies of a project—although many Python project managers support them in their [tool] table and a draft PEP exists.[5] Besides project managers, people use two approaches to fill the gap: optional dependencies and requirements files.

## Optional Dependencies

As you've seen in "Extras" on page 92, the `optional-dependencies` table contains groups of optional dependencies named extras. It has three properties that make it suitable for tracking development dependencies. First, the packages aren't installed by default, so end users don't pollute their Python environment with them. Second, it lets you group the packages under meaningful names like `tests` or `docs`. And third, the field comes with the full expressivity of dependency specifications, including version constraints and environment markers.

On the other hand, there's an impedance mismatch between development dependencies and optional dependencies. Optional dependencies are exposed to users through the package metadata—they let users opt into features that require additional packages. By contrast, users aren't meant to install development dependencies—these packages aren't required for any user-facing features.

Furthermore, you can't install extras without the project itself. By contrast, not all developer tools need your project installed. For example, linters analyze your source code for bugs and potential improvements. You can run them on a project without installing it into the environment. Besides wasting time and space, "fat" environments constrain dependency resolution unnecessarily. For example, many Python projects

---

5 Stephen Rosen, "PEP 735 – Dependency Groups in pyproject.toml" (*https://oreil.ly/KfYW0*), November 20, 2023.

could no longer upgrade important dependencies when the Flake8 linter put a version cap on `importlib-metadata`.

Keeping this in mind, extras are widely used for development dependencies and are the only method covered by a packaging standard. They're a pragmatic choice, especially if you manage linters with pre-commit (see Chapter 9). Example 4-6 shows how you'd use extras to track packages required for testing and documentation.

*Example 4-6. Using extras to represent development dependencies*

```
[project.optional-dependencies]
tests = ["pytest>=7.4.4", "pytest-sugar>=1.0.0"] ❶
docs = ["sphinx>=5.3.0"] ❷
```

❶ The `pytest-sugar` plugin enhances pytest's output with a progress bar and shows failures immediately.

❷ Sphinx is a documentation generator used by the official Python documentation and many open source projects.

You can now install the test dependencies using the `tests` extra:

```
$ uv pip install -e ".[tests]"
$ py -m pytest
```

You can also define a dev extra with all the development dependencies. This lets you set up a development environment in one go, with your project and every tool it uses:

```
$ uv pip install -e ".[dev]"
```

There's no need to repeat all the packages when you define `dev`. Instead, you can just reference the other extras, as shown in Example 4-7.

*Example 4-7. Providing a dev extra with all development dependencies*

```
[project.optional-dependencies]
tests = ["pytest>=7.4.4", "pytest-sugar>=1.0.0"]
docs = ["sphinx>=5.3.0"]
dev = ["random-wikipedia-article[tests,docs]"]
```

This style of declaring an extra is also known as a *recursive optional dependency*, since the package with the dev extra depends on itself (with `tests` and `docs` extras).

## Requirements Files

*Requirements files* are plain text files with dependency specifications on each line (Example 4-8). Additionally, they can contain URLs and paths, optionally prefixed by `-e` for an editable install, as well as global options, such as `-r` to include another requirements file or `--index-url` to use a package index other than PyPI. The file format also supports Python-style comments (with a leading # character) and line continuations (with a trailing \ character).

*Example 4-8. A simple requirements.txt file*

```
pytest>=7.4.4
pytest-sugar>=1.0.0
sphinx>=5.3.0
```

You can install the dependencies listed in a requirements file using pip or uv:

```
$ uv pip install -r requirements.txt
```

By convention, a requirements file is named *requirements.txt*. However, variations are common. You might have a *dev-requirements.txt* for development dependencies or a *requirements* directory with one file per dependency group (Example 4-9).

*Example 4-9. Using requirements files to specify development dependencies*

```
# requirements/tests.txt
-e .  ❶
pytest>=7.4.4
pytest-sugar>=1.0.0

# requirements/docs.txt
sphinx>=5.3.0  ❷

# requirements/dev.txt
-r tests.txt  ❸
-r docs.txt
```

❶ The *tests.txt* file requires an editable install of the project because the test suite needs to import the application modules.

❷ The *docs.txt* file doesn't require the project. (That's assuming you build the documentation from static files only. If you use the `autodoc` Sphinx extension to generate API documentation from docstrings in your code, you'll also need the project here.)

❸ The *dev.txt* file includes the other requirements files.

 If you include other requirements files using `-r`, their paths are evaluated relative to the including file. By contrast, paths to dependencies are evaluated relative to your current directory, which is typically the project directory.

Create and activate a virtual environment, then run the following commands to install the development dependencies and run the test suite:

```
$ uv pip install -r requirements/dev.txt
$ py -m pytest
```

Requirements files aren't part of the project metadata. You share them with other developers using the version control system, but they're invisible to your users. For development dependencies, this is exactly what you want. What's more, requirements files don't implicitly include your project in the dependencies. That shaves time from all tasks that don't need the project installed.

Requirements files also have downsides. They aren't a packaging standard and are unlikely to become one—each line of a requirements file is essentially an argument to pip install. "Whatever pip does" may remain the unwritten law for many edge cases in Python packaging, but community standards replace it more and more. Another downside is the clutter these files cause in your project when compared to a table in *pyproject.toml*.

As mentioned above, Python project managers let you declare development dependencies in *pyproject.toml*, outside of the project metadata—Rye, Hatch, PDM, and Poetry all offer this feature. See Chapter 5 for a description of Poetry's dependency groups.

# Locking Dependencies

You've installed your dependencies in a local environment or in continuous integration (CI), and you've run your test suite and any other checks you have in place. Everything looks good, and you're ready to deploy your code. But how do you install the same packages in production that you used when you ran your checks?

Using different packages in development and production has consequences. Production may end up with a package that's incompatible with your code, has a bug or security vulnerability, or—in the worst case—has been hijacked by an attacker. If your service gets a lot of exposure, this scenario is worrying—and it can involve any package in your dependency tree, not just those that you import directly.

 *Supply chain attacks* infiltrate a system by targeting its third-party dependencies. For example, in 2022, a threat actor dubbed "Juice-Ledger" uploaded malicious packages to legitimate PyPI projects after compromising them with a phishing campaign.[6]

---

6 Dan Goodin, "Actors Behind PyPI Supply Chain Attack Have Been Active Since Late 2021" (*https://oreil.ly/lIfh2*), September 2, 2022.

There are many reasons why environments end up with different packages given the same dependency specifications. Most of them fall into two categories: upstream changes and environment mismatch. First, you can get different packages if the set of available packages changes upstream:

- A new release comes in before you deploy.

- A new artifact is uploaded for an existing release. For example, maintainers sometimes upload additional wheels when a new Python release comes out.

- A maintainer deletes or yanks a release or artifact. *Yanking* is a soft delete that hides the file from dependency resolution unless you request it specifically.

Second, you can get different packages if your development environment doesn't match the production environment:

- Environment markers evaluate differently on the target interpreter (see "Environment Markers" on page 94). For example, the production environment might use an old Python version that requires a backport like `importlib-metadata`.

- Wheel compatibility tags can cause the installer to select a different wheel for the same package (see "Wheel Compatibility Tags" on page 72). For example, this can happen if you develop on a Mac with Apple silicon while production uses Linux on an x86-64 architecture.

- If the release doesn't include a wheel for the target environment, the installer builds it from the sdist on the fly. Wheels for extension modules often lag behind when a new Python version sees the light.

- If the environments don't use the same installer (or different versions of the same installer), each installer may resolve the dependencies differently. For example, uv uses the PubGrub algorithm for dependency resolution,[7] while pip uses a backtracking resolver for Python packages, `resolvelib`.

- Tooling configuration or state can also cause different results—for example, you might install from a different package index or from a local cache.

You need a way to define the exact set of packages required by your application, and you want its environment to be an exact image of this package inventory. This process is known as *locking*, or *pinning*, the project dependencies, which are listed in a *lock file*.

So far, I've talked about locking dependencies for reliable and reproducible deployments. Locking is also beneficial during development, for both applications and libraries. By sharing a lock file with your team and with contributors, you put everybody

---

7 Natalie Weizenbaum, "PubGrub: Next-Generation Version Solving" (*https://oreil.ly/NSC3t*), April 2, 2018.

on the same page: every developer uses the same dependencies when running the test suite, building the documentation, or performing other tasks. Using the lock file for mandatory checks avoids surprises where checks fail in CI after passing locally. To reap these benefits, lock files must include development dependencies, too.

As of this writing, Python lacks a packaging standard for lock files—although the topic is under active consideration.[8] Meanwhile, many Python project managers, such as Poetry, PDM, and pipenv, have implemented their own lock file formats; others, like Rye, use requirements files for locking dependencies.

In this section, I'll introduce two methods for locking dependencies using requirements files: *freezing* and *compiling requirements*. In Chapter 5, I'll describe Poetry's lock files.

---

## "Locking" Dependencies in the Project Metadata

If you want to lock the dependencies for an application, why not narrow the version constraints in *pyproject.toml*? For example, couldn't you lock the dependencies on httpx and rich as shown below?

```
[project]
dependencies = ["httpx[http2]==0.27.0", "rich==13.7.1"]
```

There are two main problems with this approach.

First, you've locked only direct dependencies. For example, random-wikipedia-article uses h2 to communicate via HTTP/2, but that package is missing from the dependency specifications.

Second, and more importantly, you've lost valuable information: the compatible version ranges for your top-level dependencies. Version constraints determine the search space for a dependency resolver. The resolver can no longer help you upgrade packages or resolve dependencies for a new environment—like when you bump the Python version in production.

You need a way to record dependencies outside of the dependencies table.

---

## Freezing Requirements with pip and uv

Requirements files are a popular format for locking dependencies. They let you keep the dependency information separate from the project metadata. Pip and uv can generate these files from an existing environment:

---

8 Brett Cannon, "Lock Files, Again (But This Time w/ Sdists!)" (*https://oreil.ly/HYLsY*), February 22, 2024.

```
$ uv pip install .
$ uv pip freeze
anyio==4.3.0
certifi==2024.2.2
h11==0.14.0
h2==4.1.0
hpack==4.0.0
httpcore==1.0.4
httpx==0.27.0
hyperframe==6.0.1
idna==3.6
markdown-it-py==3.0.0
mdurl==0.1.2
pygments==2.17.2
random-wikipedia-article @ file:///Users/user/random-wikipedia-article
rich==13.7.1
sniffio==1.3.1
```

Taking an inventory of the packages installed in an environment is known as *freezing*. Store the list in *requirements.txt* and commit the file to source control—with one change: replace the file URL with a dot for the current directory. This lets you use the requirements file anywhere, as long as you're inside the project directory.

When deploying your project to production, you can install the project and its dependencies like this:

```
$ uv pip install -r requirements.txt
```

Assuming your development environment uses a recent interpreter, the requirements file won't list `importlib-metadata`—that library is only required before Python 3.8. If your production environment runs an ancient Python version, your deployment will break. There's an important lesson here: lock your dependencies in an environment that matches the production environment.

 Lock your dependencies on the same Python version, Python implementation, operating system, and processor architecture as those used in production. If you deploy to multiple environments, generate a requirements file for each one.

Freezing requirements comes with a few limitations. First, you need to install your dependencies every time you refresh the requirements file. Second, it's easy to pollute the requirements file inadvertently if you temporarily install a package and forget to create the environment from scratch afterward.[9] Third, freezing doesn't allow you to record package hashes—it merely takes an inventory of an environment, and

---

9 Uninstalling the package isn't enough: the installation can have side effects on your dependency tree. For example, it may upgrade or downgrade other packages or pull in additional dependencies.

environments don't record hashes for the packages you install into them. (I'll cover package hashes in the next section.)

## Compiling Requirements with pip-tools and uv

The pip-tools project lets you lock dependencies without these limitations. You can compile requirements directly from *pyproject.toml*, without installing the packages. Under the hood, pip-tools leverages pip and its dependency resolver.

Pip-tools comes with two commands: `pip-compile`, to create a requirements file from dependency specifications, and `pip-sync`, to apply the requirements file to an existing environment. The uv tool provides drop-in replacements for both commands: `uv pip compile` and `uv pip sync`.

Run `pip-compile` in an environment that matches the target environment for your project. If you use pipx, specify the target Python version:

```
$ pipx run --python=3.12 --spec=pip-tools pip-compile
```

By default, `pip-compile` reads from *pyproject.toml* and writes to *requirements.txt*. You can use the `--output-file` option to specify a different destination. The tool also prints the requirements to standard error, unless you specify `--quiet` to switch off terminal output.

Uv requires you to be explicit about the input and output files:

```
$ uv pip compile --python-version=3.12 pyproject.toml -o requirements.txt
```

Pip-tools and uv annotate the file to indicate the dependent package for each dependency, as well as the command used to generate the file. There's one more difference to the output of `pip freeze`: the compiled requirements don't include your own project. You'll have to install it separately after applying the requirements file.

Requirements files allow you to specify package hashes for each dependency. These hashes add another layer of security to your deployments: they enable you to install only vetted packaging artifacts in production. The option `--generate-hashes` includes SHA-256 hashes for each package listed in the requirements file. For example, here are hashes over the sdist and wheel files for an `httpx` release:

```
httpx==0.27.0 \
--hash=sha256:71d5465162c13681bff01ad59b2cc68dd838ea1f10e51574bac27103f00c91a5 \
--hash=sha256:a0cb88a46f32dc874e04ee956e4c2764aba2aa228f650b06788ba6bda2962ab5
```

Package hashes make installations more deterministic and reproducible. They're also an important tool in organizations that require screening every artifact that goes into production. Validating the integrity of packages prevents *on-path attacks* where a threat actor ("man in the middle") intercepts a package download to supply a compromised artifact.

Hashes also have the side effect that pip refuses to install packages without them: either all packages have hashes, or none do. As a consequence, hashes protect you from installing files that aren't listed in the requirements file.

Install the requirements file in the target environment using pip or uv, followed by the project itself. You can harden the installation using a couple of options: the option `--no-deps` ensures that you only install packages listed in the requirements file, and the option `--no-cache` prevents the installer from reusing downloaded or locally built artifacts:

```
$ uv pip install -r requirements.txt
$ uv pip install --no-deps --no-cache .
```

Update your dependencies at regular intervals. Once per week may be acceptable for a mature application running in production. Daily may be more appropriate for a project under active development—or even as soon as the releases come in. Tools like Dependabot and Renovate help with this chore: they open pull requests in your repositories with automated dependency upgrades.

If you don't upgrade dependencies regularly, you may be forced to apply a "big bang" upgrade under time pressure. A single security vulnerability can force you to port your project to major releases of multiple packages, as well as Python itself.

You can upgrade your dependencies all at once, or one dependency at a time. Use the `--upgrade` option to upgrade all dependencies to their latest version, or pass a specific package with the `--upgrade-package` option (`-P`).

For example, here's how you'd upgrade Rich to the latest version:

```
$ uv pip compile -p 3.12 pyproject.toml -o requirements.txt -P rich
```

So far, you've created the target environment from scratch. You can also use `pip-sync` to synchronize the target environment with the updated requirements file. Don't install pip-tools in the target environment for this: its dependencies may conflict with those of your project. Instead, use pipx, as you did with `pip-compile`. Point `pip-sync` to the target interpreter using its `--python-executable` option:

```
$ py -m venv .venv
$ pipx run --spec=pip-tools pip-sync --python-executable=.venv/bin/python
```

The command removes the project itself since it's not listed in the requirements file. Reinstall it after synchronizing:

```
$ .venv/bin/python -m pip install --no-deps --no-cache .
```

Uv uses the environment in *.venv* by default, so you can simplify these commands:

```
$ uv pip sync requirements.txt
$ uv pip install --no-deps --no-cache .
```

In "Development Dependencies" on page 97, you saw two ways to declare development dependencies: extras and requirements files. Pip-tools and uv support both as inputs. If you track development dependencies in a dev extra, generate the *dev-requirements.txt* file like this:

```
$ uv pip compile --extra=dev pyproject.toml -o dev-requirements.txt
```

If you have finer-grained extras, the process is the same. You may want to store the requirements files in a *requirements* directory to avoid clutter.

If you specify your development dependencies in requirements files instead of extras, compile each of these files in turn. By convention, input requirements use the *.in* extension, while output requirements use the *.txt* extension (Example 4-10).

*Example 4-10. Input requirements for development dependencies*

```
# requirements/tests.in
pytest>=7.4.4
pytest-sugar>=1.0.0

# requirements/docs.in
sphinx>=5.3.0

# requirements/dev.in
-r tests.in
-r docs.in
```

Unlike Example 4-9, the input requirements don't list the project itself. If they did, the output requirements would include the path to the project—and every developer would end up with a different path. Instead, pass *pyproject.toml* together with the input requirements to lock the entire set of dependencies together:

```
$ uv pip compile requirements/tests.in pyproject.toml -o requirements/tests.txt
$ uv pip compile requirements/docs.in -o requirements/docs.txt
$ uv pip compile requirements/dev.in pyproject.toml -o requirements/dev.txt
```

Remember to install the project after you've installed the output requirements.

Why bother compiling *dev.txt* at all? Can't it just include *docs.txt* and *tests.txt*? If you install separately locked requirements on top of each other, they may well end up conflicting. Let the dependency resolver see the full picture. If you pass all the input requirements, it can give you a consistent dependency tree in return.

Table 4-3 summarizes the command-line options for `pip-compile` (and `uv pip compile`) you've seen in this chapter:

*Table 4-3. Selected command-line options for `pip-compile`*

| Option | Description |
| --- | --- |
| `--generate-hashes` | Include SHA-256 hashes for every packaging artifact |
| `--output-file` | Specify the destination file |
| `--quiet` | Do not print the requirements to standard error |
| `--upgrade` | Upgrade all dependencies to their latest version |
| `--upgrade-package=<package>` | Upgrade a specific package to its latest version |
| `--extra=<extra>` | Include dependencies from the given extra in *pyproject.toml* |

## Summary

In this chapter, you've learned how to declare project dependencies using *pyproject .toml* and how to declare development dependencies using either extras or requirements files. You've also learned how to lock dependencies for reliable deployments and reproducible checks using pip-tools and uv. In the next chapter, you'll see how the project manager Poetry helps with dependency management using dependency groups and lock files.

# CHAPTER 5

# Managing Projects with Poetry

The preceding chapters introduced the building blocks for publishing production-quality Python packages. So far, you've written a *pyproject.toml* for a project; created an environment and installed dependencies with uv, pip, or pip-tools; and built and published packages with `build` and Twine.

By standardizing project metadata and build backends, *pyproject.toml* broke the setuptools monopoly (see "The Evolution of Python Project Managers" on page 110) and brought diversity to the packaging ecosystem. Defining a Python package got easier, too: a single well-specified file with great tooling support replaces the legacy boilerplate of *setup.py* and untold configuration files.

Yet, some problems remain.

Before you can work on a *pyproject.toml*-based project, you need to research packaging workflows, configuration files, and associated tooling. You have to choose one of a number of available build backends (Table 3-2)—and many people don't know what those are, let alone how to choose them. Important aspects of Python packages remain unspecified—for example, how project sources are laid out and which files should go into the packaging artifacts.

Dependency and environment management could be easier, too. You need to hand-craft your dependency specifications and compile them with pip-tools, cluttering your project with requirements files. And it can be hard to keep track of the many Python environments on a typical developer system.

The Python project manager Poetry was addressing these problems before some of the standards governing *pyproject.toml* took shape. Its friendly command-line interface lets you perform most tasks related to packaging, dependencies, and environments. Poetry brings its own standards-compliant build backend, `poetry.core`—but you can remain blissfully unaware of this fact. It also comes with a strict dependency resolver and locks all dependencies by default, behind the scenes.

Why learn about packaging standards and low-level plumbing if Poetry abstracts away many of these details? Because, while Poetry ventures into new territory, it still works within the framework defined by packaging standards. Mechanisms like dependency specifications and virtual environments power its central features. Interoperability standards let Poetry interact with package repositories as well as other build backends and package installers.

An understanding of these underlying mechanisms helps you debug situations where Poetry's convenient abstractions break down—for example, when a misconfiguration or a bug causes a package to end up in the wrong environment. Finally, the experience of past decades teaches us that tools come and go, while standards and algorithms are here to stay.

---

## The Evolution of Python Project Managers

A decade ago, Python packaging was firmly in the hands of three tools: setuptools, virtualenv, and pip. You'd use setuptools to create Python packages, virtualenv to set up virtual environments, and pip to install packages into them. Everybody did. Around 2016—the same year that the *pyproject.toml* file became standard—things started to change.

In 2015, Thomas Kluyver began developing Flit, an alternative build tool that could create packages and publish them to PyPI. In 2016, Donald Stufft from the pip maintainer team started working on Pipfile, a proposed replacement for requirements files, including a specification of lock files. In 2017, his work led to Kenneth Reitz's Pipenv, which allows you to manage dependencies and environments for Python applications and deploy them in a reproducible way. Pipenv deliberately didn't package your application: you'd just keep a bunch of Python modules in a Git repository.

Poetry, started in 2018 by Sébastien Eustace, was the first tool to provide a unified approach to packaging, dependencies, and environments—and quickly became widely adopted. Two other tools follow a similarly holistic approach: PDM, started by Frost Ming in 2019, and Hatch by Ofek Lev in 2017. Hatch has recently grown in popularity, especially among tooling and library developers. In 2023, they were joined by Rye, a project manager written in Rust by Armin Ronacher. In addition, Hatch and Rye also manage Python installations, leveraging the Python Standalone Builds project.

Poetry, Hatch, PDM, and Rye each give you an integrated workflow for managing Python packages, environments, and dependencies. As such, they've come to be known as *Python project managers*. Keep an eye on Astral's uv as well!

---

# Installing Poetry

Install Poetry globally using pipx to keep its dependencies isolated from the rest of the system:

```
$ pipx install poetry
```

A single Poetry installation works with multiple Python versions. However, Poetry uses its own interpreter as the default Python version. For this reason, it's worthwhile to install Poetry on the latest stable Python release. When installing a new feature release of Python, reinstall Poetry like this:

```
$ pipx reinstall --python=3.12 poetry
```

You can omit the --python option if pipx already uses the new Python version (see "Configuring pipx" on page 42).

When a prerelease of Poetry becomes available, you can install it side by side with the stable version:

```
$ pipx install poetry --suffix=@preview --pip-args=--pre
```

Here, I've used the --suffix option to rename the command so you can invoke it as poetry@preview while keeping poetry as the stable version. The --pip-args option lets you pass options to pip, like --pre for including prereleases.

 Poetry also comes with an official installer (*https://oreil.ly/wYjFf*), which you can download and run with Python. It's not as flexible as pipx, but it provides a readily available alternative:

```
$ curl -sSL https://install.python-poetry.org | python3 -
```

Upgrade Poetry periodically to receive improvements and bugfixes:

```
$ pipx upgrade poetry
```

Type poetry on its own to check your installation of Poetry. Poetry prints its version and usage to the terminal, including a useful listing of all available subcommands:

```
$ poetry
```

Having successfully installed Poetry, you may want to enable tab completion for your shell. Use the command poetry help completions for shell-specific instructions. For example, the following commands enable tab completion in the Bash shell:

```
$ poetry completions bash >> ~/.bash_completion
$ echo ". ~/.bash_completion" >> ~/.bashrc
```

Restart your shell for the changes to take effect.

# Creating a Project

You can create a new project using the command `poetry new`. As an example, I'll use the `random-wikipedia-article` project from previous chapters. Run the following command in the parent directory where you want to keep your new project:

```
$ poetry new --src random-wikipedia-article
```

After running this command, you'll see that Poetry created a project directory named *random-wikipedia-article*, with the following structure:

```
random-wikipedia-article
├── README.md
├── pyproject.toml
├── src
│   └── random_wikipedia_article
│       └── __init__.py
└── tests
    └── __init__.py
```

The `--src` option instructs Poetry to place the import package in a subdirectory named *src* rather than directly in the project directory.

---

### The src Layout

Until a few years ago, package authors placed the import package directly in the project directory. These days, a project layout with *src*, *tests*, and *docs* directories at the top is becoming more common.

Keeping the import package tucked away under *src* has practical advantages. During development, the current directory often appears at the start of `sys.path`. Without an *src* layout, you may be importing your project from its source code, not from the package you've installed in the project environment. In the worst case, your tests could fail to detect issues in a release you're about to publish.

On the other hand, whenever you *want* to execute the source code itself, editable installs achieve this by design. With an *src* layout, packaging tools can implement editable installs by adding the *src* directory to `sys.path`—without the side effect of making unrelated Python files importable.

---

Let's take a look at the generated *pyproject.toml* (Example 5-1).

*Example 5-1. A pyproject.toml file for Poetry*

```
[tool.poetry]
name = "random-wikipedia-article"
version = "0.1.0"
description = ""
authors = ["Your Name <you@example.com>"]
readme = "README.md"
packages = [{include = "random_wikipedia_article", from = "src"}]

[tool.poetry.dependencies]
python = "^3.12"

[build-system]
requires = ["poetry-core"]
build-backend = "poetry.core.masonry.api"
```

Poetry has created a standard build-system table with its build backend, poetry.core. This means anybody can install your project from source using pip or uv—no need to set up, or even know about, the Poetry project manager. Similarly, you can build packages using any standard build frontend, such as build:

```
$ pipx run build
* Creating isolated environment: venv+pip...
* Installing packages in isolated environment:
  - poetry-core
* Getting build dependencies for sdist...
* Building sdist...
* Building wheel from sdist
* Creating isolated environment: venv+pip...
* Installing packages in isolated environment:
  - poetry-core
* Getting build dependencies for wheel...
* Building wheel...
Successfully built random_wikipedia_article-0.1.0.tar.gz
  and random_wikipedia_article-0.1.0-py3-none-any.whl
```

## The Project Metadata

You may be surprised to see the project metadata appear under tool.poetry instead of the familiar project table (see "Project Metadata" on page 73). The Poetry project plans to support the project metadata standard in its next major release.[1] As you can see in Table 5-1, most fields have the same name and a similar syntax and meaning.

Example 5-2 fills in the metadata for the project. I've highlighted some differences from Example 3-4. (You'll use the command-line interface to add the dependencies later.)

---

1 Sébastien Eustace, "Support for PEP 621" (*https://oreil.ly/AI1tQ*), November 6, 2020.

*Example 5-2. Metadata for a Poetry project*

```
[tool.poetry]
name = "random-wikipedia-article"
version = "0.1.0"
description = "Display extracts from random Wikipedia articles"
keywords = ["wikipedia"]
license = "MIT"  ❶
classifiers = [
    "License :: OSI Approved :: MIT License",
    "Development Status :: 3 - Alpha",
    "Environment :: Console",
    "Topic :: Games/Entertainment :: Fortune Cookies",
]
authors = ["Your Name <you@example.com>"]  ❷
readme = "README.md"  ❸
homepage = "https://yourname.dev/projects/random-wikipedia-article"  ❹
repository = "https://github.com/yourname/random-wikipedia-article"
documentation = "https://readthedocs.io/random-wikipedia-article"
packages = [{include = "random_wikipedia_article", from = "src"}]

[tool.poetry.dependencies]
python = ">=3.10"  ❺

[tool.poetry.urls]
Issues = "https://github.com/yourname/random-wikipedia-article/issues"

[tool.poetry.scripts]
random-wikipedia-article = "random_wikipedia_article:main"
```

❶ The `license` field is a string with a SPDX identifier, not a table.

❷ The `authors` field contains strings in the format `"name <email>"`, not tables. Poetry prepopulates the field with your name and email from Git.

❸ The `readme` field is a string with the file path. You can also specify multiple files as an array of strings, such as *README.md* and *CHANGELOG.md*. Poetry concatenates them with a blank line in between.

❹ Poetry has dedicated fields for some project URLs, namely its homepage, repository, and documentation; for other URLs, there's also a generic `urls` table.

❺ The `python` entry in `dependencies` lets you declare compatible Python versions. For this project, you require Python 3.10 or later.

*Table 5-1. Metadata fields in* `tool.poetry`

| Field | Type | Description | project field |
| --- | --- | --- | --- |
| name | String | The project name | name |
| version | String | The version of the project | version |
| description | String | A short description of the project | description |
| keywords | Array of strings | A list of keywords for the project | keywords |
| readme | String or array of strings | A file or list of files with the project description | readme |
| license | String | A SPDX license identifier, or "Proprietary" | license |
| authors | Array of strings | The list of authors | authors |
| maintainers | Array of strings | The list of maintainers | maintainers |
| classifiers | Array of strings | A list of classifiers describing the project | classifiers |
| homepage | String | The URL of the project homepage | urls |
| repository | String | The URL of the project repository | urls |
| documentation | String | The URL of the project documentation | urls |
| urls | Table of strings | The project URLs | urls |
| dependencies | Table of strings or tables | Required third-party packages | dependencies |
| extras | Table of tables | Optional third-party packages | optional-dependencies |
| groups | Table of tables | Dependency groups | *none* |
| scripts | Table of strings or tables | Entry-point scripts | scripts |
| plugins | Table of tables of strings | Entry-point groups | entry-points |

Some `project` fields have no direct equivalent under `tool.poetry`:

- There's no `requires-python` field; instead, you specify the required Python version in the `dependencies` table, using the `python` key.
- There's no dedicated field for GUI scripts; use `plugins.gui_scripts` instead.
- There's no `dynamic` field—all metadata is Poetry-specific, so declaring dynamic fields wouldn't make much sense.

Before we move on, let's check that the *pyproject.toml* file is valid. Poetry provides a convenient command to validate the TOML file against its configuration schema:

```
$ poetry check
All set!
```

## The Package Contents

Poetry allows you to specify which files and directories to include in the distribution—a feature still missing from the *pyproject.toml* standards (Table 5-2).

*Table 5-2. Package content fields in* `tool.poetry`

| Field | Type | Description |
|---|---|---|
| `packages` | Array of tables | Patterns for modules to include in the distribution |
| `include` | Array of strings or tables | Patterns for files to include in the distribution |
| `exclude` | Array of strings or tables | Patterns for files to exclude from the distribution |

Each table under `packages` has an `include` key with a file or directory. You can use `*` and `**` wildcards in their names and paths, respectively. The `from` key allows you to include modules from subdirectories such as *src*. Finally, you can use the `format` key to restrict modules to a specific distribution format; valid values are `sdist` and `wheel`.

The `include` and `exclude` fields allow you to list other files to include in, or exclude from, the distribution. Poetry seeds the `exclude` field using the *.gitignore* file, if present. By default, Poetry includes these additional files in source distributions only. Instead of a string, you can use a table with `path` and `format` keys to specify the distribution formats that should include the files. Example 5-3 shows how to include the test suite in source distributions.

*Example 5-3. Including the test suite in source distributions*

```
packages = [{include = "random_wikipedia_article", from = "src"}]
include = ["tests"]
```

## The Source Code

Copy the contents of Example 5-4 into the *__init__.py* file in the new project.

*Example 5-4. The source code for* `random-wikipedia-article`

```
import httpx
from rich.console import Console

from importlib.metadata import metadata

API_URL = "https://en.wikipedia.org/api/rest_v1/page/random/summary"
USER_AGENT = "{Name}/{Version} (Contact: {Author-email})"

def main():
    fields = metadata("random-wikipedia-article")
    headers = {"User-Agent": USER_AGENT.format_map(fields)}
```

```
with httpx.Client(headers=headers, http2=True) as client:
    response = client.get(API_URL, follow_redirects=True)
    response.raise_for_status()
    data = response.json()

console = Console(width=72, highlight=False)
console.print(data["title"], style="bold", end="\n\n")
console.print(data["extract"])
```

You've declared an entry-point script in the scripts section in *pyproject.toml*, so users can invoke the application as random-wikipedia-article. If you'd like to also allow users to invoke the program with py -m random_wikipedia_article, create a *__main__.py* module next to *__init__.py* as shown in Example 3-3.

# Managing Dependencies

Let's add the dependencies for random-wikipedia-article, starting with Rich, the console output library:

```
$ poetry add rich
Using version ^13.7.1 for rich

Updating dependencies
Resolving dependencies... (0.2s)

Package operations: 4 installs, 0 updates, 0 removals

  - Installing mdurl (0.1.2)
  - Installing markdown-it-py (3.0.0)
  - Installing pygments (2.17.2)
  - Installing rich (13.7.1)

Writing lock file
```

If you inspect *pyproject.toml* after running this command, you'll find that Poetry has added Rich to the dependencies table (Example 5-5).

*Example 5-5. The dependencies table after adding Rich*

```
[tool.poetry.dependencies]
python = ">=3.10"
rich = "^13.7.1"
```

Poetry also installs the package into an environment for the project. If you already have a virtual environment in *.venv*, Poetry uses that. Otherwise, it creates a virtual environment in a shared location (see "Managing Environments" on page 121).

# Caret Constraints

The caret (^) is a Poetry-specific extension to version specifiers, borrowed from npm, the package manager for Node.js. *Caret constraints* allow releases with the given minimum version, except those that may contain breaking changes according to the Semantic Versioning (*https://semver.org*) standard. After `1.0.0`, a caret constraint allows patch and minor releases, but no major releases. Before `1.0.0`, only patch releases are allowed—in the `0.*` era, minor releases are allowed to introduce breaking changes.

Caret constraints are similar to *tilde constraints* (see "Version Specifiers" on page 90), but the latter only allow the last version segment to increase. For example, the following constraints are equivalent:

```
rich = "^13.7.1"
rich = ">=13.7.1,<14"
```

On the other hand, tilde constraints typically exclude minor releases:

```
rich = "~13.7.1"
rich = ">=13.7.1,==13.7.*"
```

Caret constraints put an upper bound on the version. As explained in "Upper Version Bounds in Python" on page 91, you should avoid upper bounds if you can. Add Rich with only a lower bound instead:

```
$ poetry add "rich>=13.7.1"
```

You can use this command to remove upper bounds from existing caret constraints, as well.[2] If you specified extras or markers when you first added the dependency, you'll need to specify them again.

---

## Should You Cap Dependencies?

It's unfortunate that Poetry adds upper bounds to dependencies by default. For libraries, the practice prevents downstream users from receiving fixes and improvements, since constraints aren't scoped to the packages that introduce them, as in Node.js. Many open source projects don't have the resources to backport fixes to past releases. For applications, lock files provide a better way to achieve reliable deployments.

The situation is similar but worse for the Python requirement. Excluding Python 4 by default will cause disruption across the ecosystem when the core Python team eventually releases a new major version. It's unlikely that Python 4 will come anywhere near Python 3 in terms of incompatible changes. Poetry's constraint is contagious

---

2 The command also keeps your lock file and project environment up-to-date. If you edit the constraint in *pyproject.toml*, you'll need to do this yourself. Read on to learn more about lock files and environments.

in the sense that dependent packages must also introduce it. And it's impossible for Python package installers to satisfy—they can't downgrade the environment to an earlier version of Python.

Whenever possible, replace caret constraints with lower bounds (>=), especially for Python itself. After editing *pyproject.toml*, refresh the lock file using the command `poetry lock --no-update`.

## Extras and Environment Markers

Let's add the other dependency of `random-wikipedia-article`, the HTTP client library `httpx`. Like in Chapter 4, you'll activate the `http2` extra for HTTP/2 support:

```
$ poetry add "httpx>=0.27.0" --extras=http2
```

Poetry updates the *pyproject.toml* file accordingly:

```
[tool.poetry.dependencies]
python = ">=3.10"
rich = ">=13.7.1"
httpx = {version = ">=0.27.0", extras = ["http2"]}
```

The project requires a recent Python version, so it doesn't require the `importlib-metadata` backport. If you had to support Python versions before 3.8, here's how you'd add the library for those versions:

```
$ poetry add "importlib-metadata>=6.7.0" --python="<3.8"
```

Besides `--python`, the `poetry add` command supports a `--platform` option to restrict dependencies to a specific operating system, such as Windows. This option accepts a platform identifier in the format used by the standard `sys.platform` attribute: `linux`, `darwin`, `win32`. For other environment markers, edit *pyproject.toml* and use the `markers` property in the TOML table for the dependency:

```
[tool.poetry.dependencies]
awesome = {version = ">=1", markers = "implementation_name == 'pypy'"}
```

## The Lock File

Poetry records the current version of each dependency in a file named *poetry.lock*, including SHA-256 hashes for its packaging artifacts. If you take a peek inside the file, you'll notice TOML stanzas for `rich` and `httpx`, as well as their direct and indirect dependencies. Example 5-6 shows a simplified version of Rich's lock entry.

*Example 5-6. The TOML stanza for Rich in poetry.lock (simplified)*

```
[[package]]
name = "rich"
```

```
version = "13.7.1"
python-versions = ">=3.7.0"
dependencies = {markdown-it-py = ">=2.2.0", pygments = ">=2.13.0,<3.0.0"}
files = [
    {file = "rich-13.7.1-py3-none-any.whl", hash = "sha256:4edbae3..."},
    {file = "rich-13.7.1.tar.gz", hash = "sha256:9be308c..."},
]
```

Use the command `poetry show` to display the locked dependencies in the terminal. Here's what the output looked like after I added Rich:

```
$ poetry show
markdown-it-py 3.0.0  Python port of markdown-it. Markdown parsing, done right!
mdurl          0.1.2  Markdown URL utilities
pygments       2.17.2 Pygments is a syntax highlighting package ...
rich           13.7.1 Render rich text, tables, progress bars, ...
```

You can also display the dependencies as a tree to visualize their relationship:

```
$ poetry show --tree
rich 13.7.1 Render rich text, tables, progress bars, ...
├── markdown-it-py >=2.2.0
│   └── mdurl >=0.1,<1.0
└── pygments >=2.13.0,<3.0.0
```

If you edit *pyproject.toml* yourself, remember to update the lock file to reflect your changes:

```
$ poetry lock --no-update
Resolving dependencies... (0.1s)

Writing lock file
```

Without the `--no-update` option, Poetry upgrades each locked dependency to the latest version covered by its constraint.

You can check if the *poetry.lock* file is consistent with *pyproject.toml*:

```
$ poetry check --lock
```

Resolving dependencies up front lets you deploy applications in a reliable and reproducible manner. It also gives developers in a team a common baseline and makes checks more deterministic—avoiding surprises in continuous integration (CI). You should commit *poetry.lock* to source control to reap these benefits.

Poetry's lock file is designed to work across operating systems and Python interpreters. Having a single environment-independent, or "universal," lock file is beneficial if your code must run in diverse environments or if you're an open source maintainer with contributors from all over the world.

By contrast, compiled requirements files quickly become unwieldy. If your project supports Windows, macOS, and Linux on the four most recent feature versions of

Python, you'll need to manage a dozen requirements files. Adding another processor architecture or Python implementation only makes things worse.

Universal lock files come at a price, however. Poetry re-resolves dependencies when it installs the packages into an environment. Its lock file is essentially a shrunken world view: it records every package the project might require in a given environment. By contrast, compiled requirements are an exact image of an environment. This makes them more amenable to auditing and more attractive for secure deployments.

## Updating Dependencies

You can update all dependencies in the lock file to their latest versions using a single command:

```
$ poetry update
```

You can also provide a specific direct or indirect dependency to update:

```
$ poetry update rich
```

The `poetry update` command doesn't modify the project metadata in *pyproject.toml*. It only updates dependencies within the compatible version range. If you need to update the version range, use `poetry add` with the new constraint, including any extras and markers. Alternatively, edit *pyproject.toml* and refresh the lock file with `poetry lock --no-update`.

If you no longer need a package for your project, remove it with `poetry remove`:

```
$ poetry remove <package>
```

# Managing Environments

Poetry's `add`, `update`, and `remove` commands don't just update dependencies in the *pyproject.toml* and *poetry.lock* files. They also synchronize the project environment with the lock file by installing, updating, or removing packages. Poetry creates the virtual environment for the project on demand.

By default, Poetry stores the environments for all projects in a shared folder. Configure Poetry to keep the environment in a *.venv* directory inside the project instead:

```
$ poetry config virtualenvs.in-project true
```

This setting makes the environment discoverable for other tools in the ecosystem, such as py and uv. Having the directory in the project is convenient when you need to examine its contents. Although the setting restricts you to a single environment, this limitation is seldom a concern. Tools like Nox and tox are tailor-made for testing across multiple environments (see Chapter 8).

You can check the location of the current environment using the command poetry env info --path. If you want to create a clean slate for your project, use the following commands to remove existing environments and create a new one using the specified Python version:

```
$ poetry env remove --all
$ poetry env use 3.12
```

You can re-run the second command to re-create the environment on a different interpreter. Instead of a version like 3.12, you can also pass a command like pypy3 for the PyPy interpreter or a full path like /usr/bin/python3 for the system Python.

Before you use the environment, you should install the project. Poetry performs editable installs, so the environment reflects any code changes immediately:

```
$ poetry install
```

Enter the project environment by launching a shell session with poetry shell. Poetry activates the virtual environment using the activation script for your current shell. With the environment activated, you can run the application from the shell prompt. Just exit the shell session when you're done:

```
$ poetry shell
(random-wikipedia-article-py3.12) $ random-wikipedia-article
(random-wikipedia-article-py3.12) $ exit
```

You can also run the application in your current shell session, using the command poetry run:

```
$ poetry run random-wikipedia-article
```

The command is also handy for starting an interactive Python session in the project environment:

```
$ poetry run python
>>> from random_wikipedia_article import main
>>> main()
```

When you run a program with poetry run, Poetry activates the virtual environment without launching a shell. This works by adding the environment to the program's PATH and VIRTUAL_ENV variables (see "Activation scripts" on page 36).

 Just type py to get a Python session for your Poetry project on Linux and macOS. This requires the Python Launcher for Unix, and you must configure Poetry to use in-project environments.

# Dependency Groups

Poetry allows you to declare development dependencies, organized in dependency groups. Dependency groups aren't part of the project metadata and are invisible to end users. Let's add the dependency groups from "Development Dependencies" on page 97:

```
$ poetry add --group=tests pytest pytest-sugar
$ poetry add --group=docs sphinx
```

Poetry adds the dependency groups under the group table in *pyproject.toml*:

```
[tool.poetry.group.tests.dependencies]
pytest = "^8.1.1"
pytest-sugar = "^1.0.0"

[tool.poetry.group.docs.dependencies]
sphinx = "^7.2.6"
```

Dependency groups are installed into the project environment by default. You can mark a group as optional using its `optional` key, like this:

```
[tool.poetry.group.docs]
optional = true

[tool.poetry.group.docs.dependencies]
sphinx = "^7.2.6"
```

 Don't specify the `--optional` flag when you add a dependency group with `poetry add`—it doesn't mark the group as optional. The option designates optional dependencies that are behind an extra; it has no valid use in the context of dependency groups.

The `poetry install` command has several options that provide finer-grained control over which dependencies are installed into the project environment (Table 5-3).

*Table 5-3. Installing dependencies with `poetry install`*

| Option | Description |
| --- | --- |
| `--with=<group>` | Include a dependency group in the installation. |
| `--without=<group>` | Exclude a dependency group from the installation. |
| `--only=<group>` | Exclude all other dependency groups from the installation. |
| `--no-root` | Exclude the project itself from the installation. |
| `--only-root` | Exclude all dependencies from the installation. |
| `--sync` | Remove packages from the environment unless scheduled for installation. |

You can specify a single group or multiple groups (separated by commas). The special group main refers to packages listed in the tool.poetry.dependencies table. Use the option --only=main to exclude all development dependencies from an installation. Similarly, the option --without=main lets you restrict an installation to development dependencies.

# Package Repositories

Poetry lets you upload your packages to the Python Package Index (PyPI) and other package repositories. It also lets you configure the repositories from which you add packages to your project. This section looks at both the publisher and the consumer sides of interacting with package repositories.

If you're following along in this section, please don't upload the example project to PyPI. Use the TestPyPI repository instead—it's a playground for testing, learning, and experimentation.

## Publishing Packages to Package Repositories

Before you can upload packages to PyPI, you need an account and an API token to authenticate with the repository, as explained in "Uploading Packages with Twine" on page 65. Next, add the API token to Poetry:

```
$ poetry config pypi-token.pypi <token>
```

You can create packages for a Poetry project using standard tooling like build or with Poetry's command-line interface:

```
$ poetry build
Building random-wikipedia-article (0.1.0)
  - Building sdist
  - Built random_wikipedia_article-0.1.0.tar.gz
  - Building wheel
  - Built random_wikipedia_article-0.1.0-py3-none-any.whl
```

Like build, Poetry places the packages in the *dist* directory. You can publish the packages in *dist* using poetry publish:

```
$ poetry publish
```

You can also collapse the two commands into one:

```
$ poetry publish --build
```

Let's upload the example project to TestPyPI, a separate instance of the Python Package Index for testing distributions. If you want to upload packages to a repository other than PyPI, you need to add the repository to your Poetry configuration:

---

```
$ poetry config repositories.testpypi https://test.pypi.org/legacy/
```

First, create an account and an API token on TestPyPI. Next, configure Poetry to use that token when uploading to TestPyPI:

```
$ poetry config pypi-token.testpypi <token>
```

You can now specify the repository when publishing your project. Feel free to try this with your own version of the example project:

```
$ poetry publish --repository=testpypi
Publishing random-wikipedia-article (0.1.0) to TestPyPI
 - Uploading random_wikipedia_article-0.1.0-py3-none-any.whl 100%
 - Uploading random_wikipedia_article-0.1.0.tar.gz 100%
```

Some package repositories use HTTP basic authentication with a username and password. You can configure the credentials for such a repository like this:

```
$ poetry config http-basic.<repo> <username>
```

The command prompts you for the password and stores it in the system keyring, if available, or in the *auth.toml* file on disk.

Alternatively, you can also configure a repository via environment variables (replace *<REPO>* with the repository name in uppercase, such as PYPI):

```
$ export POETRY_REPOSITORIES_<REPO>_URL=<url>
$ export POETRY_PYPI_TOKEN_<REPO>=<token>
$ export POETRY_HTTP_BASIC_<REPO>_USERNAME=<username>
$ export POETRY_HTTP_BASIC_<REPO>_PASSWORD=<password>
```

Poetry also supports repositories that are secured by mutual TLS or use a custom certificate authority; see the official documentation (*https://oreil.ly/21oFD*) for details.

## Fetching Packages from Package Sources

You've seen how to upload your package to repositories other than PyPI. Poetry also supports alternate repositories on the consumer side: you can add packages to your project from sources other than PyPI. While upload targets are a user setting and stored in the Poetry configuration, package sources are a project setting, stored in *pyproject.toml*.

Add a package source using the command poetry source add:

```
$ poetry source add <repo> <url> --priority=supplemental
```

Poetry searches supplemental sources if the package wasn't found on PyPI. If you want to disable PyPI, configure a primary source instead (the default priority):

```
$ poetry source add <repo> <url>
```

You configure credentials for package sources just like you do for repositories:

```
$ poetry config http-basic.<repo> <username>
```

You can now add packages from the alternate source:

```
$ poetry add httpx --source=<repo>
```

The following command lists the package sources for the project:

```
$ poetry source show
```

 Specify the source when adding packages from supplemental sources. Otherwise, Poetry searches all sources when looking up a package. An attacker could upload a malicious package to PyPI with the same name as your internal package (*dependency confusion attack*).

# Extending Poetry with Plugins

Poetry comes with a plugin system that lets you extend its functionality. Use pipx to inject the plugin into Poetry's environment:

```
$ pipx inject poetry <plugin>
```

Replace *<plugin>* with the name of the plugin on PyPI.

If the plugin affects the build stage of your project, add it to the build dependencies in *pyproject.toml*, as well. See "The Dynamic Versioning Plugin" on page 129 for an example.

By default, pipx upgrades applications without the injected packages. Use the option --include-injected to also upgrade application plugins:

```
$ pipx upgrade --include-injected poetry
```

If you no longer need the plugin, remove it from the injected packages:

```
$ pipx uninject poetry <plugin>
```

If you're no longer sure which plugins you have installed, list them like this:

```
$ poetry self show plugins
```

In this section, I'll introduce you to three useful plugins for Poetry:

poetry-plugin-export
  Lets you generate requirements and constraints files

poetry-plugin-bundle
  Lets you deploy the project to a virtual environment

poetry-dynamic-versioning
  Populates the project version from the VCS

## Generating Requirements Files with the Export Plugin

Poetry's lock file is great to ensure that everybody on your team, and every deployment environment, ends up with the same dependencies. But what do you do if you can't use Poetry in some context? For example, you may need to deploy your project on a system that has only a Python interpreter and the bundled pip.

As of this writing, there's no lock file standard in the wider Python world; each packaging tool that supports lock files implements its own format.[3] None of these lock file formats has support in pip. But we do have requirements files.

Requirements files let you pin packages to an exact version, require their artifacts to match cryptographic hashes, and use environment markers to restrict packages to specific Python versions and platforms. Wouldn't it be nice if you could generate one from your *poetry.lock* for interoperability with non-Poetry environments? This is precisely what the export plugin achieves.

Install the plugin with pipx:

```
$ pipx inject poetry poetry-plugin-export
```

The plugin powers the `poetry export` command, which sports a `--format` option to specify the output format. By default, the command writes to the standard output stream; use the `--output` option to specify a destination file:

```
$ poetry export --format=requirements.txt --output=requirements.txt
```

Distribute the requirements file to the target system and use pip to install the dependencies (typically followed by installing a wheel of your project):

```
$ python3 -m pip install -r requirements.txt
```

Exporting to requirements format is useful beyond deploying. Many tools work with requirements files as the de facto industry standard. For example, you can scan a requirements file for dependencies with known security vulnerabilities using a tool like Safety (*https://oreil.ly/_nekX*).

## Deploying Environments with the Bundle Plugin

In the previous section, you saw how to deploy your project on a system without Poetry. If you do have Poetry available, you might be wondering: can you just deploy with `poetry install`? You could, but Poetry performs an editable install of your project—you'll be running your application from the source tree. That may not be acceptable in a production environment. Editable installs also limit your ability to ship the virtual environment to another destination.

---

3 Apart from Poetry's own *poetry.lock* and the closely related PDM lock file format, there's pipenv's *Pipfile.lock* and the `conda-lock` format for Conda environments.

The bundle plugin allows you to deploy your project and locked dependencies to a virtual environment of your choosing. It creates the environment, installs the dependencies from the lock file, then builds and installs a wheel of your project.

Install the plugin with pipx:

```
$ pipx inject poetry poetry-plugin-bundle
```

After installation, you'll see a new `poetry bundle` subcommand. Let's use that to bundle the project into a virtual environment in a directory named *app*. Use the `--python` option to specify the interpreter for the environment and the option `--only=main` to exclude development dependencies:

```
$ poetry bundle venv --python=/usr/bin/python3 --only=main app

  - Bundled random-wikipedia-article (0.1.0) into app
```

Test the environment by running the entry-point script for the application:[4]

```
$ app/bin/random-wikipedia-article
```

You can use the bundle plugin to create a minimal Docker image for production. Docker supports *multistage builds*, where the first stage builds the application in a full-fledged build environment, and the second stage copies the build artifacts over into a minimal runtime environment. This allows you to ship slim images to production, speeding up deployments and reducing bloat and potential vulnerabilities in your production environments.

In Example 5-7, the first stage installs Poetry and the bundle plugin, copies the Poetry project, and bundles it into a self-contained virtual environment. The second stage copies the virtual environment into a minimal Python image.

*Example 5-7. Multistage Dockerfile with Poetry*

```
FROM debian:12-slim AS builder    ❶
RUN apt-get update && \
    apt-get install --no-install-suggests --no-install-recommends --yes pipx
ENV PATH="/root/.local/bin:${PATH}"
RUN pipx install poetry
RUN pipx inject poetry poetry-plugin-bundle
WORKDIR /src
COPY . .
RUN poetry bundle venv --python=/usr/bin/python3 --only=main /venv

FROM gcr.io/distroless/python3-debian12    ❷
COPY --from=builder /venv /venv    ❸
ENTRYPOINT ["/venv/bin/random-wikipedia-article"]    ❹
```

---

4 Replace *bin* with *Scripts* if you're on Windows.

❶ The first FROM directive introduces the build stage, where you build and install your project. The base image is a slim variant of the Debian stable release.

❷ The second FROM directive defines the image that you deploy to production. The base image is a *distroless* Python image for Debian stable: Python language support minus the operating system.

❸ The COPY directive allows you to copy the virtual environment over from the build stage.

❹ The ENTRYPOINT directive lets you run the entry-point script when users invoke docker run with the image.

If you have Docker installed, you can try this out. First, create a *Dockerfile* in your project with the contents from Example 5-7. Next, build and run the Docker image:

```
$ docker build -t random-wikipedia-article .
$ docker run --rm -ti random-wikipedia-article
```

You should see the output from random-wikipedia-article in your terminal.

## The Dynamic Versioning Plugin

The dynamic versioning plugin populates the version in the project metadata from a Git tag. Keeping the version in a single place reduces churn (see "Single-Sourcing the Project Version" on page 76). The plugin is based on Dunamai, a Python library for deriving standards-compliant version strings from tags in your version control system.

Install the plugin with pipx and enable it for your project:

```
$ pipx inject poetry "poetry-dynamic-versioning[plugin]"
$ poetry dynamic-versioning enable
```

The second step enables the plugin in the tool section of *pyproject.toml*:

```
[tool.poetry-dynamic-versioning]
enable = true
```

Remember that you have installed the Poetry plugin globally. The explicit opt-in ensures that you don't accidentally start overwriting the version field in unrelated Poetry projects.

Build frontends like pip and build need the plugin when they build your project. For this reason, enabling the plugin also adds it to the build dependencies in *pyproject.toml*. The plugin brings its own build backend, which wraps the one provided by Poetry:

```
[build-system]
requires = ["poetry-core>=1.0.0", "poetry-dynamic-versioning>=1.0.0,<2.0.0"]
build-backend = "poetry_dynamic_versioning.backend"
```

Poetry still requires the `version` field in its own section. Set the field to `"0.0.0"` to indicate that it's unused:

```
[tool.poetry]
version = "0.0.0"
```

You can now add a Git tag to set your project version:

```
$ git tag v1.0.0
$ poetry build
Building random-wikipedia-article (1.0.0)
  - Building sdist
  - Built random_wikipedia_article-1.0.0.tar.gz
  - Building wheel
  - Built random_wikipedia_article-1.0.0-py3-none-any.whl
```

The plugin also replaces `__version__` attributes in Python modules. This mostly works out of the box, but you need to declare *src* layout if you use it:

```
[tool.poetry-dynamic-versioning]
enable = true
substitution.folders = [{path = "src"}]
```

Let's add a `--version` option to the application. Edit *__init__.py* in the package to add the following lines:

```
import argparse

__version__ = "0.0.0"

def main():
    parser = argparse.ArgumentParser(prog="random-wikipedia-article")
    parser.add_argument(
        "--version", action="version", version=f"%(prog)s {__version__}"
    )
    parser.parse_args()
    ...
```

Before proceeding, commit your changes, but without adding another Git tag. Let's try the option in a fresh installation of the project:

```
$ uv venv
$ uv pip install .
$ py -m random_wikipedia_article --version
random-wikipedia-article 1.0.0.post1.dev0+51c266e
```

As you can see, the plugin rewrote the `__version__` attribute during the build. Since you didn't tag the commit, Dunamai marked the version as a developmental post-release of `1.0.0` and appended the commit hash using a local version identifier.

---

# Summary

Poetry provides a unified workflow to manage packaging, dependencies, and environments. Poetry projects are interoperable with standard tooling: you can build them with build and upload them to PyPI with Twine. But the Poetry command-line interface also provides convenient shorthands for these tasks and many more.

Poetry records the precise working set of packages in its lock file, giving you deterministic deployments and checks, as well as a consistent experience when collaborating with others. Poetry can track development dependencies; it organizes them in dependency groups that you can install separately or together. You can extend Poetry with plugins—for example, to deploy the project into a virtual environment or to derive the version number from Git.

If you need reproducible deployments for an application, if your team develops on multiple operating systems, or if you just feel that standard tooling adds too much overhead to your workflows, you should give Poetry a try.

# Testing and Static Analysis

PART III
Testing and Static Analysis

# CHAPTER 6

# Testing with pytest

If you think back to when you wrote your first programs, you may recall a common experience: you had an idea for how a program could help with a real-life task and spent a sizable amount of time coding it from top to bottom, only to be confronted with screens full of disheartening error messages when you finally ran it. Or, worse, it gave you results that were subtly wrong.

There are a few lessons we've all learned from experiences like this. One is to start simple and keep it simple as you iterate on the program. Another lesson is to test early and repeatedly. Initially, this may just mean to run the program manually and validate that it does what it should. Later on, if you break the program into smaller parts, you can test those parts in isolation and automatically. As a side effect, the program gets easier to read and work on, too.

In this chapter, I'll talk about how testing can help you produce value early and consistently. Good tests amount to an executable specification of the code you own. They set you free from institutional knowledge in a team or company, and they speed up your development by giving you immediate feedback on changes.

The third-party testing framework pytest (*https://oreil.ly/HiVnu*) has become somewhat of a de facto standard in the Python world. Tests written with pytest are simple and readable: you write most tests as if there was no framework, using basic language primitives like functions and assertions. Despite its simplicity, the framework is powerful and expressive, notably through its concepts of test fixtures and parameterized tests. Pytest is extensible and comes with a rich ecosystem of plugins.

Pytest originated in the PyPy project, a Python interpreter written in Python. Early on, the PyPy developers worked on a separate standard library called std, later renamed to py. Its testing module py.test became an independent project under the name pytest.

# Writing a Test

Example 6-1 revisits the Wikipedia example from Chapter 3. The program is as simple as it gets—yet it's far from obvious how you'd write tests for it. The `main` function has no inputs and no outputs—only side effects, such as writing to the standard output stream. How would you test a function like this?

*Example 6-1. The `main` function from `random-wikipedia-article`*

```python
def main():
    with urllib.request.urlopen(API_URL) as response:
        data = json.load(response)

    print(data["title"], end="\n\n")
    print(textwrap.fill(data["extract"]))
```

Let's write an *end-to-end test* that runs the program in a subprocess and checks that it completes with nonempty output. End-to-end tests run the entire program the way an end user would (Example 6-2).

*Example 6-2. A test for `random-wikipedia-article`*

```python
import subprocess
import sys

def test_output():
    args = [sys.executable, "-m", "random_wikipedia_article"]
    process = subprocess.run(args, capture_output=True, check=True)
    assert process.stdout
```

 Tests written using pytest are functions whose names start with test. Use the built-in `assert` statement to check for expected behavior. Pytest rewrites the language construct to provide rich error reporting in case of a test failure.

Place the contents of Example 6-2 in the file *test_main.py* in a *tests* directory. Include an empty *__init__.py* file to turn the test suite into an import package. This lets you mirror the layout of the package you're testing,[1] and it gives you the option to import modules with test utilities.

At this point, your project should be structured in the following way:

---

1 Large packages can have modules with the same name—say, `gizmo.foo.registry` and `gizmo.bar.registry`. Under pytest's default import mode (*https://oreil.ly/vAPIj*), test modules must have unique fully qualified names—so you must place the `test_registry` modules in separate `tests.foo` and `tests.bar` packages.

```
random-wikipedia-article
├── pyproject.toml
├── src
│   └── random_wikipedia_article
│       ├── __init__.py
│       └── __main__.py
└── tests
    ├── __init__.py
    └── test_main.py
```

# Managing Test Dependencies

Tests must be able to import your project and its dependencies, so you need to install pytest in your project environment. For example, add a `tests` extra to your project:

```
[project.optional-dependencies]
tests = ["pytest>=8.1.1"]
```

You can now install pytest in the project environment:

```
$ uv pip install -e ".[tests]"
```

Alternatively, compile a requirements file and synchronize your environment:

```
$ uv pip compile --extra=tests pyproject.toml -o dev-requirements.txt
$ uv pip sync dev-requirements.txt
$ uv pip install -e . --no-deps
```

If you use Poetry, add pytest to your project using `poetry add` instead:

```
$ poetry add --group=tests "pytest>=8.1.1"
```

Please refer to these steps when I ask you to add test dependencies later in this chapter.

Finally, let's run the test suite. If you're on Windows, activate the environment before you run the following command:

```
$ py -m pytest
========================= test session starts =========================
platform darwin -- Python 3.12.2, pytest-8.1.1, pluggy-1.4.0
rootdir: ...
collected 1 item

tests/test_main.py .                                           [100%]
========================= 1 passed in 0.01s =========================
```

Use `py -m pytest` even in Poetry projects. It's both shorter and safer than `poetry run pytest`. If you forget to install pytest into the environment, Poetry falls back to your global environment. (The safe variant would be `poetry run python -m pytest`.)

# Designing for Testability

Writing finer-grained tests for the program is much harder. The API endpoint returns a random article, so *which* title and summary should the tests expect? Every invocation sends an HTTP request to the real Wikipedia API. Those network round-trips will make the test suite excruciatingly slow—and you can run tests only when your machine is connected to the internet.

Python programmers have an arsenal of tools at their disposal for situations like this. Most of these involve some form of *monkey patching*, which replaces functions or objects at runtime to make the code easier to test. For example, you can capture program output by replacing sys.stdout with a file-like object that writes to an internal buffer for later inspection. You can replace urlopen with a function that returns canned HTTP responses of your liking. Libraries like responses, respx, or vcr.py provide high-level interfaces that monkey patch the HTTP machinery behind the scenes. More generic approaches use the standard unittest.mock module or pytest's monkeypatch fixture.

> The term *monkey patch* for replacing code at runtime originated at Zope Corporation. Initially, people at Zope called the technique "guerilla patching," since it didn't abide by the usual rules of patch submission. People heard that as "gorilla patch"—and the more refined versions soon became known as "monkey patches."

While these tools serve their purpose, I'd encourage you to focus on the root of the problem: Example 6-1 has no separation of concerns. A single function serves as the application entry point, communicates with an external API, and presents the results on the console. This makes it hard to test its features in isolation.

The program also lacks abstraction—in two ways. First, it doesn't encapsulate implementation details when interfacing with other systems, like interacting with the Wikipedia API or writing to the terminal. Second, its central concept—the Wikipedia article—appears only as an amorphous JSON object: the program doesn't abstract its domain model in any way, such as by defining an Article class.

Example 6-3 shows a refactoring that makes the code more testable. While this version of the program is longer, it expresses its logic more clearly and is more amenable to change. Good tests don't just catch bugs: they improve the design of your code.

*Example 6-3. Refactoring for testability*

```
import sys ❶
from dataclasses import dataclass

@dataclass
class Article:
    title: str = ""
    summary: str = ""

def fetch(url):
    with urllib.request.urlopen(url) as response:
        data = json.load(response)
    return Article(data["title"], data["extract"])

def show(article, file):
    summary = textwrap.fill(article.summary)
    file.write(f"{article.title}\n\n{summary}\n")

def main():
    article = fetch(API_URL)
    show(article, sys.stdout)
```

❶  For brevity, examples in this chapter show imports on first use only.

The refactoring extracts `fetch` and `show` functions from `main`. It also defines an `Article` class as the common denominator of these functions. Let's see how these changes let you test the parts of the program in isolation and in a repeatable way.

The `show` function accepts any file-like object. While `main` passes `sys.stdout`, tests can pass an `io.StringIO` instance to store the output in memory. Example 6-4 uses this technique to check that the output ends with a newline. The final newline ensures the output doesn't run into the next shell prompt.

*Example 6-4. Testing the show function*

```
import io
from random_wikipedia_article import Article, show

def test_final_newline():
    article = Article("Lorem Ipsum", "Lorem ipsum dolor sit amet.")
    file = io.StringIO()
    show(article, file)
    assert file.getvalue().endswith("\n")
```

There's another benefit to the refactoring: the functions hide the implementation behind an interface that involves only your problem domain—URLs, articles, files. This means your tests are less likely to break when you swap out your implementation. Go ahead and change the show function to use Rich, as shown in Example 6-5.[2] You won't need to adapt your tests!

*Example 6-5. Swapping out the implementation of show*

```
from rich.console import Console

def show(article, file):
    console = Console(file=file, width=72, highlight=False)
    console.print(article.title, style="bold", end="\n\n")
    console.print(article.summary)
```

In fact, the whole point of tests is to give you confidence that your program still works after making changes like this. Mocks and monkey patches, on the other hand, are brittle: they tie your test suite to implementation details, making it increasingly hard to change your program down the road.

## Fixtures and Parameterization

Here are some other properties of the show function that you might check for:

- It should include all the words of the title and summary.
- There should be a blank line after the title.
- The summary should not exceed a line length of 72 characters.

Every test for the show function starts by setting up an output buffer. You can use a fixture to remove this code duplication. *Fixtures* are functions declared with the pytest.fixture decorator:

```
@pytest.fixture
def file():
    return io.StringIO()
```

Tests (and fixtures) can use a fixture by including a function parameter with the same name. When pytest invokes the test function, it passes the return value of the fixture function. Let's rewrite Example 6-4 to use the fixture:

```
def test_final_newline(file):
    article = Article("Lorem Ipsum", "Lorem ipsum dolor sit amet.")
    show(article, file)
    assert file.getvalue().endswith("\n")
```

---

2 Remember to add Rich to your project as described in "Specifying Dependencies for a Project" on page 90. If you use Poetry, refer to "Managing Dependencies" on page 117.

---

If you forget to add the parameter file to the test function, you get a confusing error: 'function' object has no attribute 'write'. This happens because the name file now refers to the fixture function in the same module.[3]

If every test used the same article, you'd likely miss some edge cases. For example, you don't want your program to crash if an article comes with an empty title. Example 6-6 runs the test for a number of articles with the @pytest.mark.parametrize decorator.[4]

*Example 6-6. Running tests against multiple articles*

```python
articles = [
    Article(),
    Article("test"),
    Article("Lorem Ipsum", "Lorem ipsum dolor sit amet."),
    Article(
        "Lorem ipsum dolor sit amet, consectetur adipiscing elit",
        "Nulla mattis volutpat sapien, at dapibus ipsum accumsan eu."
    ),
]

@pytest.mark.parametrize("article", articles)
def test_final_newline(article, file):
    show(article, file)
    assert file.getvalue().endswith("\n")
```

If you parameterize many tests in the same way, you can create a *parameterized fixture*, a fixture with multiple values (Example 6-7). As before, pytest runs the test once for each article in articles.

*Example 6-7. Parameterized fixture for running tests against multiple articles*

```python
@pytest.fixture(params=articles)
def article(request):
    return request.param

def test_final_newline(article, file):
    show(article, file)
    assert file.getvalue().endswith("\n")
```

---

3 My reviewer Hynek recommends a technique to avoid this pitfall and get an idiomatic NameError instead. The trick is to name the fixture explicitly with @pytest.fixture(name="file"). This lets you use a private name for the function, such as _file, that doesn't collide with the parameter.

4 Note the somewhat uncommon spelling variant *parametrize* instead of *parameterize*.

So what did you gain here? For one thing, you don't need to decorate each test with `@pytest.mark.parametrize`. There's another advantage if your tests aren't all in the same module: you can place fixtures in a file named *conftest.py* and use them across your entire test suite without imports.

The syntax for parameterized fixtures is somewhat arcane. To keep things simple, I like to define a small helper:

```
def parametrized_fixture(*params):
    return pytest.fixture(params=params)(lambda request: request.param)
```

Use the helper to simplify the fixture from Example 6-7. You can also inline the `articles` variable from Example 6-6:

```
article = parametrized_fixture(Article(), Article("test"), ...)
```

---

## The unittest Framework

The standard library includes a testing framework in the `unittest` module—inspired by JUnit, a Java testing library from the early days of test-driven development. Let's rewrite the test using `unittest` and compare it with the pytest version:

```
import unittest

class TestShow(unittest.TestCase):
    def setUp(self):
        self.article = Article("Lorem Ipsum", "Lorem ipsum dolor sit amet.")
        self.file = io.StringIO()

    def test_final_newline(self):
        show(self.article, self.file)
        self.assertEqual("\n", self.file.getvalue()[-1])
```

In `unittest`, tests are methods with names that start with `test` in a class derived from `unittest.TestCase`. The `assert*` methods let you check for expected properties. The `setUp` method prepares the *test environment* for each test—the test objects each test uses. In this case, you're setting up an `Article` instance and an output buffer for the `show` function.

Run the test suite from the project directory using the command `py -m unittest`:

```
$ py -m unittest
.
----------------------------------------------------------------------
Ran 1 test in 0.000s

OK
```

Writing tests with `unittest` saves you a third-party dependency. If you're already familiar with a JUnit-style framework from another language, you'll feel right at home. But there are several problems with its design:

---

- The class tightly couples tests and the test environment. As a result, you can't reuse test objects as easily as with pytest fixtures.

- The framework uses inheritance to provide shared functionality. This couples tests with the framework plumbing, all in a single namespace and instance.

- Placing tests in a class makes them less readable than a module with functions.

- The assertion methods lack expressivity and generality—every type of check requires a dedicated method. For example, you have `assertEqual` and `assertIn`, but there's no `assertStartsWith`.

 If you have a test suite written with `unittest`, there's no need to rewrite it to start using pytest—pytest "speaks" `unittest`, too. Use pytest as a test runner right away and you can rewrite your test suite incrementally later.

# Advanced Techniques for Fixtures

For the `fetch` function, tests can set up a local HTTP server and perform a *roundtrip* check. This is shown in Example 6-8: you serve an `Article` instance via HTTP, fetch the article from the server, and check that the served and fetched instances are equal.

*Example 6-8. Testing the `fetch` function (version 1)*

```
def test_fetch(article):
    with serve(article) as url:
        assert article == fetch(url)
```

The `serve` helper function takes an article and returns a URL for fetching the article. More precisely, it wraps the URL in a *context manager*, an object for use in a `with` block. This allows `serve` to clean up after itself when you exit the `with` block—by shutting down the server:

```
from contextlib import contextmanager

@contextmanager
def serve(article):
    ... # start the server
    yield f"http://localhost:{server.server_port}"
    ... # shut down the server
```

You can implement the `serve` function using the `http.server` module from the standard library (Example 6-9). Don't worry too much about the details, though. Later in this chapter, I'll introduce the `pytest-httpserver` plugin, which will bear the brunt of the work.

*Example 6-9. The serve function*

```
import http.server
import json
import threading

@contextmanager
def serve(article):
    data = {"title": article.title, "extract": article.summary}
    body = json.dumps(data).encode()

    class Handler(http.server.BaseHTTPRequestHandler):  ❶
        def do_GET(self):
            self.send_response(200)
            self.send_header("Content-Type", "application/json")
            self.send_header("Content-Length", str(len(body)))
            self.end_headers()
            self.wfile.write(body)

    with http.server.HTTPServer(("localhost", 0), Handler) as server:  ❷
        thread = threading.Thread(target=server.serve_forever, daemon=True)  ❸
        thread.start()
        yield f"http://localhost:{server.server_port}"
        server.shutdown()
        thread.join()
```

❶  The request handler responds to every GET request with a UTF-8 encoded JSON representation of the article.

❷  The server accepts only local connections. The operating system randomly assigns the port number.

❸  The server runs in a background thread. This allows control to return to the tests.

Firing up and shutting down a web server for every test is expensive. Would it help to turn the server into a fixture? At first glance, not much—every test gets its own instance of a fixture. However, you can instruct pytest to create a fixture only once during the entire test session, using a *session-scoped fixture*:

```
@pytest.fixture(scope="session")
def httpserver():
    ...
```

That looks more promising, but how do you shut down the server when the tests are done with it? Up to now, your fixtures have only prepared a test object and returned it. You can't run code after a `return` statement. However, you *can* run code after a `yield` statement—so pytest allows you to define a fixture as a generator.

A *generator fixture* prepares a test object, yields it, and cleans up resources at the end—similar to a context manager. You use it in the same way as an ordinary fixture that returns its test object. Pytest handles the setup and teardown phases behind the scenes and calls your test function with the yielded value.

Example 6-10 defines the `httpserver` fixture using the generator technique.

*Example 6-10. The `httpserver` fixture*

```
@pytest.fixture(scope="session")
def httpserver():
    class Handler(http.server.BaseHTTPRequestHandler):
        def do_GET(self):
            article = self.server.article ❶
            data = {"title": article.title, "extract": article.summary}
            body = json.dumps(data).encode()
            ... # as before

    with http.server.HTTPServer(("localhost", 0), Handler) as server:
        thread = threading.Thread(target=server.serve_forever, daemon=True)
        thread.start()
        yield server
        server.shutdown()
        thread.join()
```

❶ Unlike in Example 6-9, there's no `article` in scope. Instead, the request handler accesses it from the `article` attribute on the server (see Example 6-11).

There's still a missing piece: you need to define the `serve` function. The function now depends on the `httpserver` fixture to do its work, so you can't just define it at the module level. Let's move it into the test function for now (Example 6-11).

*Example 6-11. Testing the `fetch` function (version 2)*

```
def test_fetch(article, httpserver):
    def serve(article):
        httpserver.article = article ❶
        return f"http://localhost:{httpserver.server_port}"

    assert article == fetch(serve(article))
```

❶ Store the article in the server so the request handler can access it.

The `serve` function no longer returns a context manager, just a plain URL—the `httpserver` fixture handles all of the setting up and tearing down. But you can still do better. The nested function clutters the test—and every other test for the `fetch` function. Instead, let's define `serve` inside its own fixture—after all, fixtures can return any object, including functions (Example 6-12).

*Example 6-12. The serve fixture*

```
@pytest.fixture
def serve(httpserver):  ❶
    def f(article):  ❷
        httpserver.article = article
        return f"http://localhost:{httpserver.server_port}"
    return f
```

❶    The outer function defines a `serve` fixture, which depends on `httpserver`.

❷    The inner function is the `serve` function you call in your tests.

Thanks to the `serve` fixture, the test function becomes a one-liner (Example 6-13). It's also much faster, because you start and stop the server only once per session.

*Example 6-13. Testing the fetch function (version 3)*

```
def test_fetch(article, serve):
    assert article == fetch(serve(article))
```

Your test isn't tied to any particular HTTP client library. Example 6-14 swaps out the implementation of the `fetch` function to use HTTPX.[5] This would have broken any test that used monkey patching—but your test will still pass!

*Example 6-14. Swapping out the implementation of fetch*

```
import httpx

from importlib.metadata import metadata

USER_AGENT = "{Name}/{Version} (Contact: {Author-email})"

def fetch(url):
    fields = metadata("random-wikipedia-article")
    headers = {"User-Agent": USER_AGENT.format_map(fields)}

    with httpx.Client(headers=headers, http2=True) as client:
        response = client.get(url, follow_redirects=True)
        response.raise_for_status()
        data = response.json()

    return Article(data["title"], data["extract"])
```

---

5 Remember to add a dependency on `httpx[http2]` to your project.

# Extending pytest with Plugins

As you've seen in "Entry Points" on page 79, pytest's extensible design lets anybody contribute pytest plugins and publish them to PyPI,[6] so a rich ecosystem of plugins has evolved. You've already seen the `pytest-sugar` plugin, which enhances pytest's output, including adding a progress bar. In this section, you'll look at a few more.

## The pytest-httpserver Plugin

The `pytest-httpserver` plugin (*https://oreil.ly/E5eH5*) provides an `httpserver` fixture that's more versatile and battle-tested than Example 6-10. Let's use this plugin.

First, add `pytest-httpserver` to your test dependencies. Next, remove the existing `httpserver` fixture from your test module. Finally, update the `serve` fixture to use the plugin (Example 6-15).

*Example 6-15. The* serve *fixture using* `pytest-httpserver`

```
@pytest.fixture
def serve(httpserver):
    def f(article):
        json = {"title": article.title, "extract": article.summary}
        httpserver.expect_request("/").respond_with_json(json)
        return httpserver.url_for("/")
    return f
```

Example 6-15 configures the server to respond to requests to "/" with the JSON representation of the article. The plugin offers much flexibility beyond this use case—for example, you can add custom request handlers or communicate over HTTPS.

## The pytest-xdist Plugin

As your test suite grows, you'll be looking for ways to speed up test runs. Here's an easy way: utilize all your CPU cores. The `pytest-xdist` plugin (*https://oreil.ly/BH58W*) spawns a worker process on each processor and distributes tests randomly across the workers. The randomization also helps detect hidden dependencies between your tests.

---

[6] The cookiecutter pytest-plugin template (*https://oreil.ly/jdwZ_*) gives you a solid project structure for writing your own plugin.

Add `pytest-xdist` to your test dependencies and update your environment. Use the option `--numprocesses` or `-n` to specify the number of worker processes. Specify `auto` to use all physical cores on your system:

```
$ py -m pytest -n auto
```

## The factory-boy and faker Libraries

In "Fixtures and Parameterization" on page 140, you hardcoded the articles your tests run against. Let's avoid this boilerplate—it makes your tests hard to maintain.

Instead, the `factory-boy` library (*https://oreil.ly/0XqY0*) lets you create factories for test objects. You can generate batches of objects with predictable attributes, such as by using a sequence number. Alternatively, you can populate attributes randomly using the `faker` library (*https://oreil.ly/HjT4r*).

Add `factory-boy` to your test dependencies and update your environment. Example 6-16 defines a factory for randomized articles and creates a batch of ten articles for the `article` fixture. (If you want to see `pytest-xdist` in action, increase the number of articles and run pytest with `-n auto`.)

*Example 6-16. Creating a batch of articles with factory-boy and faker*

```
from factory import Factory, Faker

class ArticleFactory(Factory):
    class Meta:
        model = Article ❶

    title = Faker("sentence") ❷
    summary = Faker("paragraph")

article = parametrized_fixture(*ArticleFactory.build_batch(10)) ❸
```

❶  Specify the class of the test objects with `Meta.model`.

❷  Use a random sentence for the title and a random paragraph for the summary.

❸  Generate a batch of articles using the `build_batch` method.

This simplified factory doesn't cover edge cases particularly well. For a real-world application, you should include empty and extremely large strings, as well as unusual characters such as control characters. Another great testing library that lets you explore the search space of possible inputs is `hypothesis` (*https://oreil.ly/mqv5H*).

## Other Plugins

Pytest plugins perform a variety of functions (Table 6-1). These include executing tests in parallel or in random order, presenting or reporting test results in custom ways, and integrating with frameworks and other tools. Many plugins provide useful fixtures—such as for interacting with external systems or creating test doubles.[7]

*Table 6-1. A selection of pytest plugins*

| Plugin | Category | Description | Option |
|---|---|---|---|
| `pytest-xdist` | Execution | Distribute tests across multiple CPUs | `--numprocesses` |
| `pytest-sugar` | Presentation | Enhance output with a progress bar | |
| `pytest-icdiff` | Presentation | Show colorized diffs on test failures | |
| `anyio` | Frameworks | Use asynchronous tests with asyncio and trio | |
| `pytest-httpserver` | Fake servers | Spawn an HTTP server with canned responses | |
| `pytest-factoryboy` | Fake data | Turn factories into fixtures | |
| `pytest-datadir` | Storage | Access static data in your test suite | |
| `pytest-cov` | Coverage | Produce coverage reports with Coverage.py | `--cov` |
| `xdoctest` | Documentation | Run code examples from docstrings | `--xdoctest` |
| `typeguard` | Type checking | Type-check your code at runtime | `--typeguard-packages` |

> Find each project on PyPI at *https://pypi.org/project/<name>*. The project homepage is available under *Project links* in the navigation bar.

# Summary

In this chapter, you've learned how to test your Python projects with pytest:

- Tests are functions that exercise your code and check for expected behavior using the `assert` built-in. Prefix their names—and the names of the containing modules—with `test_`, and pytest will discover them automatically.

- Fixtures are functions or generators that set up and tear down test objects; declare them with the `@pytest.fixture` decorator. You can use a fixture in a test by including a parameter named like the fixture.

---

7 *Test double* is the umbrella term for the various kinds of objects tests use in lieu of the real objects used in production code. A good overview is "Mocks Aren't Stubs" (*https://oreil.ly/BGTot*) by Martin Fowler, January 2, 2007.

- Plugins for pytest can provide useful fixtures, as well as modify test execution, enhance reporting, and much more.

One of the prime characteristics of good software is that it's easy to change, since any piece of code used in the real world must adapt to evolving requirements and an ever-changing environment. Tests make change easier in several ways:

- They drive software design toward loosely coupled building blocks that you can test in isolation: fewer interdependencies mean fewer barriers to change.
- They document and enforce expected behavior. That gives you the freedom and confidence to continuously refactor your codebase—keeping it maintainable as it grows and transforms.
- They reduce the cost of change by detecting defects early. The earlier you catch an issue, the cheaper it is to work out the root cause and develop a fix.

End-to-end tests give you high confidence that a feature works as designed—but they're slow, flaky, and bad at isolating the causes of failures. Let most of your tests be unit tests. Avoid monkey patching to break the dependencies of your code for testability. Instead, decouple the core of your application from I/O, external systems, and third-party frameworks. Good software design and a solid testing strategy will keep your test suite blazingly fast and resilient to change.

This chapter focuses on the tooling side of things, but there's so much more to good testing practices. Luckily, other people have written fantastic texts about this topic. Here are three of my all-time favorites:

- Kent Beck, *Test-Driven Development: By Example* (London: Pearson, 2002).
- Michael Feathers, *Working Effectively with Legacy Code* (London: Pearson, 2004).
- Harry Percival and Bob Gregory, *Architecture Patterns in Python* (Sebastopol: O'Reilly, 2020).

If you want to know all about how to test with pytest, read Brian's book:

- Brian Okken, *Python Testing with pytest: Simple, Rapid, Effective, and Scalable*, Second Edition (Raleigh: The Pragmatic Bookshelf, 2022).

# CHAPTER 7

# Measuring Coverage
# with Coverage.py

How confident in a code change are you when your tests pass?

If you look at tests as a way to detect bugs, you can describe their sensitivity and specificity.

The *sensitivity* of your test suite is the probability of a test failure when there's a defect in the code. If large parts of the code are untested, or if the tests don't check for expected behavior, you have low sensitivity.

The *specificity* of your tests is the probability that they will pass if the code is free of defects. If your tests are *flaky* (they fail intermittently) or *brittle* (they fail when you change implementation details), then you have low specificity. Invariably, people stop paying attention to failing tests. This chapter isn't about specificity, though.

There's a great way to boost the sensitivity of your tests: when you add or change behavior, write a failing test before the code that makes it pass. If you do this, your test suite will capture your expectations for the code.

Another effective strategy is to test your software with the various inputs and environmental constraints that you expect it to encounter in the real world. Cover the edge cases of a function, like empty lists or negative numbers. Test common error scenarios, not just the "happy path."

*Code coverage* is a measure of the extent to which the test suite exercises your code. Full coverage doesn't guarantee high sensitivity: if your tests cover every line in your code, you can still have bugs. It's an upper bound, though. If your code coverage is 80%, then 20% of your code will *never* trigger a test failure, no matter how many bugs creep in. It's also a quantitative measure amenable to automated tools. These two properties make coverage a useful proxy for sensitivity.

In short, coverage tools record each line in your code when you run it. After completion, they report the overall percentage of executed lines with respect to the entire codebase.

Coverage tools aren't limited to measuring test coverage. For example, code coverage lets you find which modules an API endpoint in a large codebase uses. Or you could use it to determine the extent to which code examples document your project.

In this chapter, I'll explain how to measure code coverage with Coverage.py, a coverage tool for Python. In the main sections of this chapter, you'll learn how to install, configure, and run Coverage.py, as well as how to identify missing lines of source code and missing branches in the control flow. I'll explain how to measure code coverage across multiple environments and processes. Finally, I'll talk about what code coverage you should aim for and how to reach your coverage target.

How does coverage measurement work in Python? The interpreter lets you register a callback—a *trace function*—using the function `sys.settrace`. From that point onward, the interpreter invokes the callback whenever it executes a line of code—as well as in some other situations, like entering or returning from functions or raising exceptions. Coverage tools register a trace function that records each executed line of source code in a local database.

---

## The trace Module

Python's standard library includes a coverage tool in the `trace` module. Let's use it to measure test coverage for the `random-wikipedia-article` project. Run the test suite via `trace` in the active environment, as shown here:

```
$ py -m trace --count --summary --missing -C coverage --module pytest
============================ test session starts ============================
platform darwin -- Python 3.12.2, pytest-8.1.1, pluggy-1.4.0
rootdir: ...
configfile: pyproject.toml
plugins: Faker-24.2.0, anyio-4.3.0, xdist-3.5.0, pytest_httpserver-1.0.10
collected 21 items

tests/test_main.py ....................                          [100%]

============================ 21 passed in 3.75s ============================
lines   cov%   module   (path)
  26    92%    random_wikipedia_article.__init__   (...)
  33   100%    tests.test_main   (...)
...
```

The command asks `trace` to count how often each line is executed. It writes the results to *<module>.cover* files in the *coverage* directory, marking missed lines with the string >>>>>>. It also writes a summary to the terminal, with coverage percentages for every module.

The summary includes modules from the standard library and third-party packages. It's easy to miss the fact that your __main__ module doesn't appear at all. If you're curious why the __init__ module only has 92% coverage, take a look at the file

---

*random_wikipedia_article.\_\_init\_\_.cover*. (Bear with me, we'll get to those missing lines shortly.)

Measuring coverage with the standard library alone is cumbersome, even for a simple script like `random-wikipedia-article`. The `trace` module is an early proof of concept for Python code coverage. For real-world projects, you should use the third-party package Coverage.py.

# Using Coverage.py

Coverage.py (*https://oreil.ly/aiyTK*) is a mature and widely used code coverage tool for Python. Created over two decades ago—predating PyPI and setuptools—and actively maintained ever since, it has measured coverage on every interpreter since Python 2.1.

Add `coverage[toml]` to your test dependencies (see "Managing Test Dependencies" on page 137). The `toml` extra allows Coverage.py to read its configuration from *pyproject.toml* on older interpreters. Since Python 3.11, the standard library includes the `tomllib` module for parsing TOML files.

Measuring coverage is a two-step process. First, you gather coverage data during a test run with `coverage run`. Second, you compile an aggregated report from the data with `coverage report`. Each command has a table in *pyproject.toml* under `tool.coverage`.

Start by configuring which packages you want to measure—it lets Coverage.py report modules that never showed up during execution, like the \_\_main\_\_ module earlier. (Even without the setting, it won't drown you in reports about the standard library.) Specify your top-level import package as well as the test suite:

```
[tool.coverage.run]
source = ["random_wikipedia_article", "tests"]
```

Measuring code coverage for your test suite may seem strange—but you should always do it. It alerts you when tests don't run and helps you identify unreachable code within them. Treat your tests the same way you would treat any other code.[1]

You can invoke `coverage run` with a Python script, followed by its command-line arguments. Alternatively, you can use its `-m` option with an importable module. Use the second method—it ensures that you run pytest from the current environment:

---

[1] Ned Batchelder, "You Should Include Your Tests in Coverage" (*https://oreil.ly/VAR1v*), August 11, 2020.

```
$ py -m coverage run -m pytest
```

After running this command, you'll find a file named *.coverage* in the current directory. Coverage.py uses it to store the coverage data it gathered during the test run.[2]

Coverage reports display the overall percentage of code coverage, as well as a breakdown per source file. Use the show_missing setting to also include line numbers for statements missing from coverage:

```
[tool.coverage.report]
show_missing = true
```

Run coverage report to show the coverage report in the terminal:

```
$ py -m coverage report
Name                                         Stmts   Miss   Cover   Missing
-----------------------------------------------------------------------------
src/random_wikipedia_article/__init__.py        26      2     92%   37-38
src/random_wikipedia_article/__main__.py         2      2      0%   1-3
tests/__init__.py                                0      0    100%
tests/test_main.py                              33      0    100%
-----------------------------------------------------------------------------
TOTAL                                           61      4     93%
```

Overall, your project has a coverage of 93%—four statements never showed up during the tests. The test suite itself has full coverage, as you would expect.

Let's take a closer look at those missing statements. The Missing column in the coverage report lists them by line number. You can use your code editor to display the source code with line numbers, or the standard cat -n command on Linux and macOS. Again, the entire __main__ module is missing from coverage:

```
1   from random_wikipedia_article import main   # missing
2
3   main()                                       # missing
```

The missing lines in *__init__.py* correspond to the body of the main function:

```
36  def main():
37      article = fetch(API_URL)     # missing
38      show(article, sys.stdout)    # missing
```

This is surprising—the end-to-end test from Example 6-2 runs the entire program, so all of those lines are definitely being tested. For now, disable coverage measurements for the __main__ module:

```
[tool.coverage.run]
omit = ["*/__main__.py"]
```

---

2 Under the hood, the *.coverage* file is just a SQLite database. Feel free to poke around if you have the sqlite3 command-line utility ready on your system.

You can exclude the main function using a special comment:

```
def main():  # pragma: no cover
    article = fetch(API_URL)
    show(article, sys.stdout)
```

If this feels like cheating, bear with me until "Measuring in Subprocesses" on page 159, where you'll re-enable coverage measurements for these lines.

If you run both steps again, Coverage.py will report full code coverage. Let's make sure you'll notice any lines that aren't exercised by your tests. Configure Coverage.py to fail if the percentage drops below 100% again:

```
[tool.coverage.report]
fail_under = 100
```

# Branch Coverage

If an article has an empty summary, random-wikipedia-article prints a trailing blank line (yikes). Those empty summaries are rare, but they exist, and this should be a quick fix. Example 7-1 modifies show to print only nonempty summaries.

*Example 7-1. Printing only nonempty summaries in show*

```
def show(article, file):
    console = Console(file=file, width=72, highlight=False)
    console.print(article.title, style="bold", end="\n\n")
    if article.summary:
        console.print(article.summary)
```

Curiously, the coverage stays at 100%—even though you didn't write a test first.

By default, Coverage.py measures *statement coverage*—the percentage of statements in your modules that the interpreter executed during the tests. If the summary isn't empty, every statement in the function gets executed.

On the other hand, the tests exercised only one of two code paths through the function—they never skipped the if body. Coverage.py also supports *branch coverage*, which looks at all the transitions between statements in your code and measures the percentage of those traversed during the tests. You should always enable it, as it's more precise than statement coverage:

```
[tool.coverage.run]
branch = true
```

Re-run the tests, and you'll see Coverage.py flag the missing transition from the if statement on line 33 to the exit of the function:

```
$ py -m coverage run -m pytest
$ py -m coverage report
```

```
Name                    Stmts   Miss Branch BrPart  Cover   Missing
-------------------------------------------------------------------
src/.../__init__.py        24      0      6      1    97%   33->exit
tests/__init__.py           0      0      0      0   100%
tests/test_main.py         33      0      6      0   100%
-------------------------------------------------------------------
TOTAL                      57      0     12      1    99%
Coverage failure: total of 99 is less than fail-under=100
```

Example 7-2 brings coverage back to 100%. It includes an article with an empty summary and adds the missing test for trailing blank lines.

*Example 7-2. Testing articles with empty summaries*

```python
article = parametrized_fixture(
    Article("test"), *ArticleFactory.build_batch(10)
)


def test_trailing_blank_lines(article, file):
    show(article, file)
    assert not file.getvalue().endswith("\n\n")
```

Run the tests again—and they fail! Can you spot the bug in Example 7-1?

Empty summaries produce two blank lines: one to separate the title and the summary, and one from printing the empty summary. You've removed only the second one. Example 7-3 removes the first one as well. Thanks, Coverage.py!

*Example 7-3. Avoiding both trailing blank lines in show*

```python
def show(article, file):
    console = Console(file=file, width=72, highlight=False)
    console.print(article.title, style="bold")
    if article.summary:
        console.print(f"\n{article.summary}")
```

# Testing in Multiple Environments

You will often need to support a variety of Python versions. Python releases come out every year, while long term support (LTS) distros can reach back a decade into Python's history. End-of-life Python versions can have a surprising afterlife—distributors may provide security patches years after the core Python team ends support.

Let's update random-wikipedia-article to support Python 3.7, which reached its end-of-life in June 2023. I'm assuming your project requires Python 3.10, with lower bounds on all dependencies. First, relax the Python requirement in *pyproject.toml*:

```
[project]
requires-python = ">=3.7"
```

Next, check if your dependencies are compatible with the Python version. Use uv to compile a separate requirements file for a Python 3.7 environment:

```
$ uv venv -p 3.7
$ uv pip compile --extra=tests pyproject.toml -o py37-dev-requirements.txt
  × No solution found when resolving dependencies: ...
```

The error indicates that your preferred version of HTTPX has already dropped Python 3.7. Remove your lower version bound and try again. After a few similar errors and removing the lower bounds of other packages, dependency resolution finally succeeds. Restore the lower bounds using the older versions of these packages.

You'll also need the backport importlib-metadata (see "Environment Markers" on page 94). Add the following entry to the project.dependencies field:

```
importlib-metadata>=6.7.0; python_version < '3.8'
```

Update the __init__.py module to fall back to the backport:

```
if sys.version_info >= (3, 8):
    from importlib.metadata import metadata
else:
    from importlib_metadata import metadata
```

Compile the requirements one more time. Finally, update your project environment:

```
$ uv pip sync py37-dev-requirements.txt
$ uv pip install -e . --no-deps
```

# Parallel Coverage

If you now re-run Coverage.py under Python 3.7, it reports the first branch of the if statement as missing. This makes sense: your code executes the else branch and imports the backport instead of the standard library.

It may be tempting to exclude this line from coverage measurements—but don't. Third-party dependencies like the backport can break your code, too. Instead, collect coverage data from both environments.

First, switch the environment back to Python 3.12 using your original requirements:

```
$ uv venv -p 3.12
$ uv pip sync dev-requirements.txt
$ uv pip install -e . --no-deps
```

By default, `coverage run` overwrites any existing coverage data—but you can tell it to append the data instead. Re-run Coverage.py with the `--append` option and confirm you have full test coverage:

```
$ py -m coverage run --append -m pytest
$ py -m coverage report
```

With a single file for coverage data, it's easy to erase data accidentally. If you forget to pass the `--append` option, you'll have to run the tests again. You could configure Coverage.py to append by default, but that's error-prone, too: if you forget to run `coverage erase` periodically, you'll end up with stale data in your report.

There's a better way to gather coverage across multiple environments. Coverage.py lets you record coverage data in separate files on each run. Enable this behavior with the `parallel` setting:[3]

```
[tool.coverage.run]
parallel = true
```

Coverage reports are always based on a single data file, even in parallel mode. You merge the data files using the command `coverage combine`. That turns the two-step process from earlier into a three-step one: first, `coverage run`; second, `coverage combine`; third, `coverage report`.

Let's put all of this together. For each Python version, set up the environment and run the tests, as shown here for Python 3.7:

```
$ uv venv -p 3.7
$ uv pip sync py37-dev-requirements.txt
$ uv pip install -e . --no-deps
$ py -m coverage run -m pytest
```

At this point, you'll have multiple *.coverage.** files in your project. Aggregate them into a single *.coverage* file using the command `coverage combine`:

```
$ py -m coverage combine
Combined data file .coverage.somehost.26719.001909
Combined data file .coverage.somehost.26766.146311
```

Finally, produce the coverage report with `coverage report`:

```
$ py -m coverage report
```

Does it sound *incredibly* tedious to gather coverage like this? In Chapter 8, you'll learn how to automate testing across multiple Python environments. You'll run this entire process using a single three-letter command.

---

3 The name `parallel` is somewhat misleading; the setting has nothing to do with parallel execution.

# Measuring in Subprocesses

At the end of "Using Coverage.py" on page 153, you had to disable coverage for the `main` function and the `__main__` module. But the end-to-end test certainly exercises this code. Let's remove the `# pragma` comment and the `omit` setting and figure this out.

Think about how Coverage.py registers a trace function that records executed lines. Maybe you can already guess what's going on here: the end-to-end test runs your program in a separate process. Coverage.py never registered its trace function on the interpreter in that process. None of those executed lines were recorded anywhere.

Coverage.py provides a public API to enable tracing in the current process: the `coverage.process_startup` function. You could call the function when your application starts up. But there must be a better way—you shouldn't have to modify your code to support code coverage.

It turns out you don't need to. You can place a *.pth* file in the environment that calls the function during interpreter startup. This leverages a little-known Python feature (see "Site Packages" on page 49): the interpreter executes lines starting with an `import` statement in a *.pth* file.

Install a *_coverage.pth* file into the *site-packages* directory of your environment, with the following contents:

```
import coverage; coverage.process_startup()
```

You can find the *site-packages* directory under *lib/python3.x* on Linux and macOS, and under *Lib* on Windows.

Additionally, you need to set the environment variable `COVERAGE_PROCESS_START`. On Linux and macOS, use this syntax:

```
$ export COVERAGE_PROCESS_START=pyproject.toml
```

On Windows, use the following syntax instead:

```
> $env:COVERAGE_PROCESS_START = 'pyproject.toml'
```

Re-run the test suite, combine the data files, and display the coverage report. Thanks to measuring coverage in the subprocess, the program should have full coverage again.

 Measuring coverage in subprocesses works only in parallel mode. Without parallel mode, the main process overwrites the coverage data from the subprocess, because both use the same data file.

---

**The pytest-cov Plugin**

The pytest plugin `pytest-cov` enables coverage measurements with Coverage.py when you run pytest. Add the plugin to your test dependencies and run pytest with the `--cov` option to enable it. You can still configure Coverage.py in *pyproject.toml*. Alternatively, the plugin exposes `--cov-*` options for various configuration settings.

The plugin aims to make everything work out of the box, behind the scenes—including subprocess coverage. The convenience comes at the price of a layer of indirection. Running `coverage` directly provides finer-grained control.

---

# What Coverage to Aim For

Any coverage percentage below 100% means your tests won't detect bugs in some parts of your codebase. If you're working on a new project, there isn't any other meaningful coverage target.

That doesn't imply you should test every single line of code. Consider a log statement for debugging a rare situation. The statement may be difficult to exercise from a test. At the same time, it's probably low-risk, trivial code. Writing that test won't increase your confidence in the code significantly. Exclude the line from coverage using a *pragma* comment:

```
if rare_condition:
    print("got rare condition")  # pragma: no cover
```

Don't exclude code from coverage just because it's cumbersome to test. When you start working with a new library or interfacing with a new system, it usually takes some time to figure out how to test your code. But often those tests end up detecting bugs that would have gone unnoticed and caused problems in production.

Legacy projects often consist of a large codebase with minimal test coverage. As a general rule, coverage in such projects should increase *monotonically*—no individual change should lead to a drop in coverage.

You'll often find yourself in a dilemma here: to test, you need to refactor the code, but refactoring is too risky without tests. Find the minimal safe refactoring to increase testability. Often, this consists of breaking a dependency of the code under test.[4]

For example, you may be testing a large function that, among other things, also connects to the production database. Add an optional parameter that lets you pass the connection from the outside. Tests can then pass a connection to an in-memory database instead.

---

4  Martin Fowler, "Legacy Seam" (*https://oreil.ly/-K78B*), January 4, 2024.

Example 7-4 recaps the Coverage.py settings you've used in this chapter.

*Example 7-4. Configuring Coverage.py in pyproject.toml*

```
[tool.coverage.run]
source = ["random_wikipedia_article", "tests"]
branch = true
parallel = true
omit = ["*/__main__.py"]  # avoid this if you can

[tool.coverage.report]
show_missing = true
fail_under = 100
```

# Summary

You can measure the extent to which the test suite exercises your project using Coverage.py. Coverage reports are useful for discovering untested lines. Branch coverage captures the control flow of your program instead of isolated lines of source code. Parallel coverage lets you measure coverage across multiple environments. You need to combine the data files before reporting. Measuring coverage in subprocesses requires setting up a *.pth* file and an environment variable.

Measuring test coverage effectively for a project requires some amount of configuration, as well as the right tool incantations. In the next chapter, you'll see how you can automate these steps with Nox. You'll set up checks that give you confidence in your changes—while staying out of your way.

# CHAPTER 8

# Automation with Nox

When you maintain a Python project, you're faced with many chores. Running checks on your code is an important part:

- Testing helps you reduce the defect rate of your code (Chapter 6).
- Coverage reporting pinpoints untested parts of your code (Chapter 7).
- Linters analyze your source code to find ways to improve it (Chapter 9).
- Code formatters lay out the source code in a readable way (Chapter 9).
- Type checkers verify the type correctness of your code (Chapter 10).

Other chores include:

- Building and publishing packages for distribution (Chapter 3)
- Updating the dependencies of your project (Chapter 4)
- Deploying your service (see Example 5-7 in Chapter 5)
- Building the documentation for your project

Automating these tasks has many benefits. You focus on coding while the check suite covers your back. You gain confidence in the steps that take your code from development to production. You remove human error and encode each process so others can review and improve it.

Automation gives you leverage to make each step as repeatable, each result as reproducible, as possible. Checks and tasks run in the same way on developer machines and in continuous integration (CI). They run across different Python versions, operating systems, and platforms.

In this chapter, you'll learn about Nox, a Python automation framework. Nox serves as a single entry point to your checks and tasks—for your team, external contributors, and automated systems like CI runners.

You write Nox sessions in plain Python: each Nox session is a Python function that executes commands in a dedicated, isolated environment. Using Python as the automation language gives Nox great simplicity, portability, and expressivity.

# First Steps with Nox

Install Nox globally using pipx:

```
$ pipx install --python=3.12 nox
```

Specify the latest stable version of Python—Nox defaults to that version when creating environments. Pipx makes the command nox available globally, while keeping its dependencies isolated from your global Python installation (see "Installing Applications with pipx" on page 38).

Configure Nox in a Python file named *noxfile.py* in your project, next to *pyproject.toml*. Example 8-1 shows a *noxfile.py* for running the test suite. It's meant for a simple Python project with no test dependencies besides pytest.

*Example 8-1. A session for running the test suite*

```
import nox


@nox.session
def tests(session):
    session.install(".", "pytest")
    session.run("pytest")
```

*Sessions* are the central concept in Nox: each session comprises an environment and some commands to run within it. You define a session by writing a Python function decorated with @nox.session. The function receives a session object as an argument, which you can use to install packages (session.install) and run commands (session.run) in the session environment.

You can try the session with the example project from previous chapters. For now, add your test dependencies to the session.install arguments:

```
session.install(".", "pytest", "pytest-httpserver", "factory-boy")
```

Invoke nox without arguments to run all sessions in the *noxfile.py*:

```
$ nox
nox > Running session tests
nox > Creating virtual environment (virtualenv) using python in .nox/tests
nox > python -m pip install . pytest
nox > pytest
========================= tests session starts =========================
...
```

```
=========================== 21 passed in 0.94s ===========================
nox > Session tests was successful.
```

As you can see from the output, Nox starts by creating a virtual environment for the `tests` session using `virtualenv`. If you're curious, you can find this environment under the *.nox* directory in your project.

 By default, environments use the same interpreter as Nox itself. In "Working with Multiple Python Interpreters" on page 168, you'll learn how to run sessions on another interpreter, and even across multiple ones.

First, the session installs the project and pytest into its environment. The function `session.install` is just `pip install` underneath. You can pass any appropriate options and arguments to pip. For example, you can install your dependencies from a requirements file:

```
session.install("-r", "dev-requirements.txt")
session.install(".", "--no-deps")
```

If you keep your development dependencies in an extra, use the following:

```
session.install(".[tests]")
```

Above, you've used `session.install(".")` to install your project. Behind the scenes, pip builds a wheel using the build backend you've specified in *pyproject.toml*. Nox runs in the directory containing *noxfile.py*, so this command assumes both files are in the same directory.

Nox lets you use uv instead of virtualenv and pip for creating environments and installing packages. You can switch the backend to uv by setting an environment variable:

```
$ export NOX_DEFAULT_VENV_BACKEND=uv
```

Second, the session runs the `pytest` command you just installed. If a command fails, the session is marked as failed. By default, Nox continues with the next session, but it will exit with a nonzero status at the end if any session failed. In the run above, the test suite passes and Nox reports success.

Example 8-2 adds a session to build packages for the project (see Chapter 3). The session also validates the packages using Twine's `check` command.

*Example 8-2. A session for building packages*

```
import shutil
from pathlib import Path
```

```
@nox.session
def build(session):
    session.install("build", "twine")

    distdir = Path("dist")
    if distdir.exists():
        shutil.rmtree(distdir)

    session.run("python", "-m", "build")
    session.run("twine", "check", *distdir.glob("*"))
```

Example 8-2 relies on the standard library for clearing out stale packages and locating the freshly built ones: `Path.glob` matches files against wildcards, and `shutil.rmtree` removes a directory and its contents.

 Nox doesn't implicitly run commands in a shell, unlike tools such as make. Shells differ widely between platforms, so they'd make Nox sessions less portable. For the same reason, avoid Unix utilities like rm or find in your sessions—use Python's standard library instead!

The programs you invoke with `session.run` should be available inside the environment. If they're not, Nox prints a friendly warning and falls back to the system-wide environment. In the Python world, running programs outside their intended environment is a mistake that's easy to make and hard to diagnose. Turn the warning into an error! Example 8-3 shows how.

*Example 8-3. Preventing external commands in Nox sessions*

```
nox.options.error_on_external_run = True ❶
```

❶ Modify `nox.options` at the top of your *noxfile.py*, outside of sessions.

At times, you do need to run external commands, such as non-Python build tools. You can allow external commands by passing the `external` flag to `session.run`. Example 8-4 shows how to build packages using an existing Poetry installation on your system.

*Example 8-4. Using an external command to build the packages*

```
@nox.session
def build(session):
    session.install("twine")
    session.run("poetry", "build", external=True)
    session.run("twine", "check", *Path().glob("dist/*"))
```

You're trading off reliability for speed here. Example 8-2 works with any build backend declared in *pyproject.toml* and installs it in an isolated environment on each run. Example 8-4 assumes that contributors have a recent version of Poetry on their system and breaks if they don't. Prefer the first method unless every developer environment has a well-known Poetry version.

# Working with Sessions

Over time, *noxfile.py* may accumulate a number of sessions. The `--list` option gives you a quick overview of them. If you add module and function docstrings with helpful descriptions, Nox includes them in the listing as well:

```
$ nox --list
Run the checks and tasks for this project.

Sessions defined in /path/to/noxfile.py:

* tests -> Run the test suite.
* build -> Build the package.

sessions marked with * are selected, sessions marked with - are skipped.
```

Running Nox with the `--session` option lets you select individual sessions by name:

```
$ nox --session tests
```

During development, running `nox` repeatedly lets you catch errors early. On the other hand, you don't need to validate your packages each time. Fortunately, you can change which sessions run by default by setting `nox.options.sessions`:

```
nox.options.sessions = ["tests"]
```

Now, when you run `nox` without arguments, only the `tests` session runs. You can still select the `build` session using the `--session` option. Command-line options override values specified in `nox.options` in *noxfile.py*.[1]

 Keep your default sessions aligned with the mandatory checks for your project. Contributors should be able to run `nox` without arguments to check if their code changes are acceptable.

Every time a session runs, Nox creates a fresh virtual environment and installs the dependencies. This is a good default, because it makes the checks strict, deterministic,

---

[1] In case you're wondering, always use the plural form `nox.options.sessions` in *noxfile.py*. On the command line, both `--session` and `--sessions` work. You can specify any number of sessions with these options.

and repeatable. You won't miss problems with your code due to stale packages in the session environment.

However, Nox gives you a choice. Setting up environments each time might be a tad slow if you re-run your tests in quick succession while coding. You can reuse environments with the option -r or --reuse-existing-virtualenvs. Additionally, you can skip installation commands by specifying --no-install, or combine these options using the shorthand -R:

```
$ nox -R
nox > Running session tests
nox > Re-using existing virtual environment at .nox/tests.
nox > pytest
...
nox > Session tests was successful.
```

# Working with Multiple Python Interpreters

If your project supports more than a single version of Python, you should run your tests on all of them. Nox really shines when it comes to running sessions on multiple interpreters. When you define the session with @nox.session, use the python keyword to request one or more specific Python versions, as shown in Example 8-5.

*Example 8-5. Running tests across multiple Python versions*

```python
@nox.session(python=["3.12", "3.11", "3.10"])
def tests(session):
    session.install(".[tests]")
    session.run("pytest")
```

Nox creates an environment for each version and runs the commands in those environments in turn:

```
$ nox
nox > Running session tests-3.12
nox > Creating virtual environment (virtualenv) using python3.12 ...
nox > python -m pip install '.[tests]'
nox > pytest
...
nox > Session tests-3.12 was successful.
nox > Running session tests-3.11
...
nox > Running session tests-3.10
...
nox > Ran multiple sessions:
nox > * tests-3.12: success
nox > * tests-3.11: success
nox > * tests-3.10: success
```

Did you get errors from pip when you ran Nox just now? Don't use the same compiled requirements file for every Python version. You need to lock dependencies separately for each environment (see "Session Dependencies" on page 176).

You can narrow sessions by Python version using the option `--python`:

```
$ nox --python 3.12
nox > Running session tests-3.12
...
```

During development, the `--python` option comes in handy, as it lets you save time by running tests on the latest version only.

Nox discovers interpreters by searching `PATH` for commands like `python3.12`, `python3.11`, and so on. You can also specify a string like `"pypy3.10"` to request the PyPy interpreter—any command that can be resolved against `PATH` will work. On Windows, Nox also queries the Python Launcher to find available interpreters.

Suppose you've installed a prerelease of Python and want to test your project on it. The `--python` option would require that the session lists the prerelease. Instead, you can specify `--force-python`: it overrides the interpreter for a single run. For example, the following invocation runs the `tests` session on Python 3.13:

```
$ nox --session tests --force-python 3.13
```

## Session Arguments

So far, the `tests` session runs pytest without arguments:

```
session.run("pytest")
```

You *could* pass additional options—such as `--verbose`, which lists every individual test separately in the output:

```
session.run("pytest", "--verbose")
```

But you don't always want the same options for pytest. For example, the `--pdb` option launches the Python debugger on test failures. The debug prompt can be a lifesaver when you investigate a mysterious bug. But it's worse than useless in a CI context: it would hang forever since there's nobody to enter commands. Similarly, when you work on a feature, the `-k` option lets you run tests with a specific keyword in their name—but you wouldn't want to hardcode it in *noxfile.py* either.

Fortunately, Nox lets you pass additional command-line arguments for a session. The session can forward the session arguments to a command or evaluate them for its own purposes. Session arguments are available in the session as `session.posargs`. Example 8-6 shows how you forward them to a command like pytest.

*Example 8-6. Forwarding session arguments to pytest*

```
@nox.session(python=["3.12", "3.11", "3.10"])
def tests(session):
    session.install(".[tests]")
    session.run("pytest", *session.posargs)
```

You must separate session arguments from Nox's own command-line arguments with the `--` delimiter:

```
$ nox --session tests -- --verbose
```

# Automating Coverage

Coverage tools give you a sense of how much your tests exercise the codebase (see Chapter 7). In a nutshell, you install the `coverage` package and invoke pytest via `coverage run`. Example 8-7 shows how to automate this process with Nox.

*Example 8-7. Running tests with code coverage*

```
@nox.session(python=["3.12", "3.11", "3.10"])
def tests(session):
    session.install(".[tests]")
    session.run("coverage", "run", "-m", "pytest", *session.posargs)
```

When you're testing in multiple environments, you need to store the coverage data from each environment in a separate file (see "Parallel Coverage" on page 157). Add the following lines to *pyproject.toml* to enable this mode:

```
[tool.coverage.run]
parallel = true
```

In Chapter 7, you installed your project in editable mode. The Nox session builds and installs a wheel of your project instead. This ensures that you're testing the final artifact you're distributing to users. But it also means that Coverage.py needs to map the installed files back to your source tree. Configure the mapping in *pyproject.toml*:

```
[tool.coverage.paths]
source = ["src", "*/site-packages"]  ❶
```

❶ This maps files installed in the *site-packages* directory in an environment to files in your *src* directory. The key `source` is an arbitrary identifier; it's needed because you can have multiple mappings in this section.

Example 8-8 aggregates the coverage files and displays the coverage report.

*Example 8-8. Reporting the code coverage*

```
@nox.session
def coverage(session):
    session.install("coverage[toml]")
    if any(Path().glob(".coverage.*")):
        session.run("coverage", "combine")
    session.run("coverage", "report")
```

The session invokes coverage combine only if there are any coverage data files—otherwise the command would fail with an error. As a result, you can safely use nox -s coverage to inspect your test coverage without having to re-run the tests first.

Unlike Example 8-7, this session runs on the default Python version and installs only Coverage.py. You don't need to install your project to generate the coverage report.

If you run these sessions on the example project, make sure to configure Coverage.py as shown in Chapter 7. Include Python 3.7 in the tests session if your project uses the conditional import for importlib-metadata:

```
$ nox --session coverage
nox > Running session coverage
nox > Creating virtual environment (uv) using python in .nox/coverage
nox > uv pip install 'coverage[toml]'
nox > coverage combine
nox > coverage report
Name                  Stmts   Miss Branch BrPart  Cover   Missing
------------------------------------------------------------------
src/.../__init__.py      29      2      8      0    95%   42-43
src/.../__main__.py       2      2      0      0     0%   1-3
tests/__init__.py         0      0      0      0   100%
tests/test_main.py       36      0      6      0   100%
------------------------------------------------------------------
TOTAL                    67      4     14      0    95%
Coverage failure: total of 95 is less than fail-under=100
nox > Command coverage report failed with exit code 2
nox > Session coverage failed.
```

The coverage session still reports missing coverage for the main function and the __main__ module. You'll take care of that in "Automating Coverage in Subprocesses" on page 172.

# Session Notification

As it stands, this *noxfile.py* has a subtle problem. Until you run the coverage session, your project will be littered with data files waiting to be processed. And if you haven't run the tests session recently, the data in those files may be stale—so your coverage report won't reflect the latest state of the codebase.

Example 8-9 triggers the coverage session to run automatically after the test suite. Nox supports this with the session.notify method. If the notified session isn't already selected, it runs after the other sessions have completed.

*Example 8-9. Triggering coverage reports from the tests*

```
@nox.session(python=["3.12", "3.11", "3.10"])
def tests(session):
    session.install(".[tests]")
    try:
        session.run("coverage", "run", "-m", "pytest", *session.posargs)
    finally:
        session.notify("coverage")
```

The try...finally block ensures you get a coverage report even when a test fails. That's helpful when you start development with a failing test: you want to be sure the test exercises the code you're writing to make it pass.

## Automating Coverage in Subprocesses

Alan Kay, a pioneer in object-oriented programming and graphical user interface design, once said, "Simple things should be simple; complex things should be possible."[2] Many Nox sessions will be two-liners: a line to install dependencies and a line to run a command. Yet some automations require more complex logic, and Nox excels at those, too—primarily by staying out of your way and deferring to Python as a general-purpose programming language.

Let's iterate on the tests session and measure coverage in subprocesses. As you saw in Chapter 7, setting this up requires a little dance. First, you install a *.pth* file into the environment; this gives coverage a chance to initialize when the subprocess starts up. Second, you set an environment variable to point coverage to its configuration file. It's tedious and a bit tricky to get right. Let's "automate it away"!

First, you need to determine the location for the *.pth* file. The directory is named *site-packages*, but the exact path depends on your platform and the Python version. Instead of guessing, you can query the sysconfig module for it:

```
sysconfig.get_path("purelib")
```

---

2 Alan Kay, "What Is the Story Behind Alan Kay's Adage 'Simple Things Should Be Simple, Complex Things Should Be Possible'?" (*https://oreil.ly/U5o_F*), *Quora Answer*, June 19, 2020.

If you called the function directly in your session, it would return a location in the environment where you've installed Nox. Instead, you need to query the interpreter *in the session environment*. You can do this by running python with `session.run`:

```
output = session.run(
    "python",
    "-c",
    "import sysconfig; print(sysconfig.get_path('purelib'))",
    silent=True,
)
```

The `silent` keyword lets you capture the output instead of echoing it to the terminal. Thanks to `pathlib` from the standard library, writing the *.pth* file now takes only a couple of statements:

```
purelib = Path(output.strip())
(purelib / "_coverage.pth").write_text(
    "import coverage; coverage.process_startup()"
)
```

Example 8-10 extracts these statements into a helper function. The function takes a `session` argument, but it isn't a Nox session—it lacks the `@nox.session` decorator. In other words, the function won't run unless you call it from a session.

*Example 8-10. Installing _coverage.pth into the environment*

```
def install_coverage_pth(session):
    output = session.run(...)  # see above
    purelib = Path(output.strip())
    (purelib / "_coverage.pth").write_text(...)  # see above
```

You're almost done. What's left is invoking the helper function from the `tests` session and passing the environment variable to `coverage`. Example 8-11 shows the final session.

*Example 8-11. The tests session with subprocess coverage enabled*

```
@nox.session(python=["3.12", "3.11", "3.10"])
def tests(session):
    session.install(".[tests]")  ❶
    install_coverage_pth(session)

    try:
        args = ["coverage", "run", "-m", "pytest", *session.posargs]
        session.run(*args, env={"COVERAGE_PROCESS_START": "pyproject.toml"})
    finally:
        session.notify("coverage")
```

❶ Install the dependencies before the .pth file. The order matters because the .pth file imports the coverage package.

With subprocess coverage enabled, the end-to-end test produces the missing coverage data for the main function and the __main__ module. Invoke nox and watch it run your tests and generate a coverage report. Here's what the report should look like:

```
$ nox --session coverage
nox > coverage report
Name                    Stmts   Miss Branch BrPart  Cover   Missing
---------------------------------------------------------------------
src/.../__init__.py        29      0      8      0   100%
src/.../__main__.py         2      0      0      0   100%
tests/__init__.py           0      0      0      0   100%
tests/test_main.py         36      0      6      0   100%
---------------------------------------------------------------------
TOTAL                      67      0     14      0   100%
nox > Session coverage was successful.
```

# Parameterizing Sessions

The phrase "works for me" describes a common story: a user reports an issue with your code, but you can't reproduce the bug in your environment. Runtime environments in the real world differ in a myriad of ways. Testing across Python versions covers one important variable. Another common cause of surprise is the packages that your project uses directly or indirectly—its dependency tree.

Nox offers a powerful technique for testing your project against different versions of a dependency. *Parameterization* allows you to add parameters to your session functions and supply predefined values for them; Nox runs the session with each of these values.

You declare the parameter and its values in a decorator named @nox.parametrize.[3] Example 8-12 demonstrates this feature and how it allows you to test against different versions of the Django web framework.

*Example 8-12. Testing the project with multiple Django versions*

```
@nox.session
@nox.parametrize("django", ["5.*", "4.*", "3.*"])
def tests(session, django):
    session.install(".", "pytest-django", f"django=={django}")
    session.run("pytest")
```

---

3 Like pytest, Nox uses the alternate spelling "parametrize" to protect your "E" keycap from excessive wear.

Parameterized sessions are similar to parameterized tests in pytest (see Chapter 6), from which Nox borrowed the concept. You can stack `@nox.parametrize` decorators to run sessions against all combinations of parameters:

```
@nox.session
@nox.parametrize("a", ["1.0", "0.9"])
@nox.parametrize("b", ["2.2", "2.1"])
def tests(session, a, b):
    print(a, b)  # all combinations of a and b
```

If you want to check only for certain combinations, you can combine parameters in a single `@nox.parametrize` decorator:

```
@nox.session
@nox.parametrize(["a", "b"], [("1.0", "2.2"), ("0.9", "2.1")])
def tests(session, a, b):
    print(a, b)  # only the combinations listed above
```

When running a session across Python versions, you're effectively parameterizing the session by the interpreter. In fact, Nox lets you write the following instead of passing the versions to `@nox.session`:[4]

```
@nox.session
@nox.parametrize("python", ["3.12", "3.11", "3.10"])
def tests(session):
    ...
```

This syntax is useful when you want specific combinations of Python and the dependency. Here's an example: as of this writing, Django 3.2 (LTE) doesn't officially support Python versions newer than 3.10. Consequently, you need to exclude these combinations from the test matrix. Example 8-13 shows how.

*Example 8-13. Parameterizing by valid Python and Django combinations*

```
@nox.session
@nox.parametrize(
    ["python", "django"],
    [
        (python, django)
        for python in ["3.12", "3.11", "3.10"]
        for django in ["3.2.*", "4.2.*"]
        if (python, django) not in [("3.12", "3.2.*"), ("3.11", "3.2.*")]
    ]
)
def tests(session, django):
    ...
```

---

4 The eagle-eyed reader may notice that python is not a function parameter here. If you do need it in the session function, use `session.python` instead.

# Session Dependencies

If you followed Chapter 4 closely, you may see some problems with the way Examples 8-8 and 8-11 install packages. Here are the relevant parts again:

```
@nox.session
def tests(session):
    session.install(".[tests]")
    ...

@nox.session
def coverage(session):
    session.install("coverage[toml]")
    ...
```

For one, the `coverage` session doesn't specify which version of `coverage` the project requires. The `tests` session does this right: it references the `tests` extra in *pyproject .toml*, which includes the appropriate version specifiers (see "Managing Test Dependencies" on page 137).

The `coverage` session doesn't need the project, though, so an extra seems like a bad fit. But before I get to this, let me point out another problem with the sessions above: they don't lock their dependencies.

Running checks without locking dependencies has two drawbacks. First, the checks aren't deterministic: subsequent runs of the same session may install different packages. Second, if a dependency breaks your project, checks fail until you exclude the release or another release fixes the problem.[5] In other words, any project you depend on, even indirectly, has the power to block your entire CI pipeline.

On the other hand, lock file updates are a constant churn, and they clutter your Git history. Reducing their frequency comes at the price of running checks with stale dependencies. If you don't require locking for other reasons, such as secure deployments—and you're happy to quickly fix a build when an incompatible release wreaks havoc on your CI—you may prefer to keep your dependencies unlocked. There's no such thing as a free lunch.

In "Development Dependencies" on page 97, you grouped dependencies in extras and compiled requirements files from each. In this section, I'll show you a lighter-weight method for locking: *constraints files*. You need only a single extra for it. It also doesn't require installing the project itself, as extras usually do—which helps with the `coverage` session.

---

5 Here, Semantic Versioning constraints harm more than help. Bugs occur in all releases, and your upstream's definition of a breaking change may be narrower than you like. See Hynek Schlawack, "Semantic Versioning Will Not Save You" (*https://oreil.ly/GwveY*), March 2, 2021.

Constraints files look similar to requirements files: each line lists a package with a version specifier. Unlike requirements files, however, constraints files don't cause pip to install a package—they only control which version pip selects *if* it needs to install the package.

A constraints file works great for locking session dependencies. You can share it across sessions while installing only the packages each session needs. Its only drawback, compared to using a set of requirements files, is that you need to resolve all dependencies together, so there's a higher chance of dependency conflicts.

You can generate constraints files using pip-tools or uv (see "Compiling Requirements with pip-tools and uv" on page 105). Nox can automate this part, too, as shown in Example 8-14.

*Example 8-14. Locking the dependencies with uv*

```
@nox.session(venv_backend="uv")  ❶
def lock(session):
    session.run(
        "uv",
        "pip",
        "compile",
        "pyproject.toml",
        "--upgrade",
        "--quiet",
        "--all-extras",
        "--output-file=constraints.txt",
    )
```

❶ Explicitly require uv as the environment backend. (You could also install uv into the session with `session.install("uv")`, but uv supports a broader range of Python versions than you can use to install its PyPI package.)

The `--output-file` option specifies the conventional name for a constraints file, *constraints.txt*. The `--upgrade` option ensures that you get up-to-date dependencies whenever you run the session. The `--all-extras` option includes all the optional dependencies of the project.

> Don't forget to commit the constraints file to source control. You need to share this file with every contributor, and it needs to be available in CI.

Pass the constraints file to `session.install` using the `--constraint` or `-c` option. Example 8-15 shows the tests and coverage sessions with locked dependencies.

*Example 8-15. Using a constraints file to lock session dependencies*

```
@nox.session(python=["3.12", "3.11", "3.10"])
def tests(session):
    session.install("-c", "constraints.txt", ".[tests]")
    ...

@nox.session
def coverage(session):
    session.install("-c", "constraints.txt", "coverage[toml]")
    ...
```

Using a single constraints file requires that you target a well-known interpreter and platform. You can't use the same constraints file for different environments because each environment may require different packages.

If you support multiple Python versions, operating systems, or processor architectures, compile a separate constraints file for each environment. Keep the constraints files in a subdirectory to avoid clutter. Example 8-16 shows a helper function that constructs filenames like *constraints/python3.12-linux-arm64.txt*.

*Example 8-16. Constructing paths for a constraints file*

```
import platform, sys
from pathlib import Path

def constraints(session):
    filename = f"python{session.python}-{sys.platform}-{platform.machine()}.txt"
    return Path("constraints") / filename
```

Example 8-17 updates the lock session to generate the constraints files. The session now runs on every Python version. It uses the helper function to build the path for the constraints file, ensures that the target directory exists, and passes the filename to uv.

*Example 8-17. Locking dependencies on multiple Python versions*

```
@nox.session(python=["3.12", "3.11", "3.10"], venv_backend="uv")
def lock(session):
    filename = constraints(session)
    filename.parent.mkdir(exist_ok=True)
    session.run("uv", "pip", "compile", ..., f"--output-file={filename}")
```

The `tests` and `coverage` sessions can now reference the appropriate constraints file for each Python version. For this to work, you have to declare a Python version for the `coverage` session as well (Example 8-18).

*Example 8-18. The `tests` and `coverage` session with multi-Python constraints*

```
@nox.session(python=["3.12", "3.11", "3.10"])
def tests(session):
    session.install("-c", constraints(session), ".", "pytest", "coverage[toml]")
    ...


@nox.session(python="3.12")
def coverage(session):
    session.install("-c", constraints(session), "coverage[toml]")
    ...
```

# Using Nox with Poetry Projects

If you manage your project with Poetry, you organize dependencies in dependency groups (see "Dependency Groups" on page 123). Dependency groups align naturally with Nox sessions: packages for the `tests` session go into a `tests` group, those for a docs session into a `docs` group, and so on. Using Poetry as the installer means you get locked dependencies for free—all installations honor the lock file.

Before I show you how to use Poetry in Nox sessions, let me call out a couple of differences between Poetry environments and Nox environments.

First, the Poetry environment is comprehensive: by default, it includes the project, its main dependencies, and every nonoptional dependency group. Nox environments only install packages required for the task they automate.

Second, the Poetry environment uses editable installs for the project so you don't need to reinstall after every code change. Nox environments build and install a wheel so automated checks see the project the same way an end user would.

There's no right and wrong here. Poetry environments are perfect for ad-hoc interactions with your project during development, with every tool just a `poetry run` away. Nox environments, on the other hand, are optimized for reliable and repeatable checks; they aim to be as isolated and deterministic as possible.

When you use Poetry in a Nox session, it's good to be mindful of these differences. I recommend these guidelines for invoking `poetry install` with Nox:

- Use the option `--no-root` to avoid an editable install of the project. If the session needs the project to be installed (not every session does), follow the command with `session.install(".")` to build and install a wheel.

- Use the option `--only=<group>` to install the appropriate dependency group for the session. If the session needs the project to be installed, list the special group `main` as well—this ensures that every package is pinned using *poetry.lock*.

- Use the option `--sync` to remove packages from a reused session environment when your project no longer depends on them.

Example 8-19 puts this logic into a helper function that you can share across your session functions.

*Example 8-19. Installing session dependencies with Poetry*

```python
def install(session, groups, root=True):
    if root:
        groups = ["main", *groups]

    session.run_install(
        "poetry",
        "install",
        "--no-root",
        "--sync",
        f"--only={','.join(groups)}",
        external=True,
    )
    if root:
        session.install(".")
```

The helper function uses `session.run_install` instead of `session.run`. The two functions work exactly alike, but `session.run_install` marks the command as an installation. This avoids package installations when you reuse environments with `--no-install` or `-R`.

If you've followed along using Poetry in Chapters 6 and 7, your *pyproject.toml* should have a dependency group named `tests` containing pytest and coverage. Let's split the `coverage` dependency off into a separate group, since you don't need the test dependencies for the `coverage` session:[6]

```toml
[tool.poetry.group.coverage.dependencies]
coverage = {extras = ["toml"], version = ">=7.2.7"}

[tool.poetry.group.tests.dependencies]
pytest = ">=7.4.4"
```

Here's how you'd install the dependencies in the `tests` session:

```python
@nox.session(python=["3.12", "3.11", "3.10"])
def tests(session):
    install(session, groups=["coverage", "tests"])
    ...
```

---

6 Run `poetry lock --no-update` after editing *pyproject.toml* to update the *poetry.lock* file.

And here's what the `coverage` session looks like with the helper function:

```
@nox.session
def coverage(session):
    install(session, groups=["coverage"], root=False)
    ...
```

 How does Poetry know to use a Nox environment instead of the Poetry environment? Poetry installs packages into the active environment, if one exists. When Nox runs Poetry, it activates the session environment by exporting the `VIRTUAL_ENV` environment variable (see "Virtual Environments" on page 34).

# Locking Dependencies with nox-poetry

There's an alternative approach to using Nox with Poetry projects. The `nox-poetry` package is an unofficial plugin for Nox that lets you write sessions without worrying about locking, using plain `session.install`. Behind the scenes, `nox-poetry` exports a constraints file for pip using `poetry export`.

Install `nox-poetry` into the same environment as Nox:

```
$ pipx inject nox nox-poetry
```

Decorate your sessions with `@session` from the `nox-poetry` package, which is a drop-in replacement for `@nox.session`:

```
from nox_poetry import session

@session
def tests(session):
    session.install(".", "coverage[toml]", "pytest")
    ...
```

When you install packages with `session.install`, the constraints file keeps their versions in sync with `poetry.lock`. You can manage dependencies in separate dependency groups or put them into a single `dev` group.

While this approach is convenient and simplifies the resulting *noxfile.py*, it doesn't come for free. Translating Poetry's dependency information into a constraints file isn't lossless—for example, it doesn't include package hashes or the URLs of private package repositories. Another drawback is that contributors have another global dependency to worry about. When I wrote `nox-poetry` in 2020, dependency groups didn't exist. As of this writing, I recommend using Poetry directly, as described in the previous section.

# Summary

Nox lets you automate checks and tasks for a project. Its Python configuration file *noxfile.py* organizes them into one or more sessions. Sessions are functions decorated with `@nox.session`. They receive a single argument `session` providing the session API (Table 8-1). Every session runs in an isolated virtual environment. If you pass a list of Python versions to `@nox.session`, Nox runs the session across all of them.

*Table 8-1. The session object*

| Attribute | Description | Example |
|---|---|---|
| `run()` | Run a command | `session.run("coverage", "report")` |
| `install()` | Install packages with pip | `session.install(".", "pytest")` |
| `run_install()` | Run an installation command | `session.run_install("poetry", "install")` |
| `notify()` | Enqueue another session | `session.notify("coverage")` |
| `python` | The interpreter for this session | `"3.12"` |
| `posargs` | Extra command-line arguments | `nox -- --verbose --pdb` |

The command `nox` (Table 8-2) provides a single entry point to your suite of checks. Without arguments, it runs every session defined in *noxfile.py* (or those you've listed in `nox.options.sessions`). The earlier you identify issues with your code, the cheaper it is to fix them—so use Nox to run the same checks locally as in continuous integration (CI). Besides checks, you can automate many other chores, such as building packages or documentation.

*Table 8-2. Command-line options for nox*

| Option | Description | Example |
|---|---|---|
| `--list` | List the available sessions | `nox -l` |
| `--session` | Select sessions by name | `nox -s tests` |
| `--python` | Select sessions by interpreter | `nox -p 3.12` |
| `--force-python` | Override the interpreter for a session | `nox --force-python 3.13` |
| `--reuse-existing-virtualenvs` | Reuse existing virtual environments | `nox -rs tests` |
| `--no-install` | Skip installation commands | `nox -Rs tests` |

There's a lot more to Nox that this chapter didn't cover. For example, you can use Conda or Mamba to create environments and install packages. You can organize sessions using keywords and tags, and assign friendly identifiers using `nox.param`. Last but not least, Nox comes with a GitHub Action that makes it easy to run Nox sessions in CI. Take a look at the official documentation (*https://oreil.ly/6U7hB*) to learn more.

---

# Linting with Ruff and pre-commit

In 1978, Stephen C. Johnson, a researcher at Bell Labs, wrote a program that could detect a number of bugs and obscurities in C code. He named the program after the fluff on your pullover when you take it out of the washing machine: Lint. It was to become the first in a long line of *linters*, programs that analyze source code and point out problematic constructs.

Linters don't *run* a program to discover issues with it; they read and analyze its source code. This process is known as *static analysis*, as opposed to *runtime* (or *dynamic*) *analysis*. It makes linters both fast and safe—you needn't worry about side effects, such as requests to production systems. Static checks can be smart and also fairly complete—you needn't hit the right combination of edge cases to dig up a latent bug.

> Static analysis is powerful, but you should still write tests for your programs. Where static checks use deduction, tests use observation. Linters verify a limited set of generic code properties, while tests can validate that a program satisfies its requirements.

Linters are also great at enforcing a readable and consistent style, with a preference for idiomatic and modern constructs over obscure and deprecated syntax. Organizations have adopted style guides for years, such as the recommendations in PEP 8 (*https://oreil.ly/4Vjl5*) or the Google Style Guide for Python (*https://oreil.ly/ymIbA*). Linters can function as *executable* style guides: by flagging offending constructs automatically, they keep code review focused on the meaning of a change rather than stylistic nitpicks.

This chapter has three parts:

- The first part introduces the Ruff linter, a Rust implementation of Python linters that automatically fixes many of the issues it detects.

- The second part describes pre-commit, a linter framework with Git integration.

- The third part presents the Ruff code formatter, a Rust implementation of the Black code style.

But first, let's look at a typical problem that linters help you solve.

# Linting Basics

The constructs flagged by linters may not be outright illegal. More often, they just trigger your spider-sense that something might be wrong. Consider the Python code in Example 9-1.

*Example 9-1. Can you spot the problem?*

```
import subprocess

def run(command, args=[], force=False):
    if force:
        args.insert(0, "--force")
    subprocess.run([command, *args])
```

If you haven't been bitten by this bug before, you may be surprised to find that the function sometimes passes `--force` to the command when it shouldn't:

```
>>> subprocess.run = print  # print commands instead of running them
>>> run("myscript.py", force=True)
['myscript.py', '--force']
>>> run("myscript.py")
['myscript.py', '--force']
```

The bug is known as a *mutable argument default*. Python evaluates argument defaults when a function is defined, not when you call it. In other words, both of your calls used the same list as the default for `args`. The first call appended the item `"--force"`, so that item got passed to the second call as well.

Linters can detect pitfalls like this, warn you about them, and even fix them for you. Let's use a linter named Ruff on the function—you'll hear a lot more about it in this chapter. For now, just note its error message, which identifies the bug:[1]

```
$ pipx run ruff check --extend-select B
bad.py:3:23: B006 Do not use mutable data structures for argument defaults
Found 1 error.
No fixes available (1 hidden fix can be enabled with the `--unsafe-fixes` option)
```

---

1 The B short code activates a group of checks pioneered by `flake8-bugbear`, a plugin for the Flake8 linter.

# A Short History of Python Linters

Two tools have dominated linting for much of Python's history: Pylint and Flake8.

Pylint (*https://oreil.ly/IfDv4*) (2001) is the *grande dame* of Python linting. It takes an all-encompassing approach, with hundreds of checks. It requires a certain amount of upfront configuration, but it's famous for its thoroughness.

In 2010, a simpler tool with an out-of-the-box experience saw the light of day: Flake8 (*https://oreil.ly/jmxgT*). It doesn't define any checks of its own—instead, it exposes a plugin system for other linters. It runs two fundamental linters by default: Pyflakes detects syntax errors and potential bugs, while pycodestyle enforces the PEP 8 style guide. (A third linter, McCabe, limits code complexity; it's disabled by default.) Flake8 laid the groundwork for a vast and growing ecosystem of linter plugins.

In recent years, the Python code quality ecosystem has seen significant changes, spearheaded by three tools—Black, mypy, and Ruff:

- The rise of the code formatter Black (*https://oreil.ly/8hn88*) has made countless stylistic checks unnecessary. It's named after Henry Ford's adage, "any color the customer wants, as long as it's black." Black uncompromisingly applies the same code style to every project that adopts it.

- Type checkers like mypy (*https://oreil.ly/gteOH*) have taken over the large realm of type-related linter checks—for example, detecting function calls with the wrong type of argument. I'll discuss type checking in Chapter 10.

- Ruff (*https://oreil.ly/oTbbx*) reimplements an entire ecosystem of Python code-quality tooling in Rust, including Flake8, Pylint, and Black. Besides offering a unified experience, Ruff speeds up checks by up to two orders of magnitude.[2]

Historically, linters only emitted warnings about offending code, leaving the thankless task of improving it to humans. Modern linters can fix many violations automatically, including sophisticated tasks such as refactoring a Python codebase to use modern language features.

---

2 Charlie Marsh, "Python Tooling Could Be Much, Much Faster" (*https://oreil.ly/ttQUJ*), August 30, 2022.

# The Ruff Linter

Ruff is a blazingly fast open source Python linter and code formatter, written in the Rust programming language. Ruff's linter reimplements dozens of Python linters—including many Flake8 plugins, Pylint, pyupgrade, Bandit, isort, and more.

Astral, the company behind Ruff, also created the Python packaging tool uv (see "Managing Environments with uv" on page 42), and it has assumed the stewardship of Rye, a Python project manager (see "Managing Packages with Rye" on page 68). All of these tools are implemented in Rust.

 If you manage your project with Rye, the Ruff linter and code formatter are available under the commands rye lint and rye fmt, respectively.

Install Ruff globally with pipx:

```
$ pipx install ruff
```

But wait—how can pipx install a Rust program? The Ruff binary is available as a wheel on PyPI, so Python folks like you and me can install it with good old pip and pipx. You could even run it with py -m ruff.

Let's look at another example of working with Ruff. Consider this refactoring of HTTP headers, which replaces a list with a dictionary:

```
headers = [f"User-Agent: {USER_AGENT}"] # version 1
headers = {f"User-Agent": USER_AGENT}   # version 2
```

When you refactor f-strings, it's easy to leave the f prefix behind after removing placeholders. Ruff flags f-strings without placeholders—they're noisy, they confuse readers, and somebody might have forgotten to include a placeholder.

Run the command ruff check—the front-end for Ruff's linter. Without arguments, the command lints every Python file under your current directory, unless it's listed in a *.gitignore* file:

```
$ ruff check
example.py:2:12: F541 [*] f-string without any placeholders
Found 1 error.
[*] 1 fixable with the `--fix` option.
```

Figure 9-1 takes a closer look at Ruff's diagnostic message.

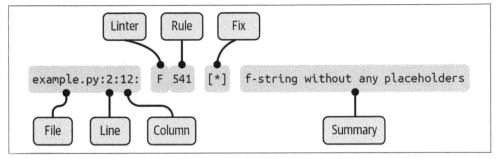

*Figure 9-1. A diagnostic message from Ruff*

Ruff tells you where the violation occurred—the file, line, and line offset—and gives you a short summary of what went wrong: *f-string without any placeholders*. Two interesting bits are sandwiched between the location and the summary: an alphanumeric code (F541) identifies the linter rule, and the sign [*] indicates that Ruff can automatically fix the issue.

If you're ever confused why you're getting a warning, you can ask Ruff to explain it using the command ruff rule:

```
$ ruff rule F541
f-string-missing-placeholders (F541)

Derived from the Pyflakes linter.

Fix is always available.

What it does
Checks for f-strings that do not contain any placeholder expressions.

Why is this bad?
f-strings are a convenient way to format strings, but they are not
necessary if there are no placeholder expressions to format.
...
```

Rule codes have a prefix of one or more letters, followed by three or more digits. The prefix identifies a specific linter—for example, the F in F541 stands for the Pyflakes linter. Ruff reimplements many more Python code-quality tools—as of this writing, it ships over 50 built-in plugins modeled after existing tools. You can find out which linters are available using the command ruff linter:

```
$ ruff linter
   F Pyflakes
 E/W pycodestyle
 C90 mccabe
   I isort
   N pep8-naming
   D pydocstyle
```

```
UP pyupgrade
... (50+ more lines)
```

You can activate linters and individual rules for your project in its *pyproject.toml* file. The setting `tool.ruff.lint.select` enables any rules whose code starts with one of the given prefixes. Out of the box, Ruff enables some basic all-around checks from Pyflakes and pycodestyle:

```
[tool.ruff.lint]
select = ["E4", "E7", "E9", "F"]
```

## Pyflakes and pycodestyle

Pyflakes (`F`) flags constructs that are almost certainly mistakes, such as unused imports or the pointless f-strings you've seen above. It steers clear of any questions of style. Pycodestyle (whose rules use the prefixes `E` and `W`), detects violations of PEP 8, the style guide originally written by Python's inventor, Guido van Rossum, together with Barry Warsaw and Alyssa Coghlan.

Ruff enables only a subset of pycodestyle by default, because code formatters have obviated many of its checks. Still, PEP 8 makes style recommendations that go beyond mere code formatting. Would you agree that `x is not None` sounds more natural than `not x is None`? The default rules detect and fix a number of such issues, leading to code that's easier to read and understand.

 If you aren't using an opinionated code formatter, consider enabling the entire `E` and `W` blocks. Their automatic fixes help ensure minimal PEP 8 compliance. They're similar to, but not yet as feature-complete as, the autopep8 formatter (see "Approaches to Code Formatting: autopep8" on page 201).[3]

## Fantastic Linters and Where to Find Them

Ruff has too many rules to describe in this book, and more are being added all the time. How do you find the good ones for your project? Try them out! Depending on your project, you may want to enable individual rules (`"B006"`), groups of rules (`"E4"`), entire plugins (`"B"`), or even every existing plugin at the same time (`"ALL"`).

---

3 As of this writing, you'll also need to enable Ruff's preview mode. Set `tool.ruff.lint.preview` to `true`.

Reserve the special ALL code for experimentation: it will implicitly enable new linters whenever you upgrade Ruff. *Beware*: some plugins require configuration to produce useful results, and some rules conflict with other rules.[4]

Besides select, Ruff has an extend-select directive that selects rules in addition to the default set (see "Linting Basics" on page 184). Generally, you should prefer the select directive, because it keeps your configuration self-contained and explicit:

```
[tool.ruff.lint]
select = ["E", "W", "F", "B006"]
```

If you're unsure where to start, Table 9-1 describes a dozen built-in plugins to try.

*Table 9-1. A dozen widely useful Ruff plugins*

| Prefix | Name | Description |
| --- | --- | --- |
| RUF | Ruff-specific rules | A collection of lints native to Ruff |
| I | isort | Group and sort import statements |
| UP | pyupgrade | Use modern language features compatible with your target Python version |
| SIM | flake8-simplify | Use idiomatic constructs to simplify code |
| FURB | refurb | Use idiomatic constructs to make good code even better |
| PIE | flake8-pie | A collection of miscellaneous lints |
| PERF | Perflint | Avoid performance antipatterns |
| C4 | flake8-comprehensions | Use list, set, and dict comprehensions |
| B | flake8-bugbear | Eliminate likely bugs and design problems |
| PL | Pylint | A large collection of rules from the mother of all Python linters |
| D | pydocstyle | Require well-formed docstrings for your functions, classes, and modules |
| S | flake8-bandit | Detect potential security vulnerabilities |

When onboarding legacy projects to Ruff, your first task will be to decide which linters provide the most useful feedback. At this stage, individual diagnostics can be quite overwhelming. It helps to zoom out using the --statistics option:

```
$ ruff check --statistics --select ALL
 123    I001    [*] Import block is un-sorted or un-formatted
  45    ARG001  [ ] Unused function argument: `bindings`
  39    UP007   [*] Use `X | Y` for type annotations
  32    TRY003  [ ] Avoid specifying long messages outside the exception class
```

---

4 My reviewer Hynek points out that setting your project to ALL can be a great way to learn about antipatterns from experienced people. You can still opt out of a rule after understanding its rationale. Enabling ALL requires a bit more work on your side, but it ensures you don't miss new rules in a Ruff release.

```
28      SIM117  [ ] Use a single `with` statement with multiple contexts
23      SLF001  [ ] Private member accessed: `_blob`
17      FBT001  [ ] Boolean-typed positional argument in function definition
10      PLR0913 [ ] Too many arguments in function definition (6 > 5)
...
```

At this point, you have two options. First, if a linter is particularly noisy, hide it from the output using the `--ignore` option. For example, if you're not ready to add type annotations and docstrings, exclude `flake8-annotations` and `pydocstyle` with `--ignore ANN,D`. Second, if you see a linter with interesting findings, enable it permanently in *pyproject.toml* and fix its warnings. Rinse and repeat.

 Work toward enforcing the same set of linters for all your projects, with the same configurations, and prefer default configurations over customizations. This will make your codebase more consistent and accessible across the entire organization.

## Disabling Rules and Warnings

The `select` setting is flexible but purely additive: it lets you opt into rules whose code starts with a given prefix. The `ignore` setting lets you fine-tune in the other direction: it disables individual rules and rule groups. Like `select`, it matches rule codes by their prefixes.

The subtractive method is handy when you need most, but not all, of a linter's rules, and when you're adopting a linter gradually. The `pydocstyle` plugin (D) checks that every module, class, and function has a well-formed docstring. Your project may be *almost* there, with the exception of module docstrings (D100). Use the `ignore` setting to disable all warnings about missing module docstrings until you've fully onboarded your project:

```
[tool.ruff.lint]
select = ["D", "E", "F"]
ignore = ["D100"]  # Don't require module docstrings for now.
```

The `per-file-ignore` setting lets you disable rules for a part of your codebase. Here's another example: the `bandit` plugin (S) has a rich inventory of checks to help you detect security vulnerabilities in your code. Its rule S101 flags every use of the `assert` keyword.[5] But you still need `assert` to express expectations in pytest (see Chapter 6). If your test suite lives in a *tests* directory, disable S101 for its files like this:

---

5 What's wrong with assertions? Nothing, but Python skips them when run with -O for optimizations— a common way to speed up production environments. So don't use `assert` to validate untrusted input!

---

```
[tool.ruff.lint.per-file-ignores]
"tests/*" = ["S101"]  # Tests can use assertions.
```

Disabling rules should be a last resort. It's usually better to suppress individual warnings by adding a special comment to offending lines. This comment has the form `# noqa:` followed by one or more rule codes.

 Always include rule codes in your `noqa` comments. Blanket `noqa` comments can hide unrelated issues. Marking violations also makes them easier to find when you're ready to fix them. Use the rule `PGH004` from the `pygrep-hooks` linter to require rule codes.

The `noqa` system lets you silence false positives as well as legitimate warnings that you choose not to prioritize at this time. For example, the MD5 message-digest algorithm is generally agreed to be insecure, and Bandit's `S324` flags its uses. But if your code interacts with a legacy system that requires you to compute an MD5 hash, you may not have a choice. Disable the warning with a `noqa` comment:

```
md5 = hashlib.md5(text.encode()).hexdigest()  # noqa: S324
```

Bandit's checks often flag constructs that deserve close scrutiny, without meaning to outright ban them. The idea is that you will vet the offending lines one by one and suppress the warning if you determine that the specific usage is innocuous.

It can be reasonable to enable a rule and suppress *all* of its warnings. This lets you enforce a rule going forward only—that is, only when you touch a region of code. Ruff supports this workflow with the `--add-noqa` option, which inserts `noqa` comments to all offending lines on your behalf:

```
$ ruff check --add-noqa
```

Like every comment, `noqa` comments can become outdated—for example, a refactoring may have inadvertently fixed the suppressed warning. Stale `noqa` comments are noisy and create friction when you're out to squash linter violations. Luckily, Ruff is in an excellent position to remediate this. Its rule `RUF100` automatically removes `noqa` comments that no longer apply.

## Automation with Nox

Without corrective measures, the code quality of large projects degrades over time. Linting, as an automated, mandatory check, helps to counteract that natural entropy. Nox (see Chapter 8) is an automation framework that lets you run linters as a part of your mandatory checks.

Here's a Nox session that runs Ruff on every Python file in the current directory:

```
@nox.session
def lint(session):
    session.install("ruff")
    session.run("ruff", "check")
```

Nox is a valid choice here, but when it comes to linting, there's a more convenient and powerful alternative: pre-commit, a cross-language linter framework with Git integration.

# The pre-commit Framework

Pre-commit is a tool and framework that lets you add third-party linters to a project with minimal boilerplate. Linters in various languages come with ready-to-use integrations for pre-commit, called *hooks*. You can run these hooks explicitly from the command line, or you can configure your local repository to run them whenever you commit changes (and on some other events).

Install pre-commit globally using pipx:

```
$ pipx install pre-commit
```

## First Steps with pre-commit

Let's add a pre-commit hook for Ruff to your project. Create a file named *.pre-commit-config.yaml* in the top-level directory, with contents as in Example 9-2. You'll find a short YAML fragment like this in the public documentation of most linters that support pre-commit.

*Example 9-2. A .pre-commit-config.yaml file with a hook for Ruff*

```
repos:
  - repo: https://github.com/astral-sh/ruff-pre-commit
    rev: v0.4.4
    hooks:
      - id: ruff
```

Authors distribute their pre-commit hooks via Git repositories. In the *.pre-commit-config.yaml* file, you specify the URL, revision, and hooks for each repository you want to use. The URL can be any location Git can clone from. The revision is most commonly a Git tag pointing to the latest release of the linter. A repository can have more than one hook—for example, Ruff provides `ruff` and `ruff-format` hooks for its linter and code formatter, respectively.

Pre-commit is intimately tied to Git, and you must invoke it from within a Git repository. Let's establish a baseline by linting every file in the repository, using the command `pre-commit run` with the `--all-files` option:

```
$ pre-commit run --all-files
[INFO] Initializing environment for https://github.com/astral-sh/ruff-pre-commit.
[INFO] Installing environment for https://github.com/astral-sh/ruff-pre-commit.
[INFO] Once installed this environment will be reused.
[INFO] This may take a few minutes...
ruff....................................................................Passed
```

When you run a hook for the first time, pre-commit clones the hook repository and installs the linter into an isolated environment. This can take some time, but you don't have to do it often: pre-commit caches the linter environments across multiple projects.

## A Hook Up Close

If you're curious how a pre-commit hook works under the hood, take a peek at Ruff's hook repository (*https://oreil.ly/BIbwL*). The file *.pre-commit-hooks.yaml* in the repository defines the hooks. Example 9-3 shows an excerpt from the file.

*Example 9-3. An excerpt from the .pre-commit-hooks.yaml file for Ruff*

```
- id: ruff
  name: ruff
  language: python
  entry: ruff check --force-exclude
  args: []
  types_or: [python, pyi]
```

Every hook comes with a unique identifier and a friendly name (`id` and `name`). Refer to hooks by their unique identifier when you interact with pre-commit. Their names appear only in console messages from the tool.

The hook definition tells pre-commit how to install and run the linter by specifying its implementation language (`language`) and its command and command-line arguments (`entry` and `args`). The Ruff hook is a Python package, so it specifies Python as the language. The `--force-exclude` option ensures that you can exclude files from linting. It tells Ruff to honor its `exclude` setting even when pre-commit passes excluded source files explicitly.

> You can override the `args` key in your *.pre-commit-config.yaml* file to pass custom command-line options to a hook. By contrast, command-line arguments in the `entry` key are mandatory—you can't override them.

Finally, the hook declares which file types the linter understands (`types_or`). The `python` file type matches files with *.py* or related extensions and executable scripts with a Python shebang. The `pyi` file type refers to stub files with type annotations (see "Distributing Types with Python Packages" on page 226).

For a Python hook, pre-commit creates a virtual environment in its cache directory. It installs the hook by running, essentially, `pip install .` inside the hook repository. When it's time to run the hook, pre-commit activates the virtual environment and invokes the command with any selected source files.

Figure 9-2 shows a developer machine with three Python projects using pre-commit hooks. Pre-commit clones the hook repositories into its cache directory and installs the hooks into isolated environments. Hook repositories define hooks in *.pre-commit-hooks.yaml* files, while projects reference the hooks in *.pre-commit-config.yaml* files.

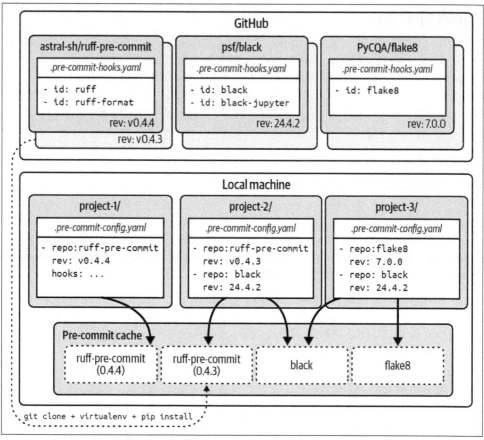

*Figure 9-2. Three projects with pre-commit hooks for Ruff, Black, and Flake8.*

---

## Automatic Fixes

Modern linters can fix many violations by modifying the offending source files in place. Linters with automatic fixes eliminate entire classes of bugs and code smells[6] at nearly zero cost. Like code formatters, they have caused a paradigm shift in software development, letting you focus on higher-level concerns without compromising on code quality.

By convention, most pre-commit hooks enable automatic fixes by default. Thanks to Git, they can apply fixes with relative safety, without risk of overwriting your work irreversibly. That said, they work best if you commit early and often.

 Automatic fixes bring tremendous benefits, but they assume some basic Git hygiene: don't pile up uncommitted changes in your repository (or stash them before linting). Pre-commit saves and restores your local modifications in some contexts, but not all.

Let's try this out. When Ruff detects the mutable argument default, it indicates that you can enable a "hidden" fix. (Ruff asks you to opt into the fix because people might conceivably depend on mutable defaults, say, for caching.) First, enable the linter rule and the fix in *pyproject.toml*:

```
[tool.ruff.lint]
extend-select = ["B006"]
extend-safe-fixes = ["B006"]
```

Ruff's pre-commit hook requires you to opt in with the `--fix` option, as shown in Example 9-4. The options `--show-fixes` and `--exit-non-zero-on-fix` ensure that all violations are displayed in the terminal and result in a nonzero exit status, even if Ruff was able to fix them.

*Example 9-4. Enabling automatic fixes for the Ruff hook*

```
repos:
  - repo: https://github.com/astral-sh/ruff-pre-commit
    rev: v0.4.4
    hooks:
      - id: ruff
        args: ["--fix", "--show-fixes", "--exit-non-zero-on-fix"]
```

---

6 Kent Beck and Martin Fowler describe *code smells* as "certain structures in the code that suggest—sometimes, scream for—the possibility of refactoring." Martin Fowler, *Refactoring: Improving the Design of Existing Code*, second edition (Boston: Addison-Wesley, 2019).

Save Example 9-1 in a file called *bad.py*, commit the file, and run pre-commit:

```
$ pre-commit run --all-files
ruff................................................................Failed
- hook id: ruff
- exit code: 1
- files were modified by this hook

Fixed 1 error:
- bad.py:
    1 × B006 (mutable-argument-default)

Found 1 error (1 fixed, 0 remaining).
```

If you inspect the modified file, you'll see that Ruff has replaced the argument default with None. The empty list is now assigned inside the function, giving every call its own instance of args:

```
def run(command, args=None, force=False):
    if args is None:
        args = []
    if force:
        args.insert(0, "--force")
    subprocess.run([command, *args])
```

Instead of inspecting the modified files, you can also run `git diff` to see the changes applied to your code. Alternatively, you can tell pre-commit to show you a diff of the fixes right away, using the option `--show-diff-on-fail`.

## Running pre-commit from Nox

Pre-commit gives you access to production-ready integrations for linters in many languages. For this reason alone, I recommend running linters from pre-commit instead of Nox. (If you still need convincing, see the next section, which presents another compelling reason to use pre-commit.)

That said, you still should include a Nox session for pre-commit itself. This ensures that you can run all the checks for your project with a single command, `nox`. Example 9-5 shows how to define the session. If your *noxfile.py* sets `nox.options .sessions`, add the session to that list, as well.

*Example 9-5. A Nox session for linting with pre-commit*

```
nox.options.sessions = ["lint", "tests"]

@nox.session
def lint(session):
    options = ["--all-files", "--show-diff-on-fail"]
    session.install("pre-commit")
    session.run("pre-commit", "run", *options, *session.posargs)
```

By default, pre-commit runs every hook you've configured for your project. You can run specific hooks by passing them as additional command-line arguments. This comes in handy when addressing complaints from a specific linter. Thanks to `session.posargs` (see "Session Arguments" on page 169), this also works from Nox:

```
$ nox --session=lint -- ruff
```

Having a single entry point to checks and tasks, including linters, greatly reduces friction for everybody working on a project. But you shouldn't stop there. Pre-commit was designed to be triggered from Git on every commit. The next section explains how to set up projects to lint changes as you commit them (and why it's great).

## Running pre-commit from Git

Running linters on each commit is a game changer, for three reasons:

- You remove the overhead and distraction of invoking checks manually. Linters run in the background, alerting you only if a violation is found.
- You run checks as early as possible. As a general rule, the earlier you spot an issue, the cheaper it is to fix. (Say goodbye to CI failures due to stylistic nitpicks.)
- It's fast: you only lint files staged for a commit, instead of the entire codebase.[7]

Set up Git to invoke pre-commit on every commit by running the following command inside your project:

```
$ pre-commit install
pre-commit installed at .git/hooks/pre-commit
```

This command installs a short wrapper script into the *.git/hooks* directory that transfers control to pre-commit (Figure 9-3). Programs in the *.git/hooks* directory are known as *Git hooks*. When you run `git commit`, Git invokes the *pre-commit* Git hook. The hook, in turn, invokes pre-commit, which runs Ruff and any other pre-commit hooks you have.

Git hooks let you trigger actions at predefined points during Git's execution. For example, the *pre-commit* and *post-commit* Git hooks run before and after Git creates a commit. You've probably guessed by now which of these Git hooks pre-commit installs by default—but it supports the other Git hooks as well, if you need them.

---

7 Running pre-commit from Git is the safest way to run linters with automatic fixes: pre-commit saves and restores any changes you haven't staged, and it rolls back the fixes if they conflict with your changes.

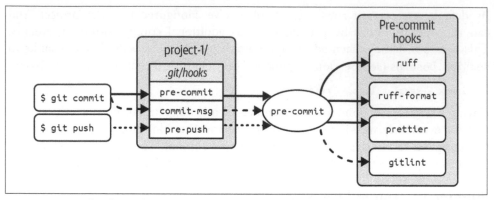

*Figure 9-3. Git hooks and pre-commit hooks*

## Pre-commit Hooks That Aren't pre-commit Hooks

Most pre-commit hooks plug into the *pre-commit* Git hook—but not all. Linters for commit messages like `commitlint` and `gitlint` use the *commit-msg* Git hook. Git calls this hook after you've composed a commit message. You can install it using the `--hook-type` or `-t` option:

```
$ pre-commit install -t commit-msg
pre-commit installed at .git/hooks/commit-msg
```

But passing this option is easy to forget. If you use Git hooks other than *pre-commit*, list them in the *.pre-commit-config.yaml* file instead:

```
default_install_hook_types: [pre-commit, commit-msg]
```

Place this directive at the top level of your pre-commit configuration.

Figure 9-4 depicts a typical workflow with pre-commit. On the left, there's a file you're editing in your project (*worktree*); the center represents the staging area for the next commit (*index*); and the current commit is on the right (HEAD).

Initially, the three areas are in sync. Suppose you remove the placeholder from the f-string, but forget to remove the f prefix from the string literal (marked as ❶ in Figure 9-4). You stage your edit using `git add` (❷) and run `git commit` to create a commit (❸a). Before your editor can pop up for the commit message, Git transfers control to pre-commit. Ruff promptly catches your mistake and fixes the string literal in your worktree (❸b).

At this point, all three areas have different contents. Your worktree contains your change with Ruff's fix, the staging area has your change without the fix, and HEAD still points to the commit before your change. This lets you audit the fix by comparing the worktree to the staging area, using `git diff`. If you're happy with what you see, you can stage the fix with `git add` (❹) and retry the commit with `git commit` (❺).

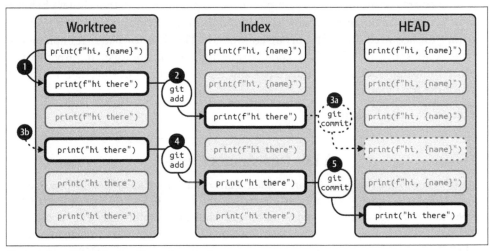

*Figure 9-4. Workflow with pre-commit*

With automatic fixes, this workflow reduces the interference of linters to a minimum, rerunning the commit. But sometimes you don't want to be distracted by linters at all—for example, you may want to record some work in progress. Git and pre-commit give you two options to get your commit past a stubborn linter. First, you can skip Git hooks entirely using the `--no-verify` or `-n` option:

```
$ git commit -n
```

Alternatively, you can skip a specific pre-commit hook using the `SKIP` environment variable (which also takes a comma-separated list, if you need to skip more than one hook):

```
$ SKIP=ruff git commit
```

Git hooks control which changes enter your local repository, but they're voluntary—they don't replace CI checks as a gatekeeper for the default branch in your shared repository. If you already run Nox in CI, the session in Example 9-5 takes care of that.

Skipping hooks doesn't help with false positives or when you want to deploy a critical fix despite minor nits: your mandatory checks would still fail in CI. In these cases, you'll need to advise the linter to ignore the specific violation (see "Disabling Rules and Warnings" on page 190).

# The Ruff Formatter

Over the course of months, Ruff reimplemented a plethora of Python linters behind the `ruff check` command and saw wide adoption in the Python world. A bit over a year in, Ruff acquired the `ruff format` command.[8] The Ruff formatter reimplements the de facto standard of Python code formatting, Black, in Rust. It provides yet another building block for the integrated and highly performant toolchain that Ruff has become for Python.

But let's start at the beginning.

---

## A Tale from Another Time

Many years ago, I was working in a small team on a C++ codebase. Our processes were simple: everybody committed directly to the main branch. There was no CI pipeline—just nightly builds and a dashboard showing compiler errors, warnings, and test failures. Every now and then, one of us went over recent changes with refactorings and style cleanups. It may sound surprising, but the codebase was in good shape. Nothing beats mutual understanding in a close-knit team.

A few years down the road, cracks appeared in our workflow. The company had grown—new engineers were unfamiliar with the coding conventions, senior engineers struggled to communicate them. On top of this, the team had inherited a legacy codebase that didn't adhere to any discernible rules at all.

We started to look at automation. Maybe tooling could take over the common chore of identifying code-quality issues and fixing them across the codebase. In 2013, a code formatter named `clang-format` had been released as part of the LLVM compiler toolkit, and it looked promising.

After a brief evaluation, I decided against it.

By design, `clang-format` completely rewrote each source file according to the configured style. I was worried about its all-or-nothing approach for a few reasons. First, despite dozens of configuration settings, it would erase many of our style conventions. Second, it would be hard to review the resulting large patch. Third, since reformatting would touch a large part of the codebase, it would become hard to establish the historical context of a line of code using the version control system.

In hindsight, I was wrong—all of these concerns can be addressed.

---

8 Charlie Marsh, "The Ruff Formatter" (*https://oreil.ly/ThaR4*), October 24, 2023.

The evolution of code formatters in Python eventually changed my mind—specifically the meteoric rise of Black. But before addressing the concerns above, let's take a step back and look at the situation in Python as it was when Black entered the scene.

## Approaches to Code Formatting: autopep8

Consider the following gem of Python code:

```python
def create_frobnicator_factory(the_factory_name,
                        interval_in_secs=100,  dbg=False,
                    use_singleton=None,frobnicate_factor=4.5):
  if dbg:print('creating frobnication factory '+the_factory_name+"...")
  if(use_singleton):   return _frob_sngltn      #we're done
  return FrobnicationFactory( the_factory_name,

    intrvl = interval_in_secs              ,f=frobnicate_factor    )
```

The function showcases various formatting issues, such as inconsistent alignment, lack or excess of whitespace, and single-line `if` constructs. Some of these clearly hurt readability. Others, such as two-space indentation, deviate from a widely accepted practice codified in PEP 8.

A minimal approach for dealing with stylistic issues of this sort is autopep8, an early pioneer of automatic linter fixes and still in use. Building on pycodestyle, it surgically corrects offenses while preserving the code layout otherwise.

Let's run autopep8 on the code example with default settings:

```
$ pipx run autopep8 example.py
```

Here's the function as formatted by autopep8:

```python
def create_frobnicator_factory(the_factory_name,
                               interval_in_secs=100,  dbg=False,
                               use_singleton=None, frobnicate_factor=4.5):
    if dbg:
        print('creating frobnication factory '+the_factory_name+"...")
    if (use_singleton):
        return _frob_sngltn  # we're done
    return FrobnicationFactory(the_factory_name,

                               intrvl=interval_in_secs, f=frobnicate_factor)
```

You'll likely find this easier on the eye. For better or worse, autopep8 didn't touch some other questionable stylistic choices, such as the rogue blank line in the `return` statement and the inconsistent quote characters. Autopep8 uses pycodestyle to detect issues, and pycodestyle had no complaint here.

Unlike most code formatters, autopep8 lets you apply selected fixes by passing `--select` with appropriate rule codes. For example, you can run `autopep8 --select=E111` to enforce four-space indentation.

## Approaches to Code Formatting: YAPF

Developed at Google in 2015, the YAPF formatter borrows its design and sophisticated formatting algorithm from `clang-format`. The name YAPF stands for "Yet Another Python Formatter."[9] YAPF reformats a codebase according to a wealth of configuration options.

Run it like this:

```
$ pipx run yapf example.py
```

Here's YAPF's version of the code, using default settings:

```
def create_frobnicator_factory(the_factory_name,
                               interval_in_secs=100,
                               dbg=False,
                               use_singleton=None,
                               frobnicate_factor=4.5):
    if dbg: print('creating frobnication factory ' + the_factory_name + "...")
    if (use_singleton): return _frob_sngltn  #we're done
    return FrobnicationFactory(the_factory_name,
                               intrvl=interval_in_secs,
                               f=frobnicate_factor)
```

YAPF's formatting rules touch more ground than autopep8—for example, it arranges the function parameters consistently and removes the bogus empty line. YAPF respects existing formatting choices as long as they're compatible with your configuration. For example, it didn't split the single-line `if` statements or eliminate parentheses around `if` conditions.

## An Uncompromising Code Formatter

In 2018, a new code formatter named Black entered the scene. Its core principle: minimal configurability!

Let's try Black on the code example:

```
$ pipx run black example.py
```

---

9 Stephen C. Johnson, the author of Lint, also established this infamous naming convention by writing Yacc (Yet Another Compiler-Compiler) in the early 1970s at Bell Labs.

Black formats the function as follows:

```
def create_frobnicator_factory(
    the_factory_name,
    interval_in_secs=100,
    dbg=False,
    use_singleton=None,
    frobnicate_factor=4.5,
):
    if dbg:
        print("creating frobnication factory " + the_factory_name + "...")
    if use_singleton:
        return _frob_sngltn  # we're done
    return FrobnicationFactory(
        the_factory_name, intrvl=interval_in_secs, f=frobnicate_factor
    )
```

Black doesn't fix individual style offenses like autopep8, nor does it enforce your style preferences like YAPF. Rather, Black reduces the source code into a canonical form, using a deterministic algorithm—mostly without taking existing formatting into account. In a certain sense, Black makes code style "disappear." This normalization massively reduces the cognitive overhead of working with Python code.

Black promotes a form of universal readability across the Python ecosystem. Code is read more often than it's being written—a transparent style helps. At the same time, Black makes code more "writable" too. When you're contributing to other people's code, there's no need to conform to a bespoke and manual code style. Even in a solo project, Black boosts your productivity: if you configure your editor to reformat on save, you can reduce your keystrokes to a minimum while coding.

Black took the Python world by storm, with project after project deciding to "blacken" their source files.

---

## Onboarding a Codebase to Black

When you onboard a large codebase to an opinionated code formatter like Black, the resulting diff can present a headache.

First, why give up conscious style choices and carefully handcrafted code? You'll have to make this decision yourself—but consider the following points: What's the ongoing cost of enforcing your style without the help of automated tools? Do your code reviews focus on the meaning of a change rather than coding style? How long does it take new engineers to get up to speed?

Second, are the changes safe? Black guarantees that the *abstract syntax tree* (AST) of the source code—that is, the parsed representation of the program, as seen by the

---

interpreter—doesn't change, except for some well-known divergences that preserve semantic equivalence.[10]

Third, when you commit the changes, how do you prevent them from cluttering up the output of `git blame`? It turns out that you can configure Git to ignore the commit when annotating files. Store the full 40-character commit hash in a file named *.git-blame-ignore-revs* in the root of the repository. Then run the following command:

```
$ git config blame.ignoreRevsFile .git-blame-ignore-revs
```

Code hosting services like GitHub increasingly support the *.git-blame-ignore-revs* file, as well.

## The Black Code Style

Black's code style becomes invisible once you've worked with it for a while. Inevitably, though, some of its choices have led to controversy, even forks. To understand its formatting rules, it helps to look at Black's goal of producing readable and consistent source code in a predictable and repeatable way.

Take the default of double quotes for string literals, for example. According to the style recommendations of PEP 257 and PEP 8, both docstrings and English text with apostrophes already require double quotes. Choosing double quotes over single quotes therefore results in a more consistent style overall.

Sometimes Black places a lone `):` after the parameters of a function. Nicknamed the "sad face," it clearly demarcates the function signature from the body without indenting parameters beyond the standard four spaces. This layout also treats parameter lists like any other bracketed constructs, such as tuples, lists, and set literals.

Black also caps lines at 88 characters (one of its few configurable settings). This tradeoff between lateral eye movement and vertical scrolling is based on a data-driven approach, tested on millions of lines of Python code at Meta.

Another goal of Black is to avoid *merge conflicts*, when concurrent changes to the same region of code cannot be combined without human intervention. The trailing comma—placing a comma behind the last item in a sequence—serves this purpose: it lets you insert before and after the last item without conflict.

---

10 "AST Before and After Formatting" (*https://oreil.ly/gW9Ef*), *Black documentation*. Last accessed: March 22, 2024.

Reducing dependencies between edits helps different people work on the same code. But it also lets you separate or reorder drive-by bugfixes or refactorings and back out tentative commits before submitting your changes for code review.

As noted, Black's algorithm is deterministic, and existing layouts hardly affect it. A "blackened" file may look as if it was generated straight from the AST.[11] In reality, this can't be the case, though. For one thing, the AST doesn't include comments, since they don't affect program execution.

Black takes some cues from the formatted source code besides comments. One example is the blank lines that divide a function body into logical partitions. Likely the most powerful way of affecting Black's output, however, is the *magic trailing comma*: if a sequence contains a trailing comma, Black splits its elements across multiple lines, even if they would fit on a single line.

Black provides an escape hatch to let you disable formatting for a region of code (Example 9-6).

*Example 9-6. Disabling formatting for a region of code*

```
@pytest.mark.parametrize(
    ("value", "expected"),
    [
        ("first test value",     "61df19525cf97aa3855b5aeb1b2bcb89"),
        ("another test value",   "5768979c48c30998c46fb21a91a5b266"),
        ("and here's another one", "e766977069039d83f01b4e3544a6a54c"),
    ]
)  # fmt: skip
def test_frobnicate(value, expected):
    assert expected == frobnicate(value)
```

Hand-formatting can be useful for program data, such as large tables with properly aligned columns.

## Formatting Code with Ruff

Code formatters can process millions of lines of code in a batch, or they can run in quick succession when triggered from your editor or on a busy CI server. Being fast was an explicit goal of Black from the start—it ships binary wheels with native code generated by mypyc, a compiler for type-annotated Python. While Black is fast, the Ruff formatter further improves performance thirtyfold, thanks to its efficient Rust implementation.

---

11 You can inspect the AST of a source file with the standard ast module, using py -m ast example.py.

Ruff aims for full compatibility with the Black code style. Unlike Black, Ruff lets you opt into single quotes and indentation using tabs. However, I'd recommend adhering to Black's widely adopted style.

When run without arguments, `ruff format` processes any Python files beneath the current directory. Instead of invoking Ruff manually, add it to your pre-commit hooks, as shown in Example 9-7.

*Example 9-7. Running Ruff from pre-commit as a linter and code formatter*

```
repos:
  - repo: https://github.com/astral-sh/ruff-pre-commit
    rev: v0.4.4
    hooks:
      - id: ruff
        args: ["--fix", "--show-fixes", "--exit-non-zero-on-fix"]
      - id: ruff-format
```

The pre-commit hook for the code formatter comes last. This gives it an opportunity to reformat any automatic fixes made by linters.

## Summary

In this chapter, you've seen how to improve and preserve the code quality in your projects using linters and code formatters. Ruff is an efficient reimplementation of many Python code-quality tools in Rust, including Flake8 and Black. While it's possible to run Ruff and other tools manually, you should automate this process and include it as a mandatory check in CI. One of the best options is pre-commit, a cross-language linter framework with Git integration. Invoke pre-commit from a Nox session to keep a single entry point for your suite of checks.

# CHAPTER 10

# Using Types for Safety and Inspection

What's a type? As a first approximation, let's say the *type* of a variable specifies the kind of values you can assign to it—for example, integers or lists of strings. When Guido van Rossum created Python, most popular programming languages fell into two camps when it came to types: static and dynamic typing.

*Statically typed* languages, like C++, require you to declare the types of variables upfront (unless the compiler is smart enough to infer them automatically). In exchange, compilers ensure a variable only ever holds compatible values. That eliminates entire classes of bugs. It also enables optimizations: compilers know how much space the variable needs to store its values.

*Dynamically typed* languages break with this paradigm: they let you assign any value to any variable. Scripting languages like JavaScript and Perl even convert values implicitly—say, from strings to numbers. This radically speeds up the process of writing code. It also gives you more leeway to shoot yourself into the foot.

Python is a dynamically typed language, yet it chose a middle ground between the opposing camps. Let's demonstrate its approach with an example:

```
import math

number = input("Enter a number: ")
number = float(number)
result = math.sqrt(number)

print(f"The square root of {number} is {result}.")
```

In Python, a variable is just a name for a value. Variables don't have types—*values* do. The program associates the same name, number, first with a value of type str, then with a value of type float. But unlike Perl and similar languages, Python never converts the values behind your back, in eager anticipation of your wishes:

```
>>> math.sqrt("1.21")
Traceback (most recent call last):
```

```
  File "<stdin>", line 1, in <module>
TypeError: must be real number, not str
```

Python isn't as forgiving as some of its contemporaries, but consider two limitations of this type check. First, you won't see a `TypeError` until you run the offending code. Second, the Python interpreter doesn't raise the error—the library function checks explicitly if something other than an integer or floating-point number was passed.

Most Python functions don't check the types of their arguments at all. Instead, they simply invoke the operations they expect their arguments to provide. Fundamentally, the type of a Python object doesn't matter as long as its behavior is correct. Taking inspiration from Vaucanson's mechanical duck from the times of Louis XV, this approach is known as *duck typing*: "If it looks like a duck and quacks like a duck, then it must be a duck."

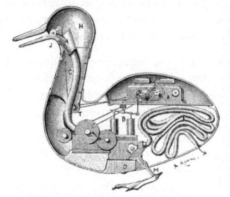

INTERIOR OF VAUCANSON'S AUTOMATIC DUCK.
*A*, clockwork; *B*, pump; *C*, mill for grinding grain; *F*, intestinal tube;
*J*, bill; *H*, head; *M*, feet.

As an example, consider the *join* operation in concurrent code. This operation lets you wait until some background work completes, "joining" the threads of control back together, as it were. Example 10-1 defines a duck-typed function that invokes `join` on a number of tasks, waiting for each in turn.

*Example 10-1. Duck typing in action*

```
def join_all(joinables):
    for task in joinables:
        task.join()
```

You can use this function with `Thread` or `Process` from the standard `threading` or `multiprocessing` modules—or with any other object that has a `join` method with the correct signature. (You can't use it with strings because `str.join` takes an argument—an iterable of strings.) Duck typing means that these classes don't need a common base class to benefit from reuse. All the types need is a `join` method with the correct signature.

Duck typing is great because the function and its callers can evolve fairly independently—a property known as *loose coupling*. Without duck typing, a function argument has to implement an explicit interface that specifies its behavior. Python gives you loose coupling for free: you can pass literally anything, as long as it satisfies the expected behavior.

Unfortunately, this freedom can make some functions hard to understand.

If you've ever had to read an entire codebase to grasp the purpose of a few lines within it, you know what I mean: it can be impossible to understand a Python function in isolation. Sometimes, the only way to decipher what's going on is to look at its callers, their callers, and so on (Example 10-2).

*Example 10-2. An obscure function*

```
def _send(objects, sender):
    """send them with the sender..."""
    for obj in objects[0].get_all():
        if p := obj.get_parent():
            sender.run(p)
        elif obj is not None and obj._next is not None:
            _send_next_object(obj._next, sender)
```

Writing out the argument and return types of the function—its type signature—dramatically reduces the amount of context you need to understand the function. Traditionally, people have done so by listing the types in a docstring. Unfortunately, docstrings are often missing, incomplete, or incorrect. More importantly, there was no formal language for describing the types in a precise and verifiable way. And without tooling to enforce the type signatures, they amounted to little more than wishful thinking.

While this kind of problem is mildly annoying in a codebase with a few hundred lines of code, it quickly turns into an existential threat when you're dealing with many millions of lines of code. Python codebases of this size are common at companies like Google, Meta, Microsoft, and Dropbox, all of which sponsored the development of static type checkers in the 2010s. A *static type checker* is a tool that verifies the type safety of a program without running it. In other words, it checks that the program doesn't perform operations on values that don't support those operations.

To some extent, type checkers can deduce the type of a function or variable automatically, using a process called *type inference*. They become much more powerful when you give programmers a way to specify types explicitly in their code. By the middle of the last decade, and thanks in particular to the foundational work of Jukka Lehtosalo and collaborators,[1] the Python language acquired a way to express the types of functions and variables in source code, called *type annotations* (Example 10-3).

*Example 10-3. A function with type annotations*

```python
def format_lines(lines: list[str], indent: int = 0) -> str:
    prefix = " " * indent
    return "\n".join(f"{prefix}{line}" for line in lines)
```

Type annotations have become the foundation of a rich ecosystem of developer tools and libraries.

On their own, type annotations mostly don't affect the runtime behavior of a program. The interpreter doesn't check that assignments are compatible with the annotated type; it merely stores the annotation inside the special __annotations__ attribute of the containing module, class, or function. While this incurs a small overhead at runtime, it means you can inspect type annotations at runtime to do exciting stuff—say, construct your domain objects from values transmitted on the wire, without any boilerplate.

One of the most important uses of type annotations, though, doesn't happen at runtime: static type checkers, like mypy, use them to verify the correctness of your code without running it.

# Benefits and Costs of Type Annotations

You don't have to use type annotations yourself to benefit from them. Type annotations are available for the standard library and many PyPI packages. Static type checkers can warn you when you use a module incorrectly, including when a breaking change in the library means your code no longer works with that library—and type checkers can warn you *before* you run your code.

Editors and IDEs leverage type annotations to give you a better coding experience, with auto-completion, tooltips, and class browsers. You can also inspect type annotations at runtime, unlocking powerful features such as data validation and serialization.

If you use type annotations in your own code, you reap more benefits. First, you're also a user of your own functions, classes, and modules—so all the benefits previously mentioned apply, like auto-completion and type checking. Additionally, you'll find it easier to reason about your code, refactor it without introducing subtle bugs, and

---

1 Jukka Lehtosalo, "Our Journey to Type Checking 4 Million Lines of Python" (*https://oreil.ly/njfdx*), September 5, 2019.

build a clean software architecture. When you are a library author, typing lets you specify an interface contract your users can rely on, while you're free to evolve the implementation.

Even a decade after their introduction, type annotations aren't free of controversy—maybe understandably so, given Python's proud stance as a dynamically typed language. Adding types to existing code poses similar challenges as introducing unit tests to a codebase that wasn't written with testing in mind. Just as you may need to refactor for testability, you may need to refactor for "typability"—replacing deeply nested primitive types and highly dynamic objects with simpler and more predictable types. You'll likely find it worth the effort.

Another challenge is the rapid evolution of the Python typing language. These days, Python type annotations are governed by the Typing Council, which maintains a single, living specification of the typing language.[2] You can expect this specification to undergo more substantial changes over the coming years. While typed Python code needs to navigate this evolution, the typing language makes no exceptions to Python's backward compatibility policy.

In this chapter, you'll learn how to verify the type safety of your Python programs using the static type checker mypy and the runtime type checker Typeguard. You'll also see how runtime inspection of type annotations can greatly enhance the functionality of your programs. But first, let's take a look at the typing language that has evolved within Python over the past decade.

# A Brief Tour of Python's Typing Language

Try out the small examples in this section on one of the type-checker playgrounds:

- mypy Playground (*https://mypy-play.net*)
- Pyright Playground (*https://pyright-play.net*)
- Pyre Playground (*https://pyre-check.org/play*)

## Variable Annotations

You can annotate a variable with the type of values that it may be assigned during the course of the program. The syntax for such type annotations consists of the variable name, a colon, and a type:

```
answer: int = 42
```

---

2 "Specification for the Python Type System" (*https://oreil.ly/Y8sDi*), last accessed January 22, 2024.

Besides the simple built-in types like `bool`, `int`, `float`, `str`, or `bytes`, you can also use standard container types in type annotations, such as `list`, `tuple`, `set`, or `dict`. For example, here's how you might initialize a variable used to store a list of lines read from a file:

```
lines: list[str] = []
```

While the previous example was somewhat redundant, this one provides actual value: without the type annotation, the type checker can't deduce that you want to store strings in the list.

The built-in containers are examples of *generic types*—types that take one or more arguments. Here's an example of a dictionary mapping strings to integers. The two arguments of `dict` specify the key and value types, respectively:

```
fruits: dict[str, int] = {
    "banana": 3,
    "apple": 2,
    "orange": 1,
}
```

Tuples are a bit special, because they come in two flavors. Tuples can be a combination of a fixed number of types, such as a pair of a string and int:

```
pair: tuple[str, int] = ("banana", 3)
```

Another example of this flavor holds coordinates in three-dimensional space:

```
coordinates: tuple[float, float, float] = (4.5, 0.1, 3.2)
```

The other common use of tuples is as an immutable sequence of arbitrary length. To accomodate for this, the typing language lets you write an ellipsis for zero or more items of the same type. For example, here's a tuple that can hold any number of integers (including none at all):

```
numbers: tuple[int, ...] = (1, 2, 3, 4, 5)
```

Any class you define in your own Python code is also a type:

```
class Parrot:
    pass

class NorwegianBlue(Parrot):
    pass


parrot: Parrot = NorwegianBlue()
```

## The Subtype Relation

The types on both sides of an assignment aren't necessarily identical. In the example above, you assign a `NorwegianBlue` value to a `Parrot` variable. This works because a

Norwegian Blue is a kind of parrot—or technically speaking, because `NorwegianBlue` is a subclass of `Parrot`.

In general, the Python typing language requires that the type on the right-hand side of a variable assignment be a *subtype* of the type on the left-hand side. A prime example of the subtype relation is the relationship of a subclass to its base class, like `NorwegianBlue` and `Parrot`.

However, subtypes are a more general concept than subclasses. For example, a tuple of ints (like `numbers`) is a subtype of a tuple of objects. Unions, introduced in the next section, are yet another example.

> Typing rules also permit assignments if the type on the right is *consistent* with that on the left. This lets you assign an `int` to a `float`, even though `int` isn't derived from `float`. The `Any` type is consistent with any other type (see "Gradual Typing" on page 214).

## Union Types

You can combine two types using the pipe operator (`|`) to construct a *union type*, which is a type whose values range over all the values of its constituent types. For example, you can use it for a user ID that's either numeric or a string:

```
user_id: int | str = "nobody"  # or 65534
```

Arguably the most important use of the union type is for "optional" values, where the missing value is encoded by `None`. Here's an example where a description is read from a *README*, provided that the file exists:

```
description: str | None = None

if readme.exists():
    description = readme.read_text()
```

Union types are another example of the subtype relation: each type involved in the union is a subtype of the union. For example, `str` and `None` are each subtypes of the union type `str | None`.

I skipped over `None` when discussing the built-in types. Strictly speaking, `None` is a value, not a type. The type of `None` is called `NoneType`, and it's available from the standard `types` module. For convenience, Python lets you write `None` in annotations to refer to the type as well.

Tony Hoare, a British computer scientist who has made foundational contributions to many programming languages, famously called the invention of null references, or `None`, his "billion-dollar mistake," due to the number of bugs they've caused since their introduction in `ALGOL` in 1965. If you've ever seen a system crash with an error like the following, you may agree with him. (Python raises this error if you attempt to access an attribute on an object that's in fact None.)

```
AttributeError: 'NoneType' object has no attribute '...'
```

The good news is that type checkers can warn you when you're using a variable that's potentially None. This can greatly reduce the risk of crashes in production systems.

How do you tell the type checker that your use of `description` is fine? Generally, you should just check that the variable isn't None. The type checker will pick up on this and allow you to use the variable:

```
if description is not None:
    for line in description.splitlines():
        print(f"    {line}")
```

There are several methods for *type narrowing*, as this technique is known. I won't discuss them all in detail here. As a rule of thumb, the control flow must reach the line in question only when the value has the right type—and type checkers must be able to infer this fact from the source code. For example, you could also use the `assert` keyword with a built-in function like `isinstance`:

```
assert isinstance(description, str)
for line in description.splitlines():
    ...
```

If you already *know* that the value has the right type, you can help out the type checker using the `cast` function from the `typing` module:

```
description_str = cast(str, description)
for line in description_str.splitlines():
    ...
```

At runtime, the `cast` function just returns its second argument. Unlike `isinstance`, it works with arbitrary type annotations.

## Gradual Typing

In Python, every type ultimately derives from `object`. This is true for user-defined classes and primitive types alike, even for types like `int` or None. In other words, `object` is a *universal supertype* in Python—you can assign literally anything to a variable of this type.

This may sound kind of powerful, but it really isn't. In terms of behavior, `object` is the smallest common denominator of all Python values, so there's precious little you can do with it, as far as type checkers are concerned:

```
number: object = 2
print(number + number)  # error: Unsupported left operand type for +
```

There's another type in Python that, like object, can hold any value. It's called Any (for obvious reasons), and it's available from the standard typing module. When it comes to behavior, Any is object's polar opposite. You can invoke any operation on a value of type Any—conceptually, it behaves like the intersection of all possible types. Any serves as an escape hatch that lets you opt out of type checking for a piece of code:

```
from typing import Any

number: Any = NorwegianBlue()
print(number + number)  # valid, but crashes at runtime!
```

In the first example, the object type results in a false positive: the code works at runtime, but type checkers will reject it. In the second example, the Any type results in a false negative: the code crashes at runtime, but type checkers won't flag it.

 When you're working in typed Python code, watch out for Any. It can disable type checking to a surprising degree. For example, if you access attributes or invoke operations on Any values, you'll end up with more Any values.

The Any type is Python's hat trick that lets you restrict type checking to portions of a codebase—formally known as *gradual typing*. In variable assignments and function calls, Any is consistent with every other type, and every type is consistent with it.

There are at least a couple of reasons why gradual typing is valuable. First, Python existed without type annotations for two decades, and Python's governing body has no plans to make type annotations obligatory. Therefore, typed and untyped Python will coexist for the foreseeable future. Second, Python's strength comes in part from its ability to be highly dynamic where needed—for example, Python makes it easy to assemble or even modify classes on the fly. In some cases, it's hard (or outright impossible) to apply strict types to such highly dynamic code.[3]

# Function Annotations

As you may recall from Example 10-3, type annotations for function arguments look quite similar to those for variables. Return types, on the other hand, are introduced with a right arrow instead of a colon—after all, the colon already introduces the function body in Python. For example, here's a type-annotated function for adding two numbers:

---

3 Tin Tvrtković, "Python Is Two Languages Now, and That's Actually Great" (*https://oreil.ly/S51aK*), February 27, 2023.

```python
def add(a: int, b: int) -> int:
    return a + b
```

Python functions that don't include a `return` statement implicitly return `None`. You might expect return type annotations to be optional in this case, too. This is not the case! As a general rule, always specify the return type when annotating a function:

```python
def greet(name: str) -> None:
    print(f"Hello, {name}")
```

Type checkers assume that a function without a return type returns Any. Likewise, function parameters without annotations default to Any. Effectively, this disables type checking for the function—exactly the behavior you'd want in a world with large bodies of untyped Python code.

Let's look at a slightly more involved function signature:

```python
import subprocess
from typing import Any

def run(*args: str, check: bool = True, **kwargs: Any) -> None:
    subprocess.run(args, check=check, **kwargs)
```

Parameters with default arguments, like `check`, use a syntax similar to variable assignments. The `*args` parameter holds the tuple of positional arguments—each argument must be a `str`. The `**kwargs` parameter holds the dictionary of keyword arguments—using Any means that the keyword arguments aren't restricted to any specific type.

In Python, you can use `yield` inside a function to define a *generator*, which is an object that produces a series of values you can use in a `for` loop. Generators support some behavior beyond iteration; when used only for iteration, they're known as *iterators*. Here's how you'd write their type:

```python
from collections.abc import Iterator

def fibonacci() -> Iterator[int]:
    a, b = 0, 1
    while True:
        yield a
        a, b = b, a + b
```

Functions are first-class citizens in Python. You can assign a function to a variable or pass it to another function—for example, to register a callback. Consequently, Python lets you express the type of a function outside of a function definition. `Callable` is a generic type that takes two arguments—a list of parameter types and the return type:

```python
from collections.abc import Callable

Serve = Callable[[Article], str]
```

# Annotating Classes

The rules for variable and function annotations also apply in the context of class definitions, where they describe instance variables and methods. You can omit the annotation for the `self` argument in a method. Type checkers can infer instance variables from assignments in a `__init__` method:

```
class Swallow:
    def __init__(self, velocity: float) -> None:
        self.velocity = velocity
```

The standard `dataclasses` module generates the canonical method definitions from the type annotations of any class decorated with `@dataclass`:

```
from dataclasses import dataclass

@dataclass
class Swallow:
    velocity: float
```

The dataclass-style definition isn't just more concise than the handwritten one; it also confers the class additional runtime behavior—such as the ability to compare instances for equality based on their attributes, or to order them.

When you're annotating classes, the problem of forward references often appears. Consider a two-dimensional point, with a method to compute its Euclidean distance from another point:

```
import math
from dataclasses import dataclass

@dataclass
class Point:
    x: float
    y: float

    def distance(self, other: Point) -> float:
        dx = self.x - other.x
        dy = self.y - other.y
        return math.sqrt(dx*dx + dy*dy)
```

While type checkers are happy with this definition, the code raises an exception when you run it with the Python interpreter:[4]

```
NameError: name 'Point' is not defined. Did you mean: 'print'?
```

Python doesn't let you use `Point` in the method definition because you're not done defining the class—the name doesn't exist yet. There are several ways to resolve

---

4 In a future Python version, this will work out of the box. See Larry Hastings, "PEP 649 – Deferred Evaluation of Annotations Using Descriptors" (*https://oreil.ly/lPvRR*), January 11, 2021.

this situation. First, you can write the forward reference as a string to avoid the NameError, a technique known as *stringized* annotations:

```
@dataclass
class Point:
    def distance(self, other: "Point") -> float:
        ...
```

Second, you can implicitly stringize all annotations in the current module using the annotations future import:

```
from __future__ import annotations

@dataclass
class Point:
    def distance(self, other: Point) -> float:
        ...
```

The third method does not help with all forward references, but it does here. You can use the special Self type to refer to the current class:

```
from typing import Self

@dataclass
class Point:
    def distance(self, other: Self) -> float:
        ...
```

Beware of a semantic difference in this third version compared to the earlier ones. If you derived a SparklyPoint class from Point, Self would refer to the derived class rather than the base class. In other words, you wouldn't be able to compute the distance of sparkly points from plain old points.

## Type Aliases

You can use the type keyword to introduce an alias for a type:[5]

```
type UserID = int | str
```

This technique is useful to make your code self-documenting and to keep it readable when the types become unwieldy, as they sometimes do. Type aliases also let you define types that otherwise would be impossible to express. Consider an inherently recursive data type such as a JSON object:

```
type JSON = None | bool | int | float | str | list[JSON] | dict[str, JSON]
```

---

5 If you see an error message like "PEP 695 type aliases are not yet supported," just omit the type keyword for now. The type checker still interprets the assignment as a type alias. If you want to be more explicit, you can use the typing.TypeAlias annotation from Python 3.10 upward.

Recursive type aliases are another example of forward references. If your Python version doesn't yet support the `type` keyword, you'll need to replace `JSON` with `"JSON"` on the righthand side to avoid a `NameError`.

## Generics

As you've seen at the beginning of this section, built-in containers like `list` are generic types. You can also define generic functions and classes yourself, and it's quite straightforward to do so. Consider a function that returns the first item in a list of strings:

```python
def first(values: list[str]) -> str:
    for value in values:
        return value
    raise ValueError("empty list")
```

There's no reason to restrict the element type to a string: the logic doesn't depend on it. Let's make the function generic for all types. First, replace `str` with the placeholder `T`. Second, mark the placeholder as a *type variable* by declaring it in square brackets after the function name. (The name `T` is just a convention; you could name it anything.) Additionally, there's no reason to restrict the function to lists, because it works with any type over which you can iterate in a `for` loop—in other words, any *iterable*:

```python
from collections.abc import Iterable

def first[T](values: Iterable[T]) -> T:
    for value in values:
        return value
    raise ValueError("no values")
```

Here's how you might use the generic function in your code:

```python
fruit: str = first(["banana", "orange", "apple"])
number: int = first({1, 2, 3})
```

You can omit the variable annotations for `fruit` and `number`, by the way—type checkers infer them from the annotation of your generic function.

 Generics with the `[T]` syntax are supported in Python 3.12+ and the Pyright type checker. If you get an error, omit the `[T]` suffix from `first` and use `TypeVar` from the `typing` module:

```python
T = TypeVar("T")
```

## Protocols

The `join_all` function from Example 10-1 works with threads, processes, or any other objects you can join. Duck typing makes your functions simple and reusable. But how can you verify the implicit contract between the functions and their callers?

*Protocols* bridge the gap between duck typing and type annotations. A protocol describes the behavior of an object without requiring the object to inherit from it. It looks somewhat like an *abstract base class*—a base class that doesn't implement any methods:

```python
from typing import Protocol

class Joinable(Protocol):
    def join(self) -> None: ...
```

The `Joinable` protocol requires the object to have a `join` method that takes no arguments and returns `None`. The `join_all` function can use the protocol to specify which objects it supports:

```python
def join_all(joinables: Iterable[Joinable]) -> None:
    for task in joinables:
        task.join()
```

Remarkably, this piece of code works with standard library types like `Thread` or `Process`, even though they don't have any knowledge of your `Joinable` protocol—a prime example of loose coupling.

This technique is known as *structural subtyping*: it's the internal structure of `Thread` and `Process` that makes them subtypes of `Joinable`. By contrast, *nominal subtyping* requires you to derive the subtype from the supertype explicitly.

## Compatibility with Older Python Versions

The description above is based on the latest Python release as of this writing, Python 3.12. Table 10-1 lists typing features that aren't yet available on older Python versions, as well as their replacements in those versions.

*Table 10-1. Availability of typing features*

| Feature | Example | Availability | Replacement |
|---|---|---|---|
| Generics in standard collections | `list[str]` | Python 3.9 | `typing.List` |
| Union operator | `str | int` | Python 3.10 | `typing.Union` |
| Self type | `Self` | Python 3.11 | `typing_extensions.Self` |
| type keyword | `type UserID = ...` | Python 3.12 | `typing.TypeAlias` (Python 3.10) |
| Type parameter syntax | `def first[T](...)` | Python 3.12 | `typing.TypeVar` |

The `typing-extensions` library provides backports for many features not available in older Python versions; see "Automating mypy with Nox" on page 225.

This concludes our brief tour of Python's typing language. While there's a lot more to typing in Python, I hope that this overview has taught you enough to make deeper forays into the exciting world of typing on your own.

# Static Type Checking with mypy

Mypy is a widely used static type checker for Python. A static type checker uses type annotations and type inference to detect bugs in a program without running it. Mypy was the original reference implementation when the typing system was codified in PEP 484. This doesn't mean that mypy is always the first type checker to implement a new feature of the typing language—for example, the `type` keyword was first implemented in Pyright. However, it's certainly a good default choice, and core members of the typing community are involved in its development.

## First Steps with mypy

Add mypy to the development dependencies of your project—for example, by adding a `typing` extra:

```
[project.optional-dependencies]
typing = ["mypy>=1.9.0"]
```

You can now install mypy in the project environment:

```
$ uv pip install -e ".[typing]"
```

If you use Poetry, add mypy to your project using `poetry add`:

```
$ poetry add --group=typing "mypy>=1.9.0"
```

Finally, run mypy on the *src* directory of your project:

```
$ py -m mypy src
Success: no issues found in 2 source files
```

Let's type-check some code with a type-related bug. Consider the following program, which passes None to a function that expects a string:

```
import textwrap

data = {"title": "Gegenes nostrodamus"}

summary = data.get("extract")
summary = textwrap.fill(summary)
```

If you run mypy on this code, it dutifully reports that the argument in the call to `textwrap.fill` isn't guaranteed to be a string:

```
$ py -m mypy example.py
example.py:5: error: Argument 1 to "fill" has incompatible type "str | None";
  expected "str"  [arg-type]
Found 1 error in 1 file (checked 1 source file)
```

## Revisiting the Wikipedia Example

Let's revisit the Wikipedia API client from Example 6-3. In a fictional scenario, sweeping censorship laws have been passed. Depending on the country you're connecting from, the Wikipedia API omits the article summary.

You could store an empty string when this happens. But let's be principled: an empty summary isn't the same as no summary at all. Let's store None when the response omits the field.

As a first step, change the `summary` default to None instead of an empty string. Use a union type to signal that the field can hold None instead of a string:

```
@dataclass
class Article:
    title: str = ""
    summary: str | None = None
```

A few lines below, the show function reformats the summary to ensure a line length of 72 characters or fewer:

```
def show(article, file):
    summary = textwrap.fill(article.summary)
    file.write(f"{article.title}\n\n{summary}\n")
```

Presumably, mypy will balk at this error, just like it did above. Yet, when you run it on the file, it's all sunshine. Can you guess why?

```
$ py -m mypy src
Success: no issues found in 2 source files
```

Mypy doesn't complain about the call because the `article` parameter doesn't have a type annotation. It considers `article` to be Any, so the expression `article.summary` also becomes Any. (Any is infectious.) As far as mypy is concerned, that expression can be `str`, None, and a pink elephant, all at the same time. This is gradual typing in action, and it's why you should be wary of Any types and missing annotations in your code.

You can help mypy detect the error by annotating the parameter as `article: Article`. Try actually fixing the bug, as well—think about how you would handle the case of summaries being None in a real program. Here's one way to solve this:

```
def show(article: Article, file):
    if article.summary is not None:
        summary = textwrap.fill(article.summary)
    else:
        summary = "[CENSORED]"
    file.write(f"{article.title}\n\n{summary}\n")
```

# Strict Mode

Mypy defaults to gradual typing by treating parameters and return values as Any if they don't have type annotations. Turn on strict mode in *pyproject.toml* to opt out of this lenient default:

```
[tool.mypy]
strict = true
```

The strict setting changes the defaults of a dozen-odd more fine-grained settings. If you run mypy on the module again, you'll notice that the type checker has become a lot more opinionated about your code. In strict mode, both defining and calling untyped functions will result in an error:[6]

```
$ py -m mypy src
__init__.py:16: error: Function is missing a type annotation
__init__.py:22: error: Function is missing a type annotation
__init__.py:27: error: Function is missing a return type annotation
__init__.py:27: note: Use "-> None" if function does not return a value
__init__.py:28: error: Call to untyped function "fetch" in typed context
__init__.py:29: error: Call to untyped function "show" in typed context
__main__.py:3: error: Call to untyped function "main" in typed context
Found 6 errors in 2 files (checked 2 source files)
```

Example 10-4 shows the module with type annotations and introduces two concepts you haven't seen yet. First, the Final annotation marks API_URL as a constant—a variable to which you can't assign another value. Second, the TextIO type is a file-like object for reading and writing strings (str), such as the standard output stream. Otherwise, the type annotations should look fairly familiar.

*Example 10-4. The Wikipedia API client with type annotations*

```
import json
import sys
import textwrap
import urllib.request
from dataclasses import dataclass
from typing import Final, TextIO

API_URL: Final = "https://en.wikipedia.org/api/rest_v1/page/random/summary"
```

---

6 For brevity, I've removed error codes and leading directories from mypy's output.

```
@dataclass
class Article:
    title: str = ""
    summary: str = ""

def fetch(url: str) -> Article:
    with urllib.request.urlopen(url) as response:
        data = json.load(response)
    return Article(data["title"], data["extract"])

def show(article: Article, file: TextIO) -> None:
    summary = textwrap.fill(article.summary)
    file.write(f"{article.title}\n\n{summary}\n")

def main() -> None:
    article = fetch(API_URL)
    show(article, sys.stdout)
```

I recommend strict mode for any new Python project because it's much easier to annotate your code as you write it. Strict checks give you more confidence in the correctness of your program because type errors are less likely to be masked by Any.

 My other favorite mypy setting in *pyproject.toml* is the `pretty` flag. It displays source snippets and indicates where the error occurred:

```
[tool.mypy]
pretty = true
```

Let mypy's strict mode be your North Star when adding types to an existing Python codebase. Mypy gives you an arsenal of finer- and coarser-grained ways to relax type checking when you're not ready to fix a type error.

Your first line of defense is a special comment of the form `# type: ignore`. Always follow it with the error code in square brackets. For example, here's a line from mypy's previous output with the error code included:

```
__main__.py:3: error: Call to untyped function "main" in typed context
    [no-untyped-call]
```

You can allow this specific call to an untyped function as follows:

```
main()  # type: ignore[no-untyped-call]
```

If you have a module with a large number of untyped calls, you can ignore the error for the entire module using the following stanza in your *pyproject.toml*:

```
[tool.mypy."<module>"]  ❶
allow_untyped_calls = true
```

❶ Replace *<module>* with the module that has the untyped calls. Use double quotes if the module's name contains any dots.

You can also ignore an error globally, like this:

```
[tool.mypy]
allow_untyped_calls = true
```

You can even disable all type errors for a given module:

```
[tool.mypy."<module>"]
ignore_errors = true
```

## Automating mypy with Nox

Throughout this book, you've automated checks for your projects using Nox. Nox sessions allow you and other contributors to run checks easily and repeatedly during local development, the same way they'd run on a continuous integration (CI) server.

Example 10-5 shows a Nox session for type checking your project with mypy.

*Example 10-5. A Nox session for type checking with mypy*

```
import nox

@nox.session(python=["3.12", "3.11", "3.10"])
def mypy(session: nox.Session) -> None:
    session.install(".[typing]")
    session.run("mypy", "src")
```

Just like you run the test suite across all supported Python versions, you should also type-check your project on every Python version. This practice is fairly effective at ensuring that your project is compatible with those versions, even when your test suite doesn't exercise that one code path where you forgot about backward compatibility.

> You can also pass the target version using mypy's `--python-version` option. However, installing the project on each version ensures that mypy checks your project against the correct dependencies. These may not be the same on all Python versions.

Inevitably, as you type-check on multiple versions, you'll get into situations where either the runtime code or the type annotations don't work across all versions. For example, Python 3.9 deprecated `typing.Iterable` in favor of `collections.abc.Iterable`. Use conditional imports based on the Python version, as shown below. Static type checkers recognize Python version checks in your code, and they will base their type checks on the code relevant for the current version:

```
import sys

if sys.version_info >= (3, 9):
    from collections.abc import Iterable
else:
    from typing import Iterable
```

Another sticking point: typing features not yet available at the low end of your supported Python version range. Fortunately, these often come with backports in a third-party library named `typing-extensions`. For example, Python 3.11 added the useful `Self` annotation, which denotes the currently enclosing class. If you support versions older than that, add `typing-extensions` to your dependencies and import `Self` from there:

```
import sys

if sys.version_info >= (3, 11):
    from typing import Self
else:
    from typing_extensions import Self
```

## Distributing Types with Python Packages

You may wonder why the Nox session in Example 10-5 installs the project into mypy's virtual environment. By nature, a static type checker operates on source code; it doesn't run your code. So why install anything but the type checker itself?

To see why this matters, consider the version of the Wikipedia project in Examples 6-5 and 6-14, where you implemented the `show` and `fetch` functions using Rich and `httpx`. How can a type checker validate your use of a specific version of a third-party package?

Rich and `httpx` are, in fact, fully type annotated. They include an empty marker file named *py.typed* next to their source files. When you install the packages into a virtual environment, the marker file allows static type checkers to locate their types.

Many Python packages distribute their types inline with *py.typed* markers. However, other mechanisms for type distribution exist. Knowing them is useful when mypy can't import the types for a package.

For example, the `factory-boy` library doesn't yet ship with types—instead, you need to install a stubs package named `types-factory-boy` from PyPI.[7] A *stubs package* is a Python package containing typing stubs, a special kind of Python source file with a *.pyi* suffix that has only type annotations and no executable code.

---

7 As of this writing, the upcoming release of `factory-boy` is expected to distribute types inline.

If you're entirely out of luck and types for your dependency simply don't exist, disable the mypy error in *pyproject.toml*, like this:

```
[tool.mypy.<package>] ❶
ignore_missing_imports = true
```

❶ Replace *<package>* with the import name of the package.

Python's standard library doesn't include type annotations. Type checkers vendor the third-party package typeshed for standard library types, so you don't have to worry about supplying them.

## Type Checking the Tests

Treat your tests like you would treat any other code. Type checking your tests helps you detect when they use your project, pytest, or testing libraries incorrectly.

Running mypy on your test suite also type-checks the public API of your project. This can be a good fallback when you're unable to fully type your implementation code for every supported Python version.

Example 10-6 extends the Nox session to type-check your test suite. Install your test dependencies so mypy has access to type information for pytest and friends.

*Example 10-6. A Nox session for type checking with mypy*

```
nox.options.sessions = ["lint", "mypy", "tests"]

@nox.session(python=["3.12", "3.11", "3.10"])
def mypy(session: nox.Session) -> None:
    session.install(".[typing,tests]")
    session.run("mypy", "src", "tests")
```

The test suite imports your package from the environment. The type checker therefore expects your package to distribute type information. Add an empty *py.typed* marker file to your import package, next to the \_\_init\_\_ and \_\_main\_\_ modules (see "Distributing Types with Python Packages" on page 226).

There isn't anything inherently special about typing a test suite. Recent versions of pytest come with high-quality type annotations. These help when your tests use one of pytest's built-in fixtures. Many test functions don't have arguments and return None. Here's a slightly more involved example using a fixture and test from Chapter 6:

```
import io
import pytest
from random_wikipedia_article import Article, show

@pytest.fixture
def file() -> io.StringIO:
    return io.StringIO()

def test_final_newline(article: Article, file: io.StringIO) -> None:
    show(article, file)
    assert file.getvalue().endswith("\n")
```

Finally, let's indulge in a bout of self-referentialism and type-check the *noxfile.py* (Example 10-7). You'll need the nox package to validate your use of Nox. I'll use a little trick here: when the session runs, there's already a suitable environment with Nox installed—you're in it! Instead of creating another environment with Nox, point mypy to the existing one using its --python-executable option.

*Example 10-7. Type checking the noxfile.py with mypy*

```
import sys

@nox.session(python=["3.12", "3.11", "3.10"])
def mypy(session: nox.Session) -> None:
    session.install(".[typing,tests]")
    session.run("mypy", "src", "tests")
    session.run("mypy", f"--python-executable={sys.executable}", "noxfile.py")
```

# Inspecting Type Annotations at Runtime

Unlike in TypeScript, where static types are available only during compilation, Python type annotations are also available at runtime. Runtime inspection of type annotations is the foundation for powerful features, and an ecosystem of third-party libraries has evolved around its use.

The interpreter stores the type annotations in a special attribute named __annotations__ on the enclosing function, class, or module. Don't access this attribute directly, however—consider it part of Python's plumbing. Python deliberately doesn't shield the attribute from you, but it provides a high-level interface that's easy to use correctly: the function inspect.get_annotations().

Let's inspect the type annotations of the Article class from Example 10-4:

```
>>> import inspect
>>> inspect.get_annotations(Article)
{'title': <class 'str'>, 'summary': <class 'str'>}
```

Recall that the `fetch` function instantiates the class like this:

```
return Article(data["title"], data["extract"])
```

If you can instantiate an `Article`, it must have a standard `__init__` method that initializes its attributes. (You can convince yourself of this fact by accessing it in the interactive session.) Where does the method come from?

The Zen of Python[8] says, "Special cases aren't special enough to break the rules." Dataclasses make no exception to this principle: they're plain Python classes without any secret sauce. Given that the class doesn't define the method itself, there's only one possible origin for it: the `@dataclass` class decorator. In fact, the decorator synthesizes the `__init__` method on the fly, along with several other methods, using your type annotations! Don't take my word for it, though. In this section, you're going to write your own miniature `@dataclass` decorator.

 Don't use this in production! Use the standard `dataclasses` module, or better: the `attrs` library. Attrs is an actively maintained, industry-strength implementation with better performance, a clean API, and additional features, and it directly inspired `dataclasses`.

## Writing a @dataclass Decorator

First of all, be a good typing citizen and think about the signature of the `@dataclass` decorator. A class decorator accepts a class and returns it, usually after transforming it in some way, such as by adding a method. In Python, classes are objects you can pass around and manipulate to your liking.

The typing language allows you to refer to, say, the `str` class by writing `type[str]`. You can read this aloud as "the type of a string." (You can't use `str` on its own here. In a type annotation, `str` just refers to an individual string.) A class decorator should work for any class object, though—it should be generic. Therefore, you'll use a type variable instead of an actual class like `str`:[9]

```
def dataclass[T](cls: type[T]) -> type[T]:
    ...
```

Type checkers need one more bit to properly understand your `@dataclass` decorator: they need to know which methods you're adding to the class and which instance variables they can expect on objects instantiated from the class. Traditionally, you had to write a type checker plugin to infuse this knowledge into the tool. These days,

---

8 Tim Peters, "PEP 20 – The Zen of Python" (*https://oreil.ly/eOLdn*), August 19, 2004.

9 As of this writing, mypy hasn't yet added support for PEP 695 type variables. If you get a mypy error, type-check the code in the Pyright playground instead or use the older `TypeVar` syntax.

the @dataclass_transform marker from the standard library lets you inform type checkers that the class exhibits dataclass-like behavior:

```
from typing import dataclass_transform

@dataclass_transform()
def dataclass[T](cls: type[T]) -> type[T]:
    ...
```

With the function signature out of the way, let's think about how to implement the decorator. You can break this into two steps. First, you'll need to assemble a string with the source code of the __init__ method, using the type annotations on the dataclass. Second, you can use Python's built-in **exec** function to evaluate that source code in the running program.

You've likely written a few __init__ methods in your career—they're pure boiler-plate. For the Article class, the method would look like this:

```
def __init__(self, title: str, summary: str) -> None:
    self.title = title
    self.summary = summary
```

Let's tackle the first step: assembling the source code from the annotations (Example 10-8). Don't fret too much about the parameter types at this point—just use the __name__ attribute of each parameter type, which will work in many cases.

*Example 10-8. Generating the code of the __init__ method*

```
def build_dataclass_init[T](cls: type[T]) -> str: ❶
    annotations = inspect.get_annotations(cls) ❷

    args: list[str] = ["self"] ❸
    body: list[str] = []

    for name, type in annotations.items():
        args.append(f"{name}: {type.__name__}")
        body.append(f"    self.{name} = {name}")

    return "def __init__({}) -> None:\n{}".format(
        ', '.join(args),
        '\n'.join(body),
    )
```

❶ Use a type variable T in the signature to make this generic for any class.

❷ Retrieve the annotations of the class as a dictionary of names and types.

❸   The variable annotation is only required for body. Most type checkers won't infer that body contains strings because it's an empty list at this point. I've annotated both variables for symmetry.

You can now pass the source code to the exec built-in. Apart from the source code, this function accepts dictionaries for the global and local variables.

The canonical way to retrieve the global variables is the globals() built-in. However, you need to evaluate the source code in the context of the module where the class is defined, rather than the context of your decorator. Python stores the name of that module in the __module__ attribute of the class, so you can look up the module object in sys.modules and retrieve the variables from its __dict__ attribute (see "The Module Cache" on page 45):

```
globals = sys.modules[cls.__module__].__dict__
```

For the local variables, you can pass an empty dictionary—this is where exec will place the method definition. All that's left is to copy the method from the locals dictionary into the class object and return the class. Without further ado, Example 10-9 shows the entire decorator.

*Example 10-9. Your own @dataclass decorator*

```
@dataclass_transform()
def dataclass[T](cls: type[T]) -> type[T]:
    sourcecode = build_dataclass_init(cls)

    globals = sys.modules[cls.__module__].__dict__  ❶
    locals = {}
    exec(sourcecode, globals, locals)  ❷

    cls.__init__ = locals["__init__"]  ❸
    return cls
```

❶   Retrieve the global variables from the module that defines the class.

❷   This is where the magic happens: let the interpreter compile the generated code on the fly.

❸   Et voilà—the class now has an __init__ method.

# Runtime Type Checking

There's more you can do with types at runtime besides generating class boilerplate. One important example is runtime type checking. To see how useful this technique is, let's take another look at the `fetch` function:

```
def fetch(url: str) -> Article:
    with urllib.request.urlopen(url) as response:
        data = json.load(response)
    return Article(data["title"], data["extract"])
```

You may have noticed that `fetch` is not type-safe. Nothing guarantees that the Wikipedia API will return a JSON payload of the expected shape. You might object that Wikipedia's OpenAPI specification (*https://oreil.ly/nh0et*) tells us exactly which data shape to expect from the endpoint. But don't base your static types on assumptions about external systems—unless you're happy with your program crashing when a bug or API change breaks those assumptions.

As you may have guessed, mypy silently passes over this issue, because `json.load` returns Any. How can we make the function type-safe? As a first step, let's replace Any with the JSON type you defined in "Type Aliases" on page 218:

```
def fetch(url: str) -> Article:
    with urllib.request.urlopen(url) as response:
        data: JSON = json.load(response)
    return Article(data["title"], data["extract"])
```

We haven't fixed the bug, but at least mypy gives us diagnostics now (edited for brevity):

```
$ py -m mypy src
error: Value of type "..." is not indexable
error: No overload variant of "__getitem__" matches argument type "str"
error: Argument 1 to "Article" has incompatible type "..."; expected "str"
error: Invalid index type "str" for "JSON"; expected type "..."
error: Argument 2 to "Article" has incompatible type "..."; expected "str"
Found 5 errors in 1 file (checked 1 source file)
```

Mypy's diagnostics boil down to two separate issues in the function. First, the code indexes `data` without verifying that it's a dictionary. Second, it passes the results to `Article` without making sure they're strings.

Let's check the type of `data` then—it has to be a dictionary with strings under the `title` and `extract` keys. You can express this concisely using structural pattern matching:

```
def fetch(url: str) -> Article:
    with urllib.request.urlopen(url) as response:
        data: JSON = json.load(response)

    match data:
```

```
        case {"title": str(title), "extract": str(extract)}:
            return Article(title, extract)

    raise ValueError("invalid response")
```

Thanks to type narrowing, the runtime type checks also appease mypy—in a way, bridging the worlds of runtime and static type checking. If you'd like to see the runtime type check in action, you can use the test harness from Chapter 6 and modify the HTTP server to return an unexpected response, such as null or "teapot".

## Serialization and Deserialization with cattrs

The function is type-safe now, but can we do better than this? The validation code duplicates the structure of the Article class—you shouldn't need to spell out the types of its fields again. If your application must validate more than one input, the boilerplate can hurt readability and maintainability. It should be possible to assemble articles from JSON objects using only the original type annotations—and it is.

The cattrs library provides flexible and type-safe serialization and deserialization for type-annotated classes such as dataclasses and attrs. It's delightfully simple to use—you pass the JSON object and the expected type to its structure function and get the assembled object back.[10] There's also a destructure function for transforming objects into primitive types for serialization.

For this last iteration on the Wikipedia example, add cattrs to your dependencies:

```
[project]
dependencies = ["cattrs>=23.2.3"]
```

Replace the fetch function with the three-liner below (don't run this yet, we'll get to the final version in a second):

```
import cattrs

def fetch(url: str) -> Article:
    with urllib.request.urlopen(url) as response:
        data: JSON = json.load(response)
    return cattrs.structure(data, Article)
```

Deserializing Article objects is now entirely determined by their type annotations. Besides being clear and concise, this version of the code is type-safe, thanks to the internal runtime checks in cattrs.

However, you still need to take care of one complication. The summary attribute doesn't match the name of its corresponding JSON field, extract. Fortunately,

---

10 In fact, the cattrs library is format-agnostic, so it doesn't matter if you read the raw object from JSON, YAML, TOML, or another data format.

cattrs is flexible enough to let you create a custom converter that renames the field on the fly:

```
import cattrs.gen

converter = cattrs.Converter()
converter.register_structure_hook(
    Article,
    cattrs.gen.make_dict_structure_fn(
        Article,
        converter,
        summary=cattrs.gen.override(rename="extract"),
    )
)
```

Finally, use the custom converter in the fetch function:

```
def fetch(url: str) -> Article:
    with urllib.request.urlopen(url) as response:
        data: JSON = json.load(response)
    return converter.structure(data, Article)
```

From a software-architecture perspective, the cattrs library has advantages over other popular data-validation libraries. It keeps serialization and deserialization separate from your *models*—the classes at the core of your application that express its problem domain and provide all the business logic. Decoupling the domain model from the data layer gives you architectural flexibility and improves the testability of your code.[11]

There are also practical advantages to the cattrs approach. You can serialize the same object in different ways if you need to. It's not intrusive—it doesn't add methods to your objects. And it works with all kinds of types: dataclasses, attrs-classes, named tuples, typed dicts, and even plain type annotations like tuple[str, int].

# Runtime Type Checking with Typeguard

Do you find the type unsafety of the original fetch function disconcerting? The issue was easy enough to spot in a short script. But how do you find similar issues in a large codebase before they cause problems? After all, you ran mypy in strict mode, and it remained silent.

Static type checkers won't catch every type-related error. In this case, gradual typing obscured the issue—specifically, json.load returning Any. Real-world code has plenty of situations like this. A library outside of your control might have overly

---

11 If you're interested in this topic, you absolutely should read *Architecture Patterns in Python* by Harry Percival and Bob Gregory (Sebastopol: O'Reilly, 2020).

permissive type annotations—or none at all. A bug in your persistence layer might load corrupted objects from disk. Maybe mypy would have caught the issue, but you silenced type errors for the module in question.

Typeguard is a third-party library and pytest plugin for runtime type checking. It can be an invaluable tool for verifying the type safety of your code in situations that elude static type checkers, such as:

*Dynamic code*
> Python code can be highly dynamic, forcing type annotations to be permissive. Your assumptions about the code may be at odds with the concrete types you end up with at runtime.

*External systems*
> Most real-world code eventually crosses the boundary to external systems such as a web service, a database, or the file system. Data you receive from these systems may not have the shape you expect it to. Its format can also unexpectedly change from one day to another.

*Third-party libraries*
> Some of your Python dependencies may not have type annotations, or their type annotations might be incomplete or overly permissive.

Add Typeguard to your dependencies in *pyproject.toml*:

```
[project]
dependencies = ["typeguard>=4.2.1"]
```

Typeguard comes with a function called check_type, which you can think of as isinstance for arbitrary type annotations. Those annotations can be quite simple—say, a list of floating-point numbers:

```
from typeguard import check_type

numbers = check_type(data, list[float])
```

The checks can also be more elaborate. For example, you can use the TypedDict construct to specify the precise shape of a JSON object you've fetched from some external service, such as the keys you expect to find and which types their associated values should have:[12]

```
from typing import Any, TypedDict

class Person(TypedDict):
    name: str
    age: int
```

---

[12] This is less useful than it may seem. TypedDict classes must list every field even if you use only a subset.

```
    @classmethod
    def check(cls, data: Any) -> "Person":
        return check_type(data, Person)
```

Here's how you might use it:

```
>>> Person.check({"name": "Alice", "age": 12})
{'name': 'Alice', 'age': 12}
>>> Person.check({"name": "Carol"})
typeguard.TypeCheckError: dict is missing required key(s): "age"
```

Typeguard also comes with a decorator named @typechecked. When used as a function decorator, it instruments the function to check the types of its arguments and return value. When used as a class decorator, it instruments every method in this way. For example, you could slap this decorator onto a function that reads Person records from a JSON file:

```
@typechecked
def load_people(path: Path) -> list[Person]:
    with path.open() as io:
        return json.load(io)
```

By default, Typeguard checks only the first item in a collection to reduce runtime overhead. You can change this strategy to check all items in the global configuration object:[13]

```
import typeguard
from typeguard import CollectionCheckStrategy

typeguard.config.collection_check_strategy = CollectionCheckStrategy.ALL_ITEMS
```

Finally, Typeguard comes with an import hook that instruments all functions and methods in a module on import. While you can use the import hook explicitly, arguably its greatest use case involves enabling Typeguard as a pytest plugin while running your test suite. Example 10-10 adds a Nox session that runs the test suite with runtime type checking.

*Example 10-10. Nox session for runtime type checking with Typeguard*

```
package = "random_wikipedia_article"

@nox.session
def typeguard(session: nox.Session) -> None:
    session.install(".[tests]", "typeguard")
    session.run("pytest", f"--typeguard-packages={package}")
```

---

13 If you call check_type directly, you'll need to pass the collection_check_strategy argument explicitly.

Running Typeguard as a pytest plugin lets you track down type-safety bugs in a large codebase—provided it has good test coverage. If it doesn't, consider enabling runtime type checking for individual functions or modules in production. Be careful here: look for false positives from the type checks, and measure their runtime overhead.

## Summary

Type annotations let you specify the types of variables and functions in your source code. You can use built-in types and user-defined classes, as well as many higher-level constructs, such as union types, `Any` for gradual typing, generics, and protocols. Stringized annotations and `Self` are useful for handling forward references. The `type` keyword lets you introduce type aliases.

Static type checkers like mypy leverage type annotations and type inference to verify the type safety of your program without running it. Mypy facilitates gradual typing by defaulting to `Any` for unannotated code. You can and should enable strict mode where possible to allow for more thorough checks. Run mypy as part of your mandatory checks, using a Nox session for automation.

Type annotations are available for inspection at runtime. They're the foundation for powerful features such as class generation with `dataclasses` or the `attrs` library, and automatic serialization and deserialization with the help of the `cattrs` library. The runtime type checker Typeguard allows you to instrument your code to verify the types of function arguments and return values at runtime. You can enable it as a pytest plugin while running your test suite.

There's a widespread sentiment that type annotations are for the sprawling codebases found at giant tech corporations—and not worth the trouble for reasonably sized projects, let alone the quick script you hacked together yesterday afternoon. I disagree. Type annotations make your programs easier to understand, debug, and maintain, no matter how large they are or how many people work on them.

Try using types for any Python code you write. Ideally, configure your editor to run a type checker in the background if it doesn't already come with typing support out of the box. If you feel that types get in your way, consider using gradual typing—but also consider whether there might be a simpler way to write your code that gives you type safety for free. If your project has any mandatory checks, type checking should be a part of them.

With this chapter, the book comes to a close.

Throughout the book, you've automated checks and tasks for your project using Nox. Nox sessions allow you and other contributors to run checks early and repeatedly during local development, in the same way they'd run on a CI server. For reference, here's a list of the Nox sessions you've defined:

- Building packages (Example 8-2)
- Running tests across multiple Python versions (Example 8-5)
- Running tests with code coverage (Example 8-9)
- Measuring coverage in subprocesses (Example 8-11)
- Generating the coverage report (Example 8-8)
- Locking the dependencies with uv (Example 8-14)
- Installing dependencies with Poetry (Example 8-19)
- Linting with pre-commit (Example 9-5)
- Static type checking with mypy (Example 10-7)
- Runtime type checking with Typeguard (Example 10-10)

There's a fundamental philosophy behind this approach, dubbed "Shift Left." Consider the software development lifecycle on a timeline extending from left to right—all the way from writing a line of code to running the program in production. (If you're Agile minded, picture the timeline as a circle where feedback from production flows back into planning and local development.)

The earlier you identify a software defect, the smaller the cost of fixing it. In the best case, you discover issues while they're still in your editor—their cost is near zero. In the worst case, you ship the bug to production. Before even starting to track down the issue in the code, you may have to roll back the bad deployment and contain its impact. For this reason, shift all your checks as far to the left on that imaginary timeline as possible.

(Run checks toward the right of the timeline as well. End-to-end tests against your production environments are invaluable for increasing confidence that your systems are operating as expected.)

Mandatory checks in CI are the main gatekeeper: they decide which code changes make it into the main branch and ship to production. But don't wait for CI. Run checks locally, as early as possible. Automating checks with Nox and pre-commit helps achieve this goal.

Integrate linters and type checkers with your editor as well! Alas, people haven't yet agreed on a single editor that everybody should use. Tools like Nox give you a common baseline for local development in your teams.

Automation also greatly reduces the cost of project maintenance. Contributors run a single command, such as nox, as an entry point to the mandatory checks. Other chores, like refreshing lock files or generating documentation, likewise only require simple commands. By encoding each process, you eliminate human error and create a basis for constant improvement.

Thank you for reading this book! While the book ends here, your journey through the ever-shifting landscape of modern Python developer tooling continues. Hopefully, the lessons from this book will remain valid and helpful, as Python continues to reinvent itself.

# Index

httpx library, 35, 38, 88-90, 92-93, 105, 119, 146, 157

## I
import packages, 55, 68
importlib library, 31, 44, 46, 47
importlib.metadata library, 31, 77, 79, 94, 95, 96, 99, 102, 104, 157, 171
inline tables (TOML), 61
inspect module, 228, 230
installation
    from Anaconda, 21-22
    with Hatch, 22-23
    interpreters, 5-8
    on Linux, 15-17
    local projects, local, 66-67
    on MacOS, 11-14
    on multiple versions of Python, 4-5
    Nox, 164
    package managers, 12
    packages, 35-36, 59, 66
    with pipx, 38, 40
    pyenv, 19
    pytest, 137
    python.org, 8, 13-14
    with Ruff, 186
    with Rye, 22-23
    on Windows, 8-9
installation schemes, 38
Installed Apps tool, 9
installers overview, 23
interpreters, 5-8, 10, 28-29
IronPython, 19
isort, 186, 189
iterators, 216

## J
join operation, 208
Jython, 19

## K
Kay, Alan, 172
Kluyver, Thomas, 110

## L
Lehtosalo, Jukka, 210
Lev, Ofek, 110
libraries, 4

(see also modules; specific library names)
    authoring, 211
    dynamic, 31, 47
    Linux and, 15
    locking dependencies, 102
    Python installation and, 4, 12, 16, 27-28, 51
    Python versions and, 4, 22, 84, 90-92, 94-97, 104, 118-120, 210, 221, 226
    shared, 30, 33
    and testing, 142-143, 152-153, 160
    third-party, 25, 87
    virtual environments, 34, 38, 49-51
linters
    activating, 188
    as executable style guide, 183
    automatic fixes and, 195-196
    available, listing, 187
    Flake8, 184, 185
    mutable argument default, 184
    pre-commit, installation, 192
    Pylint, 185
    Ruff, 186-205
Linux, 15-17
    (see also individual distributions)
locking dependencies, 91, 101-107

## M
macOS
    Anaconda/Conda support, 17, 21-22
    Coverage.py and, 154, 159
    environments, 31-38, 72
    modules, 30-31, 49
    Poetry and, 120, 122
    Python installation, 5-7, 11-14, 17, 19, 23-24, 26-28
    Python Launcher, 18-19, 44
Maturin, 65
metadata, 31
    (see also importlib-metadata; packages)
    core, 73
    project, 31, 73-85, 113-115
MicroPython, 3
Ming, Frost, 110
Miniconda, 21
    (see also Anaconda)
Miniforge, 21
modules, 25-26, 30-31, 44-46, 58-59
    (see also specific module names)
monkey patching, 138

mutable argument default, 184
mypy, 61, 96, 185, 210, 221-228

## N

namespace packages, 30
Nix, 17
nominal subtyping, 220
   (see also types)
None type, 213-214
noqa, 191
Nox, 167-182, 191, 196, 225-226
   session.install, 164, 165
   session.run, 164, 166
nox-poetry, 181
NumPy, 72

## O

overlay distribution, 12

## P

packages, 58-60
   (see also build; Hatch; hatchling; modules;
      pip; Poetry; Rye)
   building with build frontends, 62-65
   building with Nox, 165
   core metadata, 73
   dependencies, 87
   distribution packages, 55
   import packages, 55, 68
   installing, 12, 35-36, 66
   managers, 12, 68-70, 87
   namespace packages, 30
   publishing, 65
   pyproject.toml file, 60-62
   site packages, 33
   stubs package, 226
   terminology, 30
   type distribution and, 226-227
   uploading, 65
parallel coverage, 157-158
parameterization, 140-143, 174-175
PATH (see environment variables)
PathFinder, 47
   (see also modules)
PDM, 64, 65, 101, 103, 110, 127
Perflint, 189
pip, 26, 27, 34-38, 55
pip-tools, 105-107, 177

Pipenv, 103, 110, 127
Pipfile, 110
pipx, 26, 34, 38-42, 52, 66-67, 105, 111, 126,
   164, 186
plugins, 41-42, 77
   (see also entry points; specific plugin
     names)
   in metadata, 115
   nox-poetry, 181
   Poetry, 126-130
   pytest, 98, 147-149, 160
   writing, 79-81
Poetry, 109
   build-system table, 113
   caret constraints, 118
   dependency groups, 123-124
   dependency management, 117-121
   development dependencies, 123-124
   environment management, 121-122
   installation, 111
   Nox and, 179-181
   nox-poetry, 181
   packages, 112, 124-126
   plugins, 126-130
   poetry new command, 112
   poetry update command, 121
   project creation, 112-121
   project metadata, 113-115
   pytest, 137
   Python versions, 111
   src layout, 112
   tab completion, 111
   upgrading, 111
pre-commit, 99, 183, 192-199, 206, 238
project manager, 110
projects, 66
   (see also packages)
   layout, 67-68
   metadata, 73-85
protocols, 220
   (see also types)
publishing packages (see packages)
py utility, 10-11, 18
py.typed markers, 226
pycodestyle, 185, 188, 201
pydocstyle, 190
pyenv, 19-20
Pyflakes, 185, 187, 188
Pylint, 185, 186

---

## W

wheels, 64, 70-73, 102
Wikipedia API, 88-89
Windows
    Anaconda/Conda support, 17, 21-22
    Coverage.py and, 159
    environments, 33-35
    modules, 30-31, 49, 96
    Nox and, 169

Poetry and, 119, 120-121, 128
Python installation, 3, 5, 6, 8-9, 23-24,
    27-28, 31-37, 72-73
Python Launcher, 10-11, 19, 44, 169
testing, 137

## Y

yanking, 102
YAPF (Yet Another Python Formatter), 202

## About the Author

**Claudio Jolowicz** is a senior software engineer at Cloudflare with nearly two decades of industry experience in Python and C++ and an open source maintainer active in the Python community. He is the author of the *Hypermodern Python* blog and project template, and co-maintainer of Nox, a Python tool for test automation. In former lives, Claudio has worked as a legal scholar and as a musician touring from Scandinavia to West Africa. Get in touch with him on Mastodon: *@cjolowicz@fosstodon.org*.

## Colophon

The animal on the cover of *Hypermodern Python Tooling* is the Peruvian sheartail (*Thaumastura cora*), a member of the *Mellisugini* tribe of bee hummingbirds.

The males of most species in this tribe have specialized tail feathers, often used to produce sounds during courtship display. As shown on the cover of this book, male Peruvian sheartails indeed sport very long, black and white forked tails. The upperparts of both sexes are a luminous green, while males' throat feathers are a lustrous purple to magenta.

The Peruvian sheartail is one of the smallest hummingbirds, and some believe it to be the lightest of all South American hummingbirds. The sheartail makes its home among the arid coastal shrubland of Peru, as well as in farmland, gardens, and orchards, where it forages flowering plants for nectar. The population is expanding into Chile, and individuals have also been sighted in Ecuador.

Due to its stable population, the Peruvian sheartail has been classified by the IUCN as being of least concern from a conservation standpoint. Many of the animals on O'Reilly covers are endangered; all of them are important to the world.

The cover illustration is by Karen Montgomery, based on an antique line engraving from Wood's *Natural History*. The series design is by Edie Freedman, Ellie Volckhausen, and Karen Montgomery. The cover fonts are Gilroy Semibold and Guardian Sans. The text font is Adobe Minion Pro; the heading font is Adobe Myriad Condensed; and the code font is Dalton Maag's Ubuntu Mono.

Gabriela Jolowicz and Kate Dullea prepared the chapter-opening images based on illustrations from *De la terre à la lune: trajet direct en 97 heures 20 minutes* by Jules Verne (Paris: J. Hetzel, 1872); *Le vingtième siècle* by Albert Robida (Paris: Georges Decaux, 1883); *Le magasin pittoresque*, vol. 5 (Paris: Édouard Charton, 1837); and *Museum museorum* by Michael Bernhard Valentini (Frankfurt: J.D. Zunner & J.A. Jungen, 1714).